198

D1080486

WAYS OF LOVING

Other books by Brendan Gill

DEATH IN APRIL

THE TROUBLE OF ONE HOUSE

THE DAY THE MONEY STOPPED

COLE

TALLULAH

HAPPY TIMES

WAYS
OF
LOVING

Brendan Gill

Harcourt Brace Jovanovich, Inc.
New York

Printed in the United States of America

Except for "End of an Exceptionally Short Affair,"
which appeared in *Cosmopolitan,* "The Sunflower Kid,"
which appeared in *The Saturday Evening Post,* and "The Loser"
and the novellas "The Malcontents" and "Last Things,"
all the stories in this collection appeared originally
in *The New Yorker.*

Library of Congress Cataloging in Publication Data

Gill, Brendan, 1914–
Ways of loving.

CONTENTS: End of an exceptionally short affair.—
The knife.—Truth and consequences. [etc.]
I. Title.
PZ3.G399Way   813'.5'2   73-18497
ISBN 0-15-195312-0

First edition

B C D E

Contents

END OF AN EXCEPTIONALLY
SHORT AFFAIR
3

THE KNIFE
11

TRUTH AND CONSEQUENCES
20

THE MALCONTENTS
A novella
26

THE MISCHIEVOUS SINFULNESS
OF MOTHER COAKLEY
78

TOO LATE TO MARRY,
TOO SOON TO DIE
85

THE TRIUMPH
90

SIGNS
99

COUNTRY FIRE
106

THE SUNFLOWER KID
112

THE OTHER SIDE
141

THE LOSER
147

REMEMBRANCE
156

SOMETHING YOU JUST DON'T DO IN A CLUB
159

THE SACRIFICE
183

THE TOAST
193

THE CEMETERY
197

AND HOLY GHOST
208

FAT GIRL
222

LAST THINGS
A novella
250

WAYS OF LOVING

End
of an Exceptionally
Short Affair

He knew exactly what she was going to say and he dreaded it. He pressed his eyes shut in the crook of her arm, as if not seeing were a way of not having to hear. When she said that he was the very best person to make love to that she had ever known, contempt for her flooded him like pain, unstoppable. Answer her, he thought, say anything, babble the enormous trifle she is waiting to hear. But no, not a word, because for once in his life he wanted an affair without a single silly accommodating or double-crossing lie in it. Hadn't he promised himself that much—that little—a few days earlier, when the affair began? And already the promise was in jeopardy. He was angry with himself for feeling contempt for the girl, angrier still at the need to mask for the girl's sake his contempt and anger. If only she had kept silent! But like so many women he had known, she could not be sure that a thing was true until she had spoken it; and sooner or later this would lead her to the next, and much more reckless, step, which was to speak a thing in order to make it true.

Cradled in her arm, he felt his head lightly rise and fall

as her lungs breathed in, breathed out. The body was a system of cages—head, chest, pelvis—designed, not to imprison things, but to release them. It might be that holding back words was sometimes as dangerous to the body as holding one's breath. She was waiting, but he didn't yet trust himself to answer. He felt too violently the force of his contempt and anger; age was not expected to manifest strong emotions in the presence of the young. For the young assumed that with thinning hair, a thickening belly, and all the other repellent, irreversible signals of physical decline went a similar decline in the variety and strength of one's feelings. That false assumption led to a still falser one—that as a man's powers failed, self-discipline became more and more nearly a matter of course, earning for him at last, and by then quite easily, the reward of a chaste and unarousable old age. He saw now, in his middle fifties, that the contrary was the case; it was one of the nasty jack-in-the-box surprises of life that though powers failed, appetites did not. With every passing year, he found self-discipline harder to achieve and his lapses from it more unbecoming. Old age for him might well consist of a steady fumbling downward into indiscriminate lust and impromptu misdemeanors. Mockingly, he pictured himself as a white-haired old man, arrested because he had been unable to resist touching the bare backs of girls in elevators. His grandchildren would go bail for him in some squalid night court: "Your Honor, for a long time he has not been himself." (Untrue! He would never have been more himself.) The judge: "This man is a menace to society. If his family doesn't lock him up, I will."

Propping himself on one elbow over the girl, he kissed the faint lines that had been nicked into the corners of her mouth by her short lifetime of smiles. He believed in telling the young as little as possible of what he had learned, pleasant or unpleasant, about the way of the world, on the principle that nothing ought to come to them at second hand, given instead of earned. He wanted to tell her nothing, but because he must and because he could think of no other words that would serve, he said, "What a good child you are." Instantly, he sensed an airy coolness about his ribs, as her taut body, warm for hours against him, infinitesimally drew away. Not for the world would she wish to hurt his feelings by letting him perceive that he had hurt hers, but in fact there was nothing else for him to take in and measure the heavy weight of. He knew perfectly well what he had done. The crime of his providing her with no childish trade-last equal to her own hung there in the greeny, early-morning, underwaterlike room. After their night together, the tiny space that had opened between them on the bed seemed of a threatening vastness. Well, but she *is* a good child, he thought, defending the small, indisputable fact as if it were a big and doubtful one, in order to put off confronting her disappointment. Failing her, at least he had not failed himself by lying. Maybe after thirty years of craven artful dodging, he was about to have it proven to him that truth was not merely necessary in a relationship, but a greater thing than kindness. It was what he had always believed and wished to act on, so far in vain. Damn her for having felt obliged to pay him a compliment! Compliments were mine fields, equally dangerous to both sides; he had spent his life avoiding them.

She said fiercely, "Not a child."

"I was thinking of the 'good.' "

"Oh, that."

5

She was not aware of being good—it was a quality not accessible to her and valuable only to others, so she could find no consolation there. He held her head fast between his hand and a hillock of entangled pillows and sheets. It was a shapely head, and over the past few days he had come to like holding it in both hands and drawing her face down to his, slowly, slowly, until their lips just brushed and their lashes touched in butterfly kisses, tickling her and making her laugh.

She said, "I hate being called a child, especially by you. I'm twenty-five. If what everyone says about you and young girls is true, I must be the oldest mistress you ever had."

He took his hand from her head, letting her go. Every word she had spoken irritated him. He felt hostility toward her rising as steadily in him as water in a glass. It would be better for both of them if he were to be up and showered and shaved and dressed and out on the street, on his way to work. He made a move to get out of bed, and this time it was she who held him, linking her hands behind his neck. "What's so awful about what I said?"

"In the first place, you're not my mistress, but a girl I've been making love to. In the second place, what 'everyone' says about me doesn't concern me; I'm not on trial. In the third place, I don't have a thing about young girls. The record shows that I've liked women of all ages, at all my ages."

"I didn't mean to make you angry."

"*I am not angry,*" he said. It was so obvious that he was very angry that if they had known each other better and had loved each other more, they might have burst out laughing, and so the dangerous corner could have been got past in safety. But the fact was that they didn't love each other at all; so far there was only the tenuous bond between them of their having made love.

"Anyhow," she said. "*Anyhow*, I didn't mean what was so bad about calling myself your mistress. I meant the thing I said before."

He might have pretended—always before, he would have pretended—not to know what she was talking about. This time, he would tell the truth, and the experiment would be all the easier for him to make because she had angered him, not once, but twice; persisting on a wrong course was worse than having chosen it. He lifted her hands, still linked, from around his neck and placed them on her bare breasts, giving her the look of a small, solemn effigy on the tomb of some long-dead medieval queen. He sat crouched on the edge of the bed and looked down at her blanched, shadowy face. Her eyes studied his, striving to get ready for what was to come. But readiness, wariness, a means of calculating risks were still beyond her. Her eyes seemed to hold nothing in their depths except their own clear sky-blueness; they were ignorant eyes, which she closed when she made love, and it was just as well. He said, "To begin with, I don't like compliments. Even intelligent ones. And yours was stupid."

She flinched at "stupid." The pale head of the effigy rolled back and forth on its crumpled pillow, seeking to reject the word. Now that he had undertaken not only to tell the truth but to punish her with the truth, he could not stop. "Can't you see how little that compliment means?" he asked. "And therefore how little gratitude I'd be able to feel?"

"Because I haven't experience enough to make it a big one?"

"At your age, how likely that you would have?"

"I'm not totally without—"

"No, no, my God, no lists."

She was so pretty and in such distress as she lay there, her hands primly sheltering her breasts. She said, "Even if it's an awfully short list, I meant what I said."

Truth in a relationship: surely it was greater than kindness? "But not important. So better left unsaid."

"The way you left unsaid what you didn't want to say? That I wasn't the best for you?"

But kindness, too. "Something like that."

"Sorry not to have been. Incompetent me." She smiled up at him. "Practice makes perfect."

"Dear not-a-child, be reasonable! Think of the arithmetic alone. I've lived at least ten thousand days longer than you. And in a life like mine, in many ways such a crazy life, there are so many girls, all of them different. But nobody's trying out for the Olympics. Nobody's keeping track of records being made and broken. No gold medals." He bent down and kissed her paper-cool forehead. "Now I'm going to take a shower. Go back to sleep. I can let myself out."

She drew a sheet up to her chin. Of her body, only her face was visible; and of her face, mostly those blank eyes. "If you go now, you won't come back. I know you."

"No, dear one, you don't know me, and I don't know you. You and I—we were only at the beginning."

" 'Were'?"

"Said without thinking."

"Poor me! That makes it so much worse."

Patiently: "I'll need to shave, too. Are you the kind of girl who keeps the same rusty blade in a razor for years at a time?"

"New blades in the cabinet, lots of them."

"Good girl."

"But I won't be going to sleep. I'm going to lie here and worry about whether when you go away this morning you're really going away."

She had covered herself, and now he, too, felt, for the first time, a sense of being naked. There was no way for them to clamber back over all those jagged cliffs of words to where they had been on waking, but how was he to tell her so? It was something he could be certain of out of the huge sum of his life; something she must find her way to uninstructed. Nothing at second hand, nothing not earned! But earning was painful, and he would be the source of her pain. His anger and contempt were gone; he was long past wishing to punish her. The light in the room was changing. Sun filled the green garden behind the house, and a sound of street traffic came washing through the open windows from over the adjacent rooftops. A bird chittered furiously in the garden; an enemy of birds was abroad. He said, "If you mean we mightn't be seeing each other again, that's nonsense. We'll make a date right now for drinks some night next week. Tuesday at six?"

"Letting me down gently?"

"Maybe it's you who'll be letting me down. Let's wait and see about that."

"I want us to go on making love."

"About that, too."

It was then that her eyes changed. It was as if they had changed color, but that was impossible; and it was more than as if they had simply changed focus or direction. No, by some small adjustment of invisible muscles her way of seeing had changed; and it was she who had willed the change. Truth had been greater than kindness, and she

9

knew, and was finding from moment to moment that she could bear to know, that they wouldn't be making love again, that he would coax and tease her into their becoming friends, that he would meet her young men and decide whether to like them or dislike them, that he would be sleeping with girls about whom he would never say a word and about whom she would never be at liberty to speak, that they would kiss on meeting and saying good-bye and would hold hands in theatres, and that only the least rueful and playful particle of desire would be acknowledged to exist between them—oh, a cataract of things newly known and just about to be known tumbled and flooded in all round her, and he stood there, a middle-aged man, naked in sunlight at the foot of her bed ("This man is a menace to society"), and again he knew exactly what she was going to say. This time, he had no reason to dread it, because she would be telling him, in a voice steady enough to bring him relief as well as pleasure, that, as far as she could tell, next Tuesday at six would be lovely.

The Knife

Michael threw himself down, locked his hands over one of his father's knees, and began, in a whisper, " 'Our Father, who art in heaven, hallowed be thy name, kingdom come, will be done, earth as it is in heaven, give us this day—' "

Carroll folded his newspaper. Michael should have been in bed an hour ago. "Take it easy, boy," he said. "Let's try it again, slow."

Michael repeated, slowly and distinctly, " 'Our Father, who art in heaven, hallowed . . .' " Carroll saw that the boy's pajamas were dirty at the cuffs; probably he had not brushed his teeth. " '. . . as we forgive them, who trespass against us'—what does 'trespass' mean?"

"Why, hurting anybody."

"Do I trespass anybody?"

"Not much, I guess. Finish it up."

Michael drew a breath. " 'And lead us not into temptation, but deliver us from evil. Amen.' "

"Now," his father said, combing back Michael's tangled hair with his fingers, "what about a good 'Hail, Mary'?"

"All right," Michael said. "Hail, Mary" was easy. " 'Hail,

Mary, full of grace, the Lord is with thee, blessed art thou among women, and blessed is the fruit of thy womb, Jesus.' " Michael lifted his head with the intention of asking if a womb got fruit like a tree, but thought better of it. His father never answered questions seriously, the way his mother used to. He decided to wait and ask Mrs. Nolan, who was his best friend. "Is Mrs. Nolan coming tomorrow?" he asked.

"She'll be here, all right. I give you ten seconds to finish that prayer."

Michael was delighted by the ultimatum. "I thought you wanted me to go slow. 'Holy Mary, Mother of God, pray for us sinners, now and at the hour of our death. Amen.' " He unlocked his hands. "Will she?"

Carroll's attention had wandered. "Will she what?"

"Will she now and at the hour of our death, A-men?"

The words of the prayer were so familiar that Carroll had long since stopped thinking of their meaning. He repeated the prayer to himself. "Pray for us sinners"—the things children were made to say! It was hard to imagine Michael as a sinner. He said, "Yes, boy, she will." He set his pipe in a broken dish on the table beside him. He had not emptied the dish of ashes in two days. Mrs. Nolan would give him a piece of her mind tomorrow morning, as she did each week when she came in to give the apartment a general cleaning and to do the laundry.

"What good can she do?"

"Climb into bed, young ragamuffin. It's past nine."

"What *good* can she do?"

"She'll help you get anything you want. I suppose she'll help you shinny up into heaven when the time comes. You know all about heaven, don't you?"

Michael felt that he had been placed on the defensive.
"Of course."

"Well, then, get along with you."

But Michael had something difficult to reason out. "You
mean she'll ask God for anything I want and He'll give it
to her for me?"

"She's His Mother."

Michael scrambled up and kissed his father on both
cheeks. Then he marched from the room, and Carroll could
hear his bare feet crossing the hall. The little bed creaked
as he lay down in it. Carroll opened the newspaper, read
a paragraph or two, and dropped it in a white heap on the
rug. He felt tired, and was grateful to feel tired; perhaps
tonight he would be able to get some sleep. He stood up,
slipped his suspenders from his shoulders, unknotted his tie,
and kicked off his shoes. He had learned to undress quickly
in the six months since his wife had died.

His pajamas were hanging inside out on a hook in the
bathroom, where he had left them that morning. It was one
of the things he had not yet got used to—that what he had
left in a certain condition in the morning would be found in
the same condition that night. When he had undressed and
was standing at the sink, he felt Michael's toothbrush with
his thumb; the brush was dry. He should have explained to
the child—for what? the twentieth time?—what happened
to a person's teeth when he forgot to brush them every night
and morning.

Carroll stared at his face in the mirror above the sink.
He tried smiling. Nobody could tell what a man was thinking by the way he smiled. Even Michael, who was as good
as a puppy at sensing moods, could not tell. He entered
the dark bedroom on tiptoe. Feeling the sheets bunched at

the foot of the mattress, he remembered that he had made the beds in a hurry. The sheets felt fresh and cool only on Saturdays, when Mrs. Nolan changed them.

Michael was not yet asleep. "Dad?"

"Go to sleep."

He had moved Michael's bed into his bedroom for the sake of convenience—when the boy had a bad dream at night, it was easier to reach out and shake him gently into comfort than to get up and pad in darkness down the hall to him—but the convenience was sometimes also a nuisance. He had never been good with the boy at night.

"I been asking Hail Mary for something."

"Tomorrow."

"No, I been asking her right now."

Carroll lay on his back with his hands over his eyes, trying to make the darkness deeper, like a weight on him. "What've you been asking for, Mickey?"

Michael hesitated. "I thought I'd better make it something easy first. To see what happened." He sat bolt upright in bed. "A jackknife."

A few blocks away the clock in the tower of the city hall was striking ten. Michael was deep in the noisy middle of a dream. He was as strenuous and determined asleep as he was awake. Carroll listened to his breathing, then tried matching his own breath to Michael's, as a device for making sleep come. No use. It was never any use. Every night Carroll pretended to himself that he was just at the brink of falling off to sleep, but his eyes always widened with wakefulness at the effort. Now, as the clock stopped striking, Carroll got up and walked into the bathroom and dressed. Then he went into the living room, tapped the bar of the lock on the front door sideways and up into its little metal loop, let himself out, heard the bar fall back in place, locked the door of the apartment, and walked down the two flights of stairs into the street. It frightened him to leave Michael alone, but it was unbearable to remain in the apartment awake. He had explained that he might sometimes go out for a few minutes, leaving Michael in charge. Michael wasn't to be startled if he woke and found the bed beside him empty. Proud to be made temporary master of the house, Michael promised he never would be. There were times when Carroll, having left the apartment and started out on a walk, would imagine Michael suddenly screaming himself awake out of some dreadful nightmare, with nobody there to hold him tight; or worse—for once one began to think of horrors, they were quick to multiply—he would imagine the apartment building afire and Michael half suffocated by smoke and crying out for him in vain behind the locked door. And then, sweat starting rankly all over his body, Carroll would run home in panic, faster, faster, *faster,* to the sleeping child.

Shops reached out of sight along both sides of the avenue. Carroll walked uptown, as he always did. He stopped in front of each bright shopwindow, studying its contents for the fifth or sixth time. He knew by now the day when each window display was changed and by whom. Certain plastic models, certain fringed crepe papers had become old friends. There were bargains that nobody ever bought, so they could not, after all, be bargains. Prices slashed would again be slashed, and the unwanted things remained. At the top of a long slope, Carroll waited for the lights to change. On his left was a bar; on his right, across the street, a drugstore. Between the slats of the orange Venetian blinds of the bar, he could see its broad mahogany counter, the stacked bottles lit from below and doubled in number by the mirrored wall behind them, and the barman polishing a glass between orders. A man and a girl were seated at a table by the window, scarcely a foot from Carroll's eyes. Neither of them seemed to be speaking; no need to speak. The girl wore a black dress, open at the throat, and her skin was milky. The man's hands lay halfway across the table; in one hand smoldered a cigarette. The girl reached out and took the cigarette and placed it in an ashtray, then gripped both the man's hands in hers and drew them slowly toward her, and she was smiling.

Carroll turned quickly away from the bar and crossed the street to the drugstore. The owner, Sam Landsman, stood sniffing the night air under the red-and-white sign bearing his name, or part of his name: TRUST UNCLE SAM.

"Well, Mr. Carroll, nice night for March."

Carroll needed to hear a voice, any voice. "How's business?" he asked.

"Can't complain," Landsman said, then shook his head. "I got to break myself of that 'Can't complain.' I got to remember, a serious subject. Business is lousy."

Carroll leaned back against Sam's window, which was crammed with hot-water bottles, perfumes, toys, and two brightly colored cardboard girls wearing shorts and sandals. The girls had been there for two months. There was dust on their teeth and on their smooth brown legs. "You ought to clean those girls' teeth, Sam," Carroll said, "and run your hand up and down their legs from time to time."

"You walk a lot," Sam said. "I figure on you, ten or eleven, most nights."

"I guess I do."

Sam slapped his belly, which was round and apparently as hard as stone. "Nothing like exercise, keep a man in shape."

Carroll nodded impatiently. It turned out, as it always turned out, that it was not a matter of any voice. "Let me have a milk shake, Sam."

They walked into the store. Carroll sat down on one of the stools at the fountain and watched Sam pouring milk into the shaker. Sam said, " 'Take out the fountain,' my accountant says. 'You're losing your shirt on the fountain.' I like a fountain, I tell him. What's a drugstore without a fountain, right?" The hands of the electric clock above the door were at ten-forty-five. Carroll could not go to bed before twelve. He swung back and forth on the stool, studying the glass showcases at either end of the fountain. "Sell any jackknives, Sam?"

"Listen, me, I sell everything. Nothing like keeping a thing in stock to kill demand." He poured out the milk shake in front of Carroll, then brought a tray of jackknives from somewhere at the rear of the store. "A nice selection," Sam said. "Beauties. A dollar up."

As he drank the shake, Carroll fingered one or another of the knives. He chose one at last. "Such expensive tastes!" Sam said. "That'll be two bucks fifty, plus tax."

Carroll paid for the knife and milk shake and walked out into the street. In another hour and a half he would have been able to walk six miles. By that time his body would be tired enough so he could sleep. By that time, he hoped, no voice could rouse him.

When Carroll woke, it was morning. He lay staring straight up, listening to the sound of the March rain against the windows. April showers might bring you May flowers, but March rains brought you nothing; they were ice-cold and they shut you in your room without any hope of escape.

Michael and Mrs. Nolan were talking together in the kitchen. Michael's voice was high with excitement. "Look at it, Mrs. Nolan! Isn't it beautiful?"

"It is that," said Mrs. Nolan. Carroll raised himself on one elbow. It was too late to give her warning.

"Under my *pillow,*" Michael said, and then, "Do *you* ask for things when you say your prayers?"

"I do, now." A pan clattered to the floor. "I've seen many a nice clean sty I'd swap for this dirty kitchen," Mrs. Nolan said. "You live like a couple of savages from week to week. God love you."

"You always get what you ask for?"

"It all depends. I sort of try to guess what the good Lord wants to give me, then ask for that."

"That's how I got this knife," Michael said. "It's got a big blade and a little blade and a screwdriver and a thing to punch holes in leather with and a file."

"You must have said yourself the grand prayer," said Mrs. Nolan. There was no hint of surprise in her voice.

"It was only a 'Hail, Mary,' but I did it slow, the way Dad told me to." Michael was silent for a moment; a knife blade clicked shut. "I'm asking for the real thing tonight. The knife was just to see. Someone's going to be here when you come next week."

Mrs. Nolan made a clucking sound. "Someone instead of me?"

"She was here with Dad and me before you came," Michael said, his voice thin with its burden, "and she's coming back."

"Michael!" Carroll called.

Michael ran to the bedroom doorway. The knife gleamed in his fist. "Look what I was showing Mrs. Nolan."

"Come here, boy," Carroll said. When Michael reached the edge of the bed, Carroll bent over and fastened his arms behind the child's back. There was only one thing to say, and one way to say it, and that was fast. "I'm glad you like it," he said. "I bought it for you last night at Uncle Sam's. The biggest and shiniest one he had."

Truth
and
Consequences

She had straight blond hair and a red mouth, and she was lame. Every day she played golf and went swimming in the center of a crowd of boys. Sitting with his mother on the hotel porch, Charles watched her and nodded while his mother repeated, "Isn't it extraordinary, a girl like that? I wonder what they see in her." He took to walking past the pool during the morning as the girl and the boys lay there side by side, laughing. He listened with interest to her voice. It was low, unhurried, forceful. So was her language. Every other word seemed to Charles to be "damn," "hell," and worse. She spoke of God, to whom Charles was preparing to dedicate his life, as if He were a disreputable friend in the next block. "I swear to God," the girl said. "I must have told you this one, for Christ's sake." Charles walked out of range of the jokes that followed. He would like to have heard them without the necessity of listening to them. He was eighteen and he was spending this last vacation with his mother before entering a seminary. In eight more summers he would be a priest. The timbre of the girl's voice and the nature of her language excited him. He had never seen or heard anyone like her in his life.

One evening after dinner, while his mother was upstairs swallowing one of the long series of pills that carried her with an air of purposeful busyness through the day, the girl sat down beside him on the hotel verandah. Her lips were smiling, and her eyes were the color of her blue, partly unbuttoned blouse. "We ought to know each other," she said. "You ought to join the rest of us at the pool."

"I'm with Mother."

The girl reached over and covered his hand with hers. He could see the delicate blue veins that ran to the base of her fingers; her hand was brown above his white one. She said, "Well, Jesus, you're old enough to go swimming by yourself, aren't you?"

Charles felt that he ought to explain before it was too late, before she had said something he could never forget. "I'm going to be a priest," he said.

The girl kept smiling, though her eyes were puzzled. "With a turn-around collar and all?"

He nodded.

"So you can't come swimming with me and the gang?"

"That hasn't anything to do with it. I just thought I'd tell you. I always do tell people."

"You could still come dancing with us if you wanted to?"

"Of course."

"Could take me to a movie if you wanted to?"

"Sure."

"I never met a boy who was going to be a priest. Could you take me out for a ride tonight? If you wanted to?"

He said quickly, "We didn't bring our car."

"Oh, shit, I meant in my car. I meant just for example. I

didn't say I'd *go*." She stared at him, her eyes moving over his body from head to foot. Lightly, with her fingers, she tickled the back of his hand. "It would be funny, with a boy who was going to be a priest."

His mother would be coming downstairs at any moment; she would make short shrift of the girl. By way of warning, Charles said, "The words you use—my mother would have a fit."

The girl ran her hand up and down the bare brown leg that was shorter than the other. "Like what?"

"Like 'Jesus,' like 'Christ.' That's taking the name of the Lord in vain. It's one of the Ten Commandments."

"I'm an awful damn fool. I talk dirty to keep people from thinking about my leg. But I didn't know you were going to be a priest."

For the girl's sake as much as his own, Charles wanted to get rid of her before his mother came. He stood up and said, "You shouldn't worry about things like that. I hadn't even noticed."

She stood up beside him. Her eyes shone in the late twilight that poured, violet and sea-green, with a salting of stars, over the shoulder of the mountain. "Damn you, please don't lie to me," she said. "Of course you've noticed. But does it bother you? Make you sick? Make you want to stay away from me?"

He said, "Oh, God, no!"

His "God" made them laugh—they could not stop laughing. She slipped her hand under his arm. She managed to say, at last, "Thanks for saying it so nice and hard. I haven't asked anybody that in a long time."

Without having willed it, Charles found himself walking the length of the verandah beside the girl. At first he walked too fast, and every few moments she would have to take a little skip to catch up with him. Her blond hair touched the shoulder of his jacket. Looking down at her, he could scarcely tell that she was lame. He bent his head to smell her perfume. She must be older than he—nobody in the whole world was younger than he—and if so she must be in college. "Where do you go to school?"

"Nowhere at the moment. Dropped out of college my very first year. Which was last year. This year I spent six months in a kibbutz, picking grapefruit. Those kibbutzim, they really smother you. You want a candy bar every day, they pencil in a candy bar. So now I'm looking around."

Like an older brother, like an uncle, he said severely, "You're bright. You got to use your brains."

"Oh, hell, yes, I'm very bright—right off the chart! So what? I'm not into having a big career. I'm not *into* anything. I'll be on the loose like this for a couple of years. Then some boy my family didn't like me sleeping with will get around to marrying me, big deal. And Daddy, who's loaded, will give us a house to play house in, and after that who knows? It stinks the way I say it, but I bet it won't be bad. It was Daddy who gave me the gimp. He smashed up a Porsche with me on the front seat. At six."

Charles felt himself stumbling. She had told him so much. She had told him the truth, which was more than he'd wanted to hear. They reached the end of the immense verandah and stood facing the valley in which, invisibly now, a river dropped, mile after mile, over smooth shelves of granite. Two old men were playing croquet in the gathering darkness, the wooden mallets and balls knocking softly together, the white trousers of the men moving like disembodied spirits across the lawn. Below them, in the kitchen,

Charles and the girl could hear the clatter of dishes being washed and stacked, and the high, whining voices of the waitresses.

"Now you," the girl said. "You really think you want that kookie thing? To be a priest?"

"Of course."

"It wasn't just some damn-fool vow your mother made when she was carrying you?"

Charles laughed. He was surprised at how easily she made him laugh. "It's true she always wanted me to be one. Especially after Dad died, when we went abroad to live. Paris. Rome. She's *very* Catholic. She claims a cardinal fell in love with her in Rome, but they didn't do much of anything about it."

"Tough tittie."

Startled, he threw his head back. "Yes. Well. I've always been to Catholic schools. I just graduated from one. I liked it. I'm going to the seminary in the fall. I'll like that, too."

"There must be more to it than that. Bells ringing in your head, something like that?"

"You mean a vocation? I guess I have one."

Out in the dark, one of the old men cried bitterly, "You missed the wicket, you damned old cheat!"

"But how can you be sure?"

Charles held fast to the railing of the verandah. It was the question he had never been able to answer, the question he never stopped asking. Only his mother had always been sure of his vocation. For the first time, he heard himself saying, "I can't be sure."

Out in the dark, the other old man was bawling, "Liar! Liar! Too damn blind to see your own spit!"

24

The girl said, "Then you won't be a priest. Jesus! Why are you afraid to face a simple thing like that?"

Charles turned and saw his mother walking heavily along the verandah. He studied her as if she were a stranger. What an enormous old woman she was, and how strong she was, and how she had driven him! He felt the girl's arm resting contentedly in the crook of his arm. She made no effort to take it away. He felt the verandah trembling under his mother's approach.

The Malcontents

How they quarreled, those three! It was as if, with the best intentions in the world, they were helpless not to. Like the alcoholic striving to resist the temptation of the first deliciously scalding shot of gin, they strove to withhold the first wounding word, and they always failed. One reason for their wrangling was that although they were members of the same family, they knew nothing whatever about family life. Grandmother, mother, and son, each was an only child. They might almost as well have been brought up in incubators, their existence regulated by clocks and valves, as to have been brought up as they were, in big houses, among innumerable servants, with never the bitter boon of being deprived of something, or cheated out of something, by one or another of a crew of piratical sisters and brothers. They lacked any sense of the give-and-take by which the silent enmities of a generation of a family are forged and then, with luck, transformed into affection and sometimes, with even more luck, into love. The three of them bickered and battled and sulked, and they were as close and wary and as much at odds as so many venomous lizards in a pail.

If, for each of them, being an only child was bad enough, what made matters worse was the exceptional disparity in their ages. Mrs. Fennelly had waited until she was thirty to have Claire, and Claire had waited five years longer than her mother before peremptorily rapping out poor little Nicky. Now Nicky was fifteen, Claire fifty, and her mother eighty. With so great a gulf of time between them, it wasn't to be wondered at that relations between Nicky and his mother and grandmother were uneasy. Mrs. Fennelly heightened the difficulty by being, in a thoroughly old-fashioned way, not a moment younger than her years. Nowadays, any number of lively old women are to be seen racketing about the world; one is often outdistanced by them in the long reaches of airport corridors, or one races them to the last available seat in a train or bus. In their clouds of blue-white curly hair, their jaunty lipsticks and trim bodies, and especially in their flood of topical chatter (much of it shrewd and some of it witty), they might be members of an altogether new race—a race doomed, not to eternal youth, but to eternal old age, and cheerfully ac-cepting and exploiting that doom. Mrs. Fennelly was far from being such an international go-getter. She was a dun-colored, shapeless little creature, with a collapsed bosom and a head that seemed always about to be tucked pro-tectively under a wing. Her wattled good looks were those of another century, and so was her scarcely audible voice, with its hint of some postbellum plantation baking in torpor under a brass-bright, steel-hard Carolina sun.

Meeting Mrs. Fennelly at a cocktail party in New York or Venice or Bar Harbor, you would think at once what an extremely nice old lady she was, and then you would think of some convenient excuse for having to move on.

What had you to say to each other, after all, once the indispensable topic of weather—very seasonable, very unseasonable—had been disposed of? If it was through Claire that you met Mrs. Fennelly, the auspices would be still less favorable; the pretty daughter would encourage you to believe, quite wrongly, that her mother was not merely old but senile. "Poor lamb!" Claire would say, leading you into the celebrated lemon-yellow, silk-walled dining room of the big old house facing Gramercy Park. "You see what comes of being treated like a member of the family? I've put you on Mother's left, but it won't be *too* bad—General Dodd, who adores Mother and is exactly her age, is on her right, and they'll be nattering away at each other from start to finish. Moreover, I've taken care to put the latest in blond bombshells on your other side. *Such* breasts, and they say she screws like a rabbit."

It will serve as a footnote to "rabbit" to mention that Claire was in the habit of describing all women under the age of thirty as bombshells and of endowing them with appetites as unappeasable as she liked you to assume hers were. In fact, her appetites were not all that urgent. Once you became her lover, it was startling to discover how easily she could be satisfied, with the supposed fierceness of her lust deteriorating, from one moment to the next, into girlish gratitude, complete even to a whispered "Thank you." For this reason, among others, few people ever slept with Claire for long. Her bitchy conversation contained more ardor than her slender, honey-colored candy bar of a body, and the best of her love-making might well consist, for you, of the provocativeness with which, on her first date with you, she lured you on and then refused you. She played to perfection the role of the lascivious puritan tease; the role of a pleasing pagan bed-companion appeared to be beyond her. Or so the common gossip went, and Claire was not above vouching for its truth. "I keep being told I'm absolutely rotten in bed," she would say, in her lovely voice. "I blame it on my terrible upbringing. The simplest things are coming to me last."

As for Mrs. Fennelly's mind in age, it was far from approaching dotage. Her responses in conversation were acute and fearless, and in the course of her incessant joustings with Claire and Nicky she gave as good as she got. Indeed, she often gave better, having the advantage over her daughter and grandson of so many more years in which to have mastered the ruthless tactics of the only child. She had been trained in a hard school, which is to say in no school at all. In the South, in the late nineties, Lily Larkin's adoring parents were quick to perceive that the quality of education available in the usual public and private schools could only harm their exquisite child; they chose to educate her at home, with the help of a succession of governesses and tutors—Fräulein this and Mademoiselle that, to teach her German and French (not to mention such skills as sewing a fine seam and painting admirable forget-me-nots upon porcelain), and an occasional itinerant professor so-and-so, to provide her with a smattering of history, mathematics, and philosophy. Lily never passed an hour in a classroom or schoolyard, never acquired a chum, never knew what it was to walk home from school through the autumn twilight, kicking at fallen leaves and holding hands with the person one loved best in all the world. She ought to have been a lonely little girl, but looking back upon those years Mrs. Fennelly would say that she remembered not a single unhappy moment. "My blessed mummy and daddy thought only of my good," she said. "I was raised in a house of love."

"You make it sound, dear Mother of mine," Claire said, "as if you had been born in a brothel."

When Mrs. Fennelly lost her temper, she took care to lower her voice. She said, "Your remarks are often less amusing than you suppose. If you were capable of being a fiftieth as devoted to Nicky as my parents were to me, Nicky would be a very happy child. And we know, do we not, that he is not a very happy child? And we know why?"

So little had Mrs. Fennelly missed, in youth, the rough-and-tumble of school life that she attempted to provide Claire with an upbringing identical to her own. But times had changed by the thirties; fewer governesses and tutors were prepared to give up their lives to little charges in great houses, and in the end Mrs. Fennelly decided to take Claire abroad. In Europe they would be able to locate suitable instructors on, so to speak, their home grounds, in settings that would be an education in themselves. Mrs. Fennelly was, besides, newly widowed, and Europe was the conventional solace of widows of wealth and breeding. There was another advantage to going to Europe, not to be spoken of before Claire. The late Mr. Fennelly was about to be the center of a scandal, and the farther away Mrs. Fennelly and Claire were when the scandal broke, the better. More than most widows, Mrs. Fennelly was eager to obliterate every memory of her husband. She had not much liked him in life, and she had found reason to dislike him intensely in death. Having no means of his own, the self-important little man had appeared content to live on an allowance granted him by Mrs. Fennelly from the ever-increasing resources of the Larkin estate. His contentment had been a deception. His heart and as much of his purse as he could manage had been elsewhere. For the payment of household expenses, the Fennellys had long made use of a joint checking account, and it turned out, upon Mr. Fennelly's unexpected death (he was stung by a bee, and the sting so frightened him that he suffered an immediate, fatal heart attack, keeling over without a word into a nearby rosebush), that he had been transferring thousands of dollars a year out of their joint account and into an account unknown to Mrs. Fennelly. It was an account that he had opened in the name of his mistress, also unknown to Mrs. Fennelly. When the family lawyers broke the news to Mrs. Fennelly that her late husband was not merely a thief but a philanderer, she was quick to act. She had his body exhumed from the Larkin family plot and placed in a plot at the farthest possible distance from it, in a section of the cemetery filled with nondescript newcomers; she then ordered the bill for the plot to be sent directly to the mistress. She swept Claire off to Paris, and when, from time to time, the child had occasion to speak of her father, Mrs. Fennelly would purse her lips and say, "That is a closed story." She was glad that she had trusted her feelings and behaved harshly toward the mistress. She believed in punishment, for herself and everyone. The only time her blessed daddy had ever whipped her, for some tiny transgression, she had felt an overwhelming gratitude to him. Afterward, how they had hugged each other!

Mrs. Fennelly and Claire spent several years abroad. Claire learned bits and pieces of four or five languages, speaking them mostly in the infinitive tense; she learned to cook a variety of national dishes, which soon converged into a single careless international approximation of shepherd's pie; and she learned exceptionally good manners. Unlike her mother, she collected plenty of chums, for the Fennellys moved from hotel to hotel in season, and hotels offer even greater opportunities for quick friendships and secret love affairs than boarding schools do. Claire had crushes on scores of girls, met in summer in the windy belly of some huge beached monster of a seaside hotel, or in winter by an open fire in the lobby of a dark Alpine inn. She would flirt with these gawky transient girls, using only her marvelous green eyes to make them want to touch her and be touched by her. The most satisfactory adventure was to bring them to the point of seduction without a word having been spoken; that way, one remained in jeopardy of rebuff up to the last possible moment. Claire liked, above all, to take chances; the greater the risk of failure, the more exhilarating one's success. The conquest of older girls was obviously more thrilling than the conquest of younger ones; it was, perhaps, in the course of making love to older girls that she acquired the habit of saying "Thank you" in that breathless, babyish voice. In her late teens, with reluctance, she began to save more and more of her love-making for men. It was men who tricked her into that unwelcome deprivation, by threats that she later discovered to be without substance. They were importunate lovers, greedy for their own good; what they wished to secure was immediate and uninterrupted possession of her. If only they had been content to have her without trafficking in her ignorance! Men, they said (speaking as if not for themselves, and yet claiming to speak for all men), would find her undesirable if it became known that she slept with women. For a time, she dared not disbelieve them, but soon enough she learned that the facts were otherwise: without exception, her sleeping with women excited men. Indeed, it often turned them into better lovers than they had hitherto known how to be; some silly schoolboy notion of the forbidden became their infallible aphrodisiac. Women lovers needed no hint of something illicit to arouse them; they sought from Claire what every lover seeks from another—to be the best beloved—and the sex of their rivals was a matter of indifference to them. Claire never forgave men for having lied to her at that critical moment in her life, and it may have been in part to avenge herself upon them that she would appear so ardent in the opening stages of a courtship and then prove so passive in the deed. When she boasted of being rotten in bed, it was men she was thinking of having disappointed and not women.

Nicky Gault, the third only child in the family, may well have wished to imitate his grandmother and mother in escaping school, but he was born too late. If times had changed between Mrs. Fennelly's generation and Claire's, they had changed even more between Claire's and Nicky's. It was no longer imaginable that a child should be educated at home; still more unimaginable if the child was a boy. Men had careers to achieve, and, in the Fennelly-Gault world of gentlemanly making good, a career began, not with the last school that one attended, but with the first. At six, Nicky entered Hubbard, the properest of the many proper schools for boys in New York. The school occupied a hideous yellow-brick building in the East Sixties, with a cagelike exercise yard on the roof and a smell of disinfectant in the tiled corridors that would always make Nicky feel slightly sick to his stomach. He was a good-looking little boy, very thin, with his father's large nearsighted dark eyes and dark hair and his mother's honey coloring. His grandmother feared that Nicky's slightness prefigured an eventual lack of height—how irritating it would be if that long-dead popinjay of a Fennelly grandfather had managed to impose his diminutive body on a grandson he had never seen! Though Nicky gave the impression of being highly intelligent, in his first tests he scored so badly that Mr. Phimister, headmaster of Hubbard, felt obliged to summon Claire to a grim early-morning discussion of the problem. From behind the usual clouds of pedagogical pipe smoke, he warned her that if Nicky were to prove incapable of measuring up to the high Hubbard standard, the just and merciful thing would be to remove him from the school as quickly as possible. "His is what I would describe as a borderline case," Phimister said, with the air of a man who has given considerable thought to the invention of the word "borderline." "But he's only six!" Claire cried, in her most enchanting voice. She had made up so prettily—and at such an hour—in order to please Phimister. She smiled radiantly at him, thinking, Ah, what a miserable, sexless little shit you are. Phimister said, "Here at Hubbard we don't think of six as all that young. We might have hoped to do a better job with Nicky if"—Phimister worked his hands, kneading an imaginary ball—"we'd had the shaping of the lad at four."

As things turned out, Nicky did well enough at Hubbard to be kept on, though he was never to do as well as was expected of him. From the start he was oppressed by a sense of being considered a failure even when, by the only standards known to him—Hubbard standards—he was a success: he got adequate grades, he played games well enough to get by without being scorned, he wrote an occasional article, no lumpier than those by his fellows, for the weekly school newspaper. He was a dutiful child but not a happy one. He wore a continuous, wary smile, listening to other boys' jokes with patience, and volunteering none of his own. On every term report, one or another of his teachers was sure to write "Always well prepared but seems unwilling to participate in impromptu discussions." Once or twice a year, the school psychiatrist would call him in for a chat. "Something of a loner, aren't you, Gault?" he would ask, giving the little boy—at eight, at ten!—the dignity of a manly last name.

"Sir?"

"Don't mix much with the other boys—that sort of thing?"

"Oh, I don't know, sir."

"Weekends, say—you go off to friends' houses? They come to yours?"

"Weekends, one day I go with my father and the other with Mother. Sometimes Dad takes a friend and me to a ball game."

A fresh tack, hoping to catch the boy off guard: "I hear you like snakes."

"Yes, sir, very much."

"You keep some as pets at home?"

"Not as pets, sir."

"Aha. I stand corrected. The scientific view. What do you feed them on?"

"Mice, sir."

"You raise mice, too?"

"Yes, sir."

"And what do you feed the mice on?"

"I try to give them a balanced diet."

"Healthy mice make healthy snakes, is that it? Ha, ha!"

The boy stared. The psychiatrist scribbled a note to himself: "Mutilated sense of humor. Perhaps a hint of latent autism here?" "How does your mother feel about having snakes around the house?"

"She doesn't mind."

"Sensible mother."

"Yes, sir. Is that all, sir?"

"Dear me, Gault, have I been keeping you from some more important engagement?" The psychiatrist gave a hearty laugh, but the most that the boy could provide in response was a wan smile. Rigid. Holding everything in. Oh, that damnable infantile anal retentiveness! How common it was among the rich! "Yes, yes, Gault, that'll be all for now." Scribble, scribble, scribble. "Have a good day!"

During Nicky's years at Hubbard, the family situation remained astonishingly stable: nobody was being born or dying, nobody was becoming very rich or very poor. Time passed with only the rudimentary punctuation of birthdays and holidays, and so seemed scarcely to pass at all. Mrs. Fennelly was entering her seventies—an age after which, for women, there is little medical or other reason that they should ever die. She spent much of the year on the old Larkin place in western North Carolina, surrounded by servants as old and liverish as herself, whom she bullied and who were quick to return her unkindnesses blow for blow. Having been divorced from Nicholas Gault the autumn that Nicky entered Hubbard, Claire bought the old Harlow house on Gramercy Park and spent several years contentedly reconstructing the interior and furnishing it with what she called "amusing bits," meaning the choicest of English and Irish eighteenth-century porters' chairs, hunt tables, partners' desks, and Chippendale wine coolers and knife boxes. Old silver, china, and pewter flowed in a glinting stream into Gramercy Park from London, Dublin, and Madison Avenue. Claire enjoyed living alone with Nicky in their huge, echoing doll's house, full of such charming toys. She liked being divorced and answerable to no one— liked it so much, indeed, that she came to like Nicholas Gault as well, thinking of him as the instrument of her freedom because he had consented to give her a divorce and forgetting that he had earlier been the instrument of her imprisonment in marriage. But, as to that, she believed the failure of the marriage to have been entirely her fault. She had married Nicholas in part because he had curly hair and skin that tasted like Necco wafers, and in part because he had so much wanted her to do so. He had been like a child in the touching pertinacity of his pleading. She ought not to have given in to him—to one as ready to experiment as she had always been, what could be so novel and compelling about the taste of Necco wafers? About simple begging? Especially since she was no longer a schoolgirl, no longer even a very young woman. She was thirty-one, and she had never been married. Well, and so there it was: that was, of course, the chief reason that she had married him. She had wanted the experience not so much of being married as of having been married. It was a relationship that she felt an intense curiosity about and not the least confidence in, and for all the interest she took in the marriage vows as she repeated them, they might have been in Choctaw. Thus it befell that Gault, believing himself to be the beneficiary of her kindness, became her victim. Four years later, she had Nicky, and again it was a question less of wanting a child than of wanting the sensation of having had a child. It was motherhood that she was determined to take the measure of before it was too late, as once she had been determined to take the measure of marriage. The defect of motherhood was that its consequences remained adamantly present, requiring to be dealt with, while marriage was but a piece of paper, canceled by a second piece of paper. She had been hard on Gault and she was often hard on Nicky; it took her a long time to forgive him for surviving the experiment in which he had played a leading role.

The years in Gramercy Park were the most tranquil of her life. She indulged herself to the full, aware that in doing so she greatly diminished her bitchiness. She was almost, she thought, conventionally nice. She stared at her image in the great gilt mirror above the drawing-room mantel. In the depths of the intricately carved frame of the mirror, elderly mandarins holding parasols sauntered through latticed pavilions, dreaming that they were butterflies. The mantel and mirror—all that survived of a red-brick Georgian house in the ferny depths of Sussex—had come up at auction in London, and Claire had outbid the richest shipping magnate in the world in order to make them hers. The gilded mandarins were her household gods. Merely to look at them made her feel as if something pleasing and entirely unexpected was just about to happen. Behind Claire's reflection in the dusk of the two-hundred-year-old glass lay reflected the drawing-room windows, and through the windows, still more duskily, could be glimpsed the reflected park, with its high black iron palings and green parterre. Claire bowed to her image among the mandarins, and said, "Well! So I am quite a nice person, after all!" Then she laughed aloud, delighted to have come without warning on this high opinion of herself.

Every summer, the three of them would travel abroad. Tirelessly, the ill-assorted little band rummaged about in the attic of Europe, seeking the ideal place in which to spend a holiday. There was certainly no chance that they would find it. Being so different in age and temperament and being, moreover, so eager to quarrel over any topic that came to hand, how likely was it that they would ever be willing to share a common opinion of a house, a town, a district, a country? That would be, for them, like playing tennis with the net down. Their purpose was not to find the ideal place to visit, but to dispose, one by one, of the ideal places suggested by others. Much of the relish that Mrs. Fennelly took in travel consisted of ridiculing what her friends had found reason to praise; for her part, Claire would side with the friends against her mother, while Nicky would weigh the advantages to him from moment to moment of siding now with his grandmother, now with his mother. It made an exhilarating game, in which sooner or later blood was sure to be drawn.

They traveled in style. On the earliest of their summer excursions, Mrs. Fennelly would have her Rolls shipped to some port convenient to their eventual destination, but as the number of ships crossing the Atlantic declined, it occurred to her that it would be wise to maintain two Rollses —one for use in the States, the other for use abroad. Bailey, her chauffeur, was shipped back and forth by air. A sullen, elderly black man, Bailey was indispensable to Mrs. Fennelly; she treated him like a slave and he responded like a slave, storing up his resentment of her possession of him to spend upon others. Summer after summer, Bailey managed to conduct the little party safely across Europe, speaking no language except English, and of English only a handful of curt words of abuse. In his hotel room at night, he would master the portion of the road map with which the following day's run would be concerned. Once under way, he would stop at intervals to check the route with passers-by. He would indicate with a finger on the map some sought-for village or town, and all he wished in reply was the passer-by's finger pointing in the correct direction. If, out of kindness, the passer-by attempted to add a few helpful words, Bailey would make a fist in his face. "No goddam foreigner goin' to give *me* shit!" he would say, and stalk back to the Rolls. Sometimes the passer-by would have an understanding of English and sometimes not; in any event, the sudden violence of the old man would sink uneasily into memory as something that might not actually have happened; perhaps the angry figure, so black inside his black uniform, had been only an apparition, created by some trick of summer heat and shimmering sunlight.

"What on earth did that rude man say to you?" Mrs. Fennelly would ask when Bailey got back in the car.

"Don't go givin' it a thought, ma'am," Bailey would say. "Veezelee, here we come!"

Fennelly, Gault & Son spent one of their summers in a high-roofed, ochre-colored villa on the Brenta Canal, a few miles from Venice. The exterior of the house had changed little since Palladio had designed it for a wealthy merchant family, some four hundred years earlier. A few bathrooms had been tucked here and there in the walls—when a toilet was flushed, pipes shuddered and snapped all over the house—and the lofty interiors were illuminated at night by dim, unshaded electric-light bulbs, which dangled at the ends of long cords in odd corners of the rooms, not because they were useful there, but because the ceiling had proved

easy to penetrate at those points. The canal in front of the
house had also scarcely changed in the course of time. It
had been known to stink in the sixteenth century, and it
certainly stank in the twentieth, when Mrs. Fennelly, Claire,
and Nicky made their way down the steps of the portico to
examine a dining terrace fashioned, a few years earlier, out
of an abandoned landing stage. In Palladio's day, the canal
had been full of flotsam that, being mostly of wood, soon
rotted away and sank from sight. The flotsam that Mrs.
Fennelly and her family observed was made of plastic and
remained immortally buoyant; syringes, fragments of
kitchen utensils, and chubby dolls' arms and legs bobbed in
the rushes along the banks of the canal. Handkerchiefs
pressed to their noses, the family agreed that it would not be
wise to risk eating out of doors. Instead, they took their
meals in a clammy basement dining room, with serpents of
punk burning in saucers along the floor to keep at bay
mosquitoes so big that by candlelight they cast shadows
like miniature aircraft up and down the table.

The villa on the Brenta was not a success. Mrs. Fennelly
was unable to imagine what her friends the Hetheringtons
had seen in the place, renting it year after year. Claire admitted that the house was inconvenient, the staff unmanage-
able, and the drive to Venice by way of Mestre suffocating,
but she liked the sense of being a part of ancient, prodigal,
sensuous Venice. "I am a red-haired courtesan," she said.
"I have a lovely big bosom out of Veronese. A dozen
swarthy lovers wait to leap into my bed and suck my
nipples. I sell my favors to the highest bidder."

"No doubt you would have enjoyed a great success," her
mother said. "Your gifts lie in a different direction from
mine."

A disappointment equal to that of the Palladian villa con-
fronted them one summer in Norway, where, in the mountains some two hours' drive from Oslo, they rented an
estate that had been laid out to resemble an eighteenth-
century village. A dozen or so log farmhouses and barns
had been plucked from sites farther up in the mountains and
scattered as if at random on a grassy hillside looking out
over a lake as blue as Como. The owner of the estate, a rich
American of Norwegian descent, had taken care to equip
the buildings with the latest in heating and plumbing; one
could be very snug under those quaint sod roofs, one could
sweat in luxury in the ancient, electrified sauna. The estate
had at least one advantage over the villa on the Brenta; there
were no mosquitoes, perhaps because the temperature remained at an arctic level throughout their stay. There were
also no neighbors, and this was not an advantage. Except
for the servants on the property, it appeared that the entire
district was without human life—indeed, without life of any
kind. From the pretty flowered terrace, nothing could be
seen to move anywhere in the vast prospect of fields and
birchwood and sky. No sailboat ever broke the smooth surface of the lake; its waters were so icy that anyone falling
into them would survive for fifteen minutes at most. Goats
and cows roamed at will somewhere on the mountains that
rose behind the estate, but even they could not be seen and
patted into neighborly tameness; the constant far-off tinny
clanking of bells heightened the lonely look of the nearby
empty pastures. The servants, who spoke no English, kept
to themselves. Claire gave them instructions with the help of
an English-Norwegian dictionary; they were eager to please,
but she understood not a word they said to her in their
harsh seesaw tongue. Bailey sat among them at night,

drinking aquavit and abusing them with sour gusto. He would roar at them that they were a bunch of goddam low-life blond blue-eyed bastards, and they would smile and fill his glass. He was the first black they had ever seen, and they found him charming.

Mrs. Fennelly recalled that the people who had recommended the estate had described it with rapture as "unspoiled." Glaring down the hillside toward the exquisite, unusable lake, Mrs. Fennelly said, "A place that has nothing in it capable of being spoiled is not entitled to be called unspoiled. It is time we made other plans." She and Claire quarreled over which of them had first proposed renting the estate; Nicky sided with Claire in putting the blame on Mrs. Fennelly, who retired to her bedroom in tears. Claire lay in the sauna, letting her body bake as she idly made love to it. Nicky was of an age to be engaged in sexual adventures of his own; no doubt the sauna served him as it did her, as a secret, makeshift, personal trysting place. The three of them bickered at dinner over where they might go next. Bailey could drive them to the airport at Oslo, then take the Rolls on, by ship, to some handy port in southern Europe. They heard Bailey ranting away drunkenly in the kitchen; for his sake as well as theirs, they must make good their escape as soon as possible. Claire put in a call to an old lover of hers, who lived on a big farm near Málaga. He had often invited her to come and stay with him *en famille*. Their affair had taken place many years earlier, and it was rare for them nowadays to make love; it would certainly be no hardship to them to be merely devoted friends for as long as her mother and son were with them. She made it a rule not to mingle her sex life and her family life, especially during the weeks of the long summer holiday. She had tried that ex-

43

periment once or twice in the past, with unlucky results. Claire's old lover was delighted to hear from her. They must come to Málaga at once. The house was full of delightful people. There was a cottage on the grounds that would be exactly right for them. There was even a cottage for Bailey and a shed for the Rolls. How old was the boy by now? Thirteen? He would enjoy the tennis court, the Ping-Pong tables, the swimming pool. There were bridge players and backgammon players for her mother—she was please to give his affectionate regards to the old bitch. As for Claire, he would make love to her all night. No? Not the way it was going to be this time? Very well, he would keep on the girl with whom he had been consoling himself all summer. She could neither read nor write—at any rate, he had no evidence that she could do so—but she had an incomparable body. Every inch of it was covered with almost invisible golden down, which here and there became fleece. Delectable. Claire would have to see for herself. He would expect them within twenty-four hours.

Off they went, joyously squabbling, their threatened summer restored to promise.

Mrs. Fennelly at eighty, though to the casual eye she might look as well as ever, saw signs that age was nicking away at her. She felt changes of temperature more than she used to, and would carry a shawl with her even in the hottest weather. She had no use for the findings of medical science and all the fiddle-faddle of statistics—she knew for a certainty that drafts and wet feet gave her colds. For that reason, and therefore not alone because she enjoyed disagreeing with Claire, she expressed grave doubts about an adventure that Claire was eager to have them undertake.

44

From some new acquaintance at a dinner party, Claire had got wind of a marvelous old house in the west of Ireland, and with her usual headlong enthusiasm, she was bound that Mrs. Fennelly, Nicky, and she should spend a month's holiday there. In a querulous voice, Mrs. Fennelly wanted to know if it wasn't the case that it did nothing but rain in Ireland. She would come down with rheumatism, sure as fate; it was in the family.

"Mother, what nonsense! There's lovely sun."

As to the prevalence of rain or sun in Ireland, Claire knew no more than her mother. But their ignorance was a point in favor of the adventure; Ireland was one of the few countries left in Europe that neither Claire nor her mother had ever visited. It was time that they got it under their belts. People were constantly raving about how pretty and little visited it was, especially in the West Country; this was Mrs. Fennelly's golden opportunity to discover that people were wrong and tell them so. Moreover, Nicky at fifteen had added to his passion for snakes a passion for horses. It was unfortunate that, according to legend, there were no snakes in Ireland, but there were certainly tens of thousands of horses. Where could one hope to ride better? If the boy behaved well, perhaps Claire might buy him a hunter there.

Ireland had still another claim upon them. For the first time in all their holidays, this summer Nicky was to be supplied with a companion, and the companion's preferences would have to be taken into consideration. The companion had been selected at the request—indeed, at the express command—of tiresome little Mr. Phimister and his no less tiresome colleague, the school psychiatrist. According to them, Nicky's tendency to be a loner had increased to an alarming degree. Unless the tendency was checked and reversed, the consequences might well be dire. Nicky must be brought out of himself at all costs, and this was unlikely to happen as long as he was obliged to spend another summer in the company of—Mr. Phimister broke off, knocking the dottle from his pipe into the palm of one hand. Mrs. Fennelly was a most remarkable lady, and Mr. Phimister would yield to no one in his admiration for her, but she *was* eighty, was she not? And Claire herself, again not to put the matter too bluntly, was, was she not . . . ? The dottle was deftly transferred from hand to wastepaper basket. Mr. Phimister put it to Claire that the ideal companion for Nicky would be some extroverted, healthy young athlete, a few years older than Nicky, whom he could look up to and emulate. There were hundreds of such splendid young men studying on scholarships in colleges throughout the country; they would like nothing better than to spend a holiday in Europe and at the same time pick up a few hundred dollars in much-needed cash. Claire had only to drop a note to the proper party at Harvard, Princeton, or wherever she pleased, and arrange a few interviews. From the point of view of the Hubbard School, it would be helpful if the companion were able to tutor Nicky in geometry and English, but the emphasis must be upon his personality—sunny, outgoing, energetic. Claire regarded Mr. Phimister with astonishment. What on earth, she wondered, did that little gray slug know of sunlight, except to scuttle out of it?

Following Mr. Phimister's instructions, Claire conducted several interviews, one of which proved highly successful. The interview took place in the small study off the drawing room in the house on Gramercy Park. The candidate was a twenty-year-old undergraduate at Yale named John Kelly. What an amusing name, Claire thought—it will hold its ground ably enough against Nicky's formidable Nicholas Van Sinderen Gault IV. He was a sturdy young man, with light-blue eyes, curly black hair, and a snub nose, which even now (for the season was early spring) had a surprising patch of sunburn at its very tip. Claire and John Kelly sat alone in the cozy little room, over tea and sandwiches, and of course she could not resist flirting with him. She lay back in depths of flowered chintz, behind the winking tea things, and smiled up at him through a scrim of cigarette smoke. Perhaps the smoke would serve to take a few years off her age; no doubt John thought of her as being a hundred. "You're never called Jack?"

"No, ma'am."

"You must surely be Irish, with that coloring?"

"Yes, ma'am."

"Lots of brothers and sisters?"

"That, too."

"Where do you come in the family?"

"Three older, three younger."

"Oh, God! That doesn't give you claustrophobia?"

"No, I like it."

"Ever been to Ireland?"

"Never been out of this country."

"Do you think you might find it amusing to spend a month there?"

"Sounds great."

"You might even discover a long-lost Kelly cousin or two, tucked away under a hedge somewhere."

"That'd be great, too."

Plainly, conversation was not going to prove John's strong point, and he was unlikely to prove, even on the most innocent level, an easy conquest, but his credentials in respect to geometry, English, and disposition were impeccable. Nicky liked him at once, which is to say that he volunteered afterward that John was O.K.; it was as much praise as Nicky bestowed on anyone. John and Nicky met in the study, formally shaking hands and staring each other in the eye. As they exchanged the wary monosyllables of the young, it became obvious that they would get on better without the burden of Claire's presence. She excused herself and from her bedroom put in a call to her mother in North Carolina. "My dear, our problems are solved. I've found the most darling boy for Nicky. *Very* straight arrow and with the nicest blue eyes. And there is only one condition to his coming with us—a pleasant condition, almost an omen. He's Irish, and it turns out that he had already set his heart on catching a glimpse of his ancestral domain this summer."

"You must have put him up to it."

"Never said a word! What a suspicious nature you have."

"It will rain every day."

"The sun will shine. John Kelly says so."

"Is that the young man's name? You know I don't like Irish names." And with reason: the name Fennelly could only be Irish, and one of the many things for which Mrs. Fennelly would never forgive her cockalorum of a husband was his causing her to lose her maiden name, almost as precious to her as her virginity. Lily Larkin was so charming, all honeysuckle and camellias; Lily Fennelly might have been the daughter of some coarse immigrant family, newly come upon its lace curtains and not yet at ease with them.

The European Rolls, having wintered in the south of France, was shipped by sea to Ireland. As for Bailey, he was shipped by air from North Carolina, and when the little party of four arrived at Shannon, there he stood at the airport exit, growling and content. For to Bailey's relief there was much to grumble at in Ireland: having to drive on the left-hand side of the road; having to drive on roads that were far too narrow and abruptly winding for a Rolls; having to drive among a people who appeared to favor fowl over cattle, cattle over pedestrians, and pedestrians over motorists. He would be able to be in radiant bad temper from morning to night, with the advantage of there being always a pub at hand, with an assured audience of morose and mostly silent listeners.

They drove up through mild Clare, sea-green Galway, the heights of Connemara. A mist hung over the stony fields, and the sun seemed always upon the brink of bursting forth, but it never did. Ireland was a tiny country of immense distances; everything was much farther away than Bailey's road maps indicated, because of the difficulty of the terrain. From time to time, they stopped by the wayside for a thermos of tea and some Boland biscuits. In the distance, an arm of the Atlantic, pewter-colored; nearby, a thread of smoke from a turf fire smoldering in some hidden cottage. Mrs. Fennelly held out a hand from under her shawl; acidly, she affirmed that she felt raindrops. Claire called attention to the fact that her body was casting a shadow on the graveled roadway; ergo, the sun must be out. Nicky refrained from taking sides in these trifling disputes. They had lost their savor for him, largely because he was so busy imitating John. Meanwhile, Bailey would take advantage of the recess to stalk off into the bracken to relieve himself. With every year, the frequency with which he performed this errand increased and the trouble he took to disguise its purpose diminished. More than once, Mrs. Fennelly had to complain that he was not only visible but audible. "Farther, Bailey, farther!" she would call out to him, in a shrill, birdy voice, and Bailey, legs spread, would roar back with relish over his shoulder, "Too late, ma'am, too late!"

John was everything that Mr. Phimister could have wished—sunny, outgoing, and a coiled spring for energy. He was a natural athlete, unhappy only when he was obliged to sit still. While others rested, he was busy doing knee bends and sit-ups and push-ups. Though he enjoyed all sports, basketball was his favorite. Whenever the family stopped for tea, John jumped from the car and started jogging, Nicky at his side. As he jogged, John would dribble an imaginary basketball in front of him or between his legs, then suddenly break away and start shooting hoops in the direction of an adjacent tree—*swish! swish!*—the imaginary ball never so much as touching the rim of the imaginary basket. In a makeshift form of fox-and-hounds, John and Nicky would see how far ahead of the Rolls they could run in the course of a tea recess; their reward would be the astonishment of Bailey and the ladies over the distance they invariably managed to cover. As the boys would come into sight far along the road, Mrs. Fennelly would say, "I hope that boy isn't exhausting poor Nicky. John is built like a truck, Nicky a watch. The difference could be very dangerous."

"You and your imagination of disaster! It never sleeps."

"My father had a very weak heart when he was still only in his twenties."

"Grampa lived to be seventy-four."

"But, then, he always took such wonderful care of himself."

Bailey would stop the car and the boys would tumble joyously aboard. "My dear young heroes," Claire would say, "you smell like a locker room at Yankee Stadium." John would look abashed and Nicky proud. Irritated with Claire—sweat was not a permissible topic of conversation —but seeking to achieve the last word, Mrs. Fennelly would address herself to her grandson: "How your mother can know what such a locker room smells like is her secret."

The demesne of Plumes lay a few miles south of Sligo. It occupied most of a long peninsula that ran far out into the Atlantic, with sandy beaches along its sheltered southern front and with steep, rocky cliffs to the north, where the great storms broke in winter, sending icy sea spray hundreds of yards inland. Between the Gothic cottage that served as a gatehouse on the public highway and the mansion overlooking the sea was a weedy ribbon of drive, perhaps five miles in length. Once, the drive had run pleasantly enough among open fields and meadows, but early in the nineteenth century some hard-pressed ancestral Merriot, hoping to recoup the family fortune, had gambled what little remained of the fortune upon the planting of conifers— hundreds of acres of pines and firs, for which, he imagined, his descendants would bless him as they drew a splendid annual income from the wise harvesting of timber. Nothing of the sort had happened, or was likely to happen, and if the ancestor was thought of at all, it was in order that his name be damned, not praised. From one generation of Merriots to the next, the plantations had been savagely ransacked for the payment of damages in some intolerable lawsuit or other (the Merriots had been famously litigious) and were now left to grow untended. Winter gales blew down uncounted thousands of trees, which, labor being unavailable to salvage them, were left to rot on the ground; subsequently, fires would break out in the dead timber and spread into neighboring stands of living trees. The present generation of Merriots had no money with which to put the plantations in order. They could only shake their fists in despair over the wild growth that kept stealthily creeping in upon the main house. By now, even on the brightest days the towering firs cast a darkness downward over the lawn, upward against the sky, filling the air with a palpable green gloom.

Claire had taken care to telephone Plumes the day before, announcing their imminent arrival, and Major Merriot had seemed to say most heartily—the connection was bad—that everything would be in readiness for them. The arrangements for a month's rental of Plumes had been notably informal, Major Merriot being loath to put anything in writing and being, it appeared, equally loath to read what anyone else had put in writing. Weeks passed before a letter from Claire would receive an answer, and then the answer was likely to be but a word or two scrawled in whatever empty space the Major had managed to find at the bottom of Claire's letter: "Good." "Will see to." "July 10th will be excellent."

As the Rolls made its way through the demesne of Plumes, rocking like a Spanish caravel whenever it struck a rut or bump—"God*dam* this road," Bailey exclaimed, "shaking my poor old baby to pieces!"—Mrs. Fennelly observed that the outlook struck her as distinctly Carpathian. "It would come as no surprise to me," she said, "if Major Merriot should turn out to be a lineal descendant of Count Dracula."

"Ah, Nicky! John!" Claire said. "Wouldn't that be lovely?

A vampire instead of a leprechaun?" It was not much of a joke, and she told it as much for her own sake as for theirs; she was trying to keep her spirits up. This Irish adventure, if it failed, would be known to have been entirely her fault.

The drive ran up a gradual slope between the dark firs and came out upon a paved courtyard directly in front of an immense pile of reddish-gray stone—a somber eighteenth-century mansion, with a lichenous portico and upwards of a hundred small-paned windows placed at regular intervals along its gaunt façade. Seated on the broad front steps, ruffling the neck of an Irish wolfhound, was a slender, middle-aged man in a Norfolk jacket. The jacket was of a color that almost matched the house, and the tweed had plainly been woven for him with that match in mind. The man stood up as the Rolls swung round in front of him, and it had scarcely come to a stop before he opened the rear door, bowed, and said with a smile, "Merriot here. Welcome to Plumes!"

"How kind of you," said Mrs. Fennelly in her coldest tone. She deduced at once that Major Merriot was a charmer, and she had no intention of being charmed by him. Claire, of course, given her tastes, might be in his bed within a week. "This is my daughter, Mrs. Gault, with whom you have corresponded," Mrs. Fennelly said. "My grandson, Nicky. Our friend John Kelly. And this is Bailey."

"Good Irish names," said the Major, unaware that he had struck an ideally unsuitable note.

In haste, protectively, Claire said, "What a beautiful place!" (Her heart sinking: it was not in the least beautiful.) "I had no idea of its size."

Merriot spoke in short bursts, not unlike his writing. "Far too big. The staff complains. Not, however, I trust, to you."

He gestured vaguely toward the nearby woods. "My wife and I. In a cottage yonder. During the course of your stay." He drew a long breath. His garrulousness had evidently exhausted him. "Will be available to help you in any way." Merriot led the way up the broad steps to the open front door. In front of them glimmered in its own marbly dusk a vast three-story-high hall. On the stone flags of the courtyard behind them, as Bailey began the familiar task of unloading the Rolls, they heard the first patterings of rain.

Nothing about Plumes was as Claire had imagined it would be. A sunny Georgian mansion set among smooth green lawns, with a blue sea at the foot of the garden—that had been her Plumes, the Plumes she had sketched with delight for her mother and son in the months before their arrival, and the reality was hard to adjust to. The house was a tomb, and not alone because of the hollowness of the family's footfalls along the paved corridors, or the sound of their voices echoing bleakly in the high-ceilinged rooms; it was a tomb also in the scantiness of its furnishings. In their daily explorations, they were astonished to discover that, although the six bedrooms at their disposal held a sufficient quantity of beds, chests, chairs, and dressing tables, the remaining twenty-odd bedrooms had long since been stripped to the walls; tatters of draperies hung at the permanently shuttered windows, and the dainty paw marks of innumerable generations of mice were etched in the dust of the bare floors. Of the big downstairs rooms, the drawing room, the dining room, the library, the billiard room, and the so-called morning room were still habitable, as was the shadowy enfilade of kitchen, butler's pantry, scullery, laundry, and storage rooms that made up the service wing,

but the ballroom, which had most of a wing of the house to
itself, and a dozen or more other rooms intended for entertainment were carpetless, pictureless, and without a stick
of furniture—grand, desolate chambers, with crystal chan-
deliers bagged in rotting muslin, waiting in vain in a continuous twilight throughout the years for doors to be flung
open and crowds of merrymakers to come tumbling through.
How many years they had waited thus only Horne, the grave,
elderly butler, could tell with precision. Major Merriot had
been selling off family things from the very day that he came
into possession of his inheritance at the age of twenty-one,
and Horne reckoned that that event had taken place thirty-
four years and seven months earlier. Horne himself had been
among the family things that the Major had inherited, and
by now he was much more nearly the archivist and historian
of Plumes than a mere keeper of its keys. Horne and Bailey
would sit for hours in a grottolike basement room beneath
the kitchen, looking out through barred windows onto a
sunken areaway high with weeds and mossy refuse. They
would face each other at a deal table, with a bottle of whiskey between them, and exchange tales of their long lifetimes
of enslavement. Horne was happy to say that the Major had
been the best of masters, and Bailey was happy to say that
Mrs. Fennelly had been the worst of mistresses. Each took
pleasure in the other's unfamiliar mode of viewing things—
Horne startled Bailey with his genuine pride in Plumes and
the long, sad Merriot history, and Bailey startled Horne
with his affectation of contempt for the human race in general and for his crosspatch employer in particular. Over the
whiskey, they became in a short while fast friends. They
were the same age, and they were lonely. By the time a
bottle of the Irish was finished of a late summer's evening,

they were, though they didn't know it, as near as might be in each other's arms.

The family's explorations of the house were a necessity laid upon them by the weather. No outdoor activity was possible in the days following their arrival at Plumes, for the rain that had begun falling as they entered the house continued to fall without intermission from that moment forward. Its persistence was uncanny. Day after day, they woke to a slur of rain washing, not in rivulets, but in ropes of water down the panes of their bedroom windows. Winds from far out in the Atlantic shook the wet ivy that gripped the house; from time to time, an unusually strong gust of wind would force its way down a flue and send smoke curling out into the room, a wraith that smelled of both sea and fire. Mrs. Fennelly and Claire were served breakfast in bed by a stout housemaid named Agnes, distinguished for tiny, red-rimmed eyes and a mountainous disarray of gray, brown, and yellow hair. Nicky and John took breakfast in the dim nave of the dining room, perched on chairs— wivern-backed, lion-footed—worthy in scale of a race of giant kings. Horne encouraged them to consume large quantities of oatmeal, eggs, bacon, coarse brown bread, and milk, on the grounds, repeated every morning, that they were growing boys. (Orange juice was unknown at Plumes. "There were orange trees in the conservatory when I was a lad," Horne said. "They were meant to be looked at, not squeezed.") Bailey ate his breakfast in the kitchen, within arm's reach of the immense stove upon which the cook, Mrs. Begley, kept several iron pots simmering all day over tremulous coals—one for porridge, one for water for tea, and one for soup, which, though its flavor altered but little from day to day, every day on the handwritten menu prepared by Horne bore a different name. Horne, Mrs. Begley, and Agnes were all that remained of the large indoor staff that had once filled the attic of Plumes. The other two members of the present indoor staff were maids of perhaps half Agnes's weight and years. They were flibbertigibbets who refused to live in. They preferred cycling over from a nearby village, and the hours they kept were so unreliable that debates about them provided the main topic of conversation belowstairs. "Listen whilst I give those two tarts a piece of my mind," Horne would say to Bailey, and without putting it into so many words he would succeed in expressing his conviction that at least once upon every journey to and from Plumes the girls were off their bicycles and under a hedge with some lustful lout of a farmer's son. The girls accepted his reproofs like praise; better than anyone, they knew that they were virgins and that all night in their movie-riddled dreams they burned with longing not to be.

Nowadays, the outdoor staff consisted of a gardener and a groom. Such lawn as the forest had not yet invaded the gardener kept in rough order with a cumbersome horse-drawn mower, which clanked and whimpered and chewed at the grass instead of cutting it. The groom was on hand to attend to the horse and to observe with resignation that his neglect of his duties had caused fifteen of the sixteen box stalls of the stables to be sealed off with cobwebs; heavy with dust, the webs ran from post to post and in them hung the withered corpses of hundreds of long-dead spiders and their uneaten prey. Nicky and John were hopeful that, if the weather were ever to clear, a couple of horses could be rented from some fox-hunting farmer in the neighborhood. The Major, on one of his earliest visits to the house, had assured them that there would be. No difficulty. In that department. So the groom had been ordered to prepare two box stalls for occupancy and to lay in fresh straw and feed. It was the first strenuous work he had been called upon to perform in a decade; daily, he pointed out that stable dust was well known to give him asthma and that many a good man with asthma had waked up one morning to find himself dead.

Until the horses could be brought in, Nicky and John contented themselves with devising a variety of indoor games. The billiard room became their sports center. Here, for an hour every morning, they jogged in place, did push-ups, and Indian-wrestled on the threadbare carpet, out of which from time to time emerged a startled moth. When they took off the cover of the pool table, they discovered that the green felt surface had sprouted spores from dampness. Perhaps the spores were the beginnings of mushrooms, perhaps not; the naturalist in Nicky gave way to the games player in John, and with one of Mrs. Begley's scrub brushes they swept the felt so clear of growth that in places the slate bed of the table was unexpectedly exposed. Balls and cues were found and a pool tournament was organized, in which the Major, Horne, Bailey, John, and Nicky were participants. Only the Major had ever played pool before, and he had not played in thirty years. With his usual competitiveness, John spent hour after hour in hard practice and acquired sufficient skill within a week to outscore the Major. Nicky was beside himself with pride in John's victory, and the Major appeared not to take his humiliation too much to heart. "Very good show," he said, shaking John's hand. "Thank you, sir," John said, with an embarrassed air. He was sorry to have beaten an older man, but he would have been sorrier still to have been beaten by him. For John, winning was the first rule of life; he was sometimes impatient with Nicky for not seeming to recognize a rule so obvious and so easy to follow.

"Somebody has to lose," Nicky would say, and John would reply at once, "Yes, but not you, not me! Losers are dead and they don't even know it."

Nicky thought otherwise, but he loved John too much to say so. Because it was the first time he had been in love, he couldn't be sure how far one was allowed to go in the matter of disagreements. He would have to find his way. It appeared that everything about the feeling of loving somebody included having to find one's way from one treacherous moment to the next. And this made one happy, as the solving of any difficult puzzle does. As for John, if he happened to notice that Nicky loved him, he never gave a sign. There had always been Nickys who looked up to him and loved him, and there always would be. It was something no more remarkable to him than the sweetness of the air he breathed.

Major Merriot was a small, shapely man, with graying hair and a limp—the result, so Horne had informed them, of a fall from a horse many years earlier. The old injury gave the Major no pain, except in winter, but it made it impossible for him to wander long distances about the countryside, as he had once liked to do. He had made Horne his companion in those days; they had had high old times together. Nicky asked Horne what it was that the Major *did,* and Horne replied, "He is a gentleman." That, Nicky saw, sufficed. It was after his accident that the Major had married. The girl was a cousin of his, daughter of an invalid parson in a neighboring parish. *Those* Merriots, Horne indicated with some delicacy, were even poorer than the Merriots of Plumes, who were *the* Merriots. With still more delicacy, Horne indicated that the Major must have been hoping for an heir, but nothing of the kind had occurred. A painful subject. On the Major's death, Plumes would pass to a nephew, a brilliant young man who, thanks be to God, not only cherished Plumes but was also doing very well in a big bank in London. The lad knew where his responsibilities lay. Fifty years from now, Horne said, his old face alight, Plumes would again be the finest holding in all of the West Country, from Donegal to Galway Bay.

In the first few days of the family's stay at Plumes, the Major was reluctant to make frequent visits to the house. Claire asked him to bring his wife round for cocktails a day or so hence, and at first he demurred. "Mustn't be underfoot, you know. Your house now." Still, he accepted the invitation when Claire proffered it for the third time— "My wife says you're extremely kind. We don't get to see. As many people as we ought. For her sake, you know. She's very young." Promptly at six, he and his wife were ushered into the morning room by Horne. "Major and Mrs. Merriot," Horne said gravely, as if he had never laid eyes on them before.

Kate Merriot was small like her husband, but with ample flesh on her bones; her body moved freely inside a trifle of a dress, offering itself to the world as if unclothed, and she shook hands with vigor. Claire had learned from Horne that Mrs. Merriot was twenty years younger than her husband, which is to say that she must be somewhere in the middle thirties; even for a woman of that age she looked exceptionally young. The Major was all self-effacing decorum; his charm lay in part in his being so difficult to confront head on. One pursued him and made him turn round and give one the benefit of those shy, unprovokable brown eyes. His wife was insouciant. Her grace as she swung round the room, openly sizing up her new acquaintances, made a pleasing demand on one's attention. How she must have rejoiced to escape the invalid parson! Liking her at once, Claire said, "We're making your morning room into our morning-noon-and-night room. We find it so much cozier here than in the drawing room."

"Ah, but this is where *we* live, too, don't we, love?" Kate Merriot said. "It's why the chairs are all sat out and the sofa springs so disgustingly disemboweled."

"Very hard use. The furniture gets," said her husband, with a glance toward Mrs. Fennelly. He would not wish her upset by the vividness of his wife's figures of speech.

No fear—something about the Merriots had put Mrs. Fennelly in a good mood. She had held them somehow to blame for the weather and the chill with which she was threatened, but she sensed now that they, too, were victims and would always take her side. She said, "It's a charming room. Once upon a time, it must have enjoyed a delightful view of the sea."

"The view's still there but for those rotten damn trees," Kate said.

For that was the pity of it: the house had been sited to face the illimitable Atlantic, and now it faced only a nearby scruffy growth of seventy-year-old poplars. The sea view from the morning room had once been thought especially fine; early nineteenth-century travelers in Ireland had given the room and the view a certain celebrity. The room was lit by a semicircular bay in the Gothic style. Six

61

pointed windows looked out over a graveled terrace to the poplars, whose highest branches were alive with rooks, damnably cawing. The embrasure of the bay was a step above the rest of the room and had something of the air of a memorial chapel in some tiny country church. On seeing it, Claire's first thought was that it was in want of an altar; characteristically, she then thought that it would prove the ideal place in which to install a bar. With her gift for improvising much out of little, that afternoon she helped John and Nicky carry in from the laundry an old flatiron-scarred wooden table, which she covered with a bed sheet that fell on all four sides to the floor. On the table she placed a dozen or so bottles, a couple of silver shakers, some silver candlesticks, an ice bucket, and a score of gleaming, assorted tumblers and goblets and wine glasses. The fire on the hearth at one side of the room cast a yellow glow into the depths of the silver and glassware in the embrasure; more light fell into their depths from the candles on the bar itself. Standing in the room, one looked past the place of libation, winking with reflected firelight and candlelight, out into the cold rain that marched in slanting pencil strokes across the lawn and pelted the windows, and one felt as snug and warm and safe as if one were in the cabin of some stout ship at sea.

Kate clapped her hands in admiration. "Ah, how lovely, how *reassuring* that bar is! Why did we never think, Richard, trolls that we are, of inventing such a thing?"

"Haven't the touch," said the Major. "One has to have. The touch."

Kate said, "If I were a goddess, I'd bathe there naked in a tub of vodka, thumbing my nose at the world."

"My wife can say," said the Major to Mrs. Fennelly, "extraordinary things."

"You'd catch your death," said Mrs. Fennelly, that sensible woman, tightening her shawl about her shoulders.

Reaching up, Kate took John's face between her hands and gave it a close scrutiny. "You're as Irish as Paddy's pig," she said. "I hope you'll like it here."

"We're having a great time," John said, feeling his cheeks ablaze against the smoothness of her palms. "Aren't we, Nicky?" It was a cry for help, John's first cry, and Nicky said, "Let's you and me go get some Cokes." He tugged at John's sleeve and began to draw him backward out of the room.

Claire said, "Dear John—be an angel and bring us back some cheese and biscuits?" With the boys still within earshot, to the Merriots she added, "Adorable boy! My Nicky worships him."

Nicky ought to have been furious with his mother for telling the truth to strangers and therefore seeming to value the truth so lightly, but instead he felt grateful: more important to him than anything else was to hear the words spoken that he could not speak himself. He hoped that John had heard them and would let him know—oh, sometime, somewhere!—that he had heard.

"These days, being so poor, we drink mostly wine," Kate said, "but I dote upon spirits. Gin—oh, God, what bliss!" She held a bottle aloft, turning it round in the candlelight. "Richard, love, I'm going to ask Mrs. Gault to make me a Martini and so must you."

Claire said, "Just what I was planning to make for Mother and me. Major, why don't you do the honors for all four of us?"

"Very glad to," said the Major, "but you Americans." He gestured apologetically toward Mrs. Fennelly; what a blithering idiot he was! He took pains to speak slowly in order not to make clumsy errors, and yet he always made them. Not for the world would he wish Mrs. Fennelly to suppose that he thought of her first as an American and then as an individual. "Have very different ideas. To ours, about proportions."

"When we were married, Richard used to make Martinis two to one. Perhaps it was that and not poverty that caused us to try wine instead."

Claire caught Kate's eye; at that instant they were ready to form a secret society, the sole purpose of which would be to play agreeable pranks on the world. The society would have but two members. "This first time," Claire said, "let me make us all a nice American Martini. Next time, we'll ask you, Major, to make us a nice Irish one."

"Now, Claire!" said Mrs. Fennelly. She recognized a note of exultation in Claire's voice that in the past had often spelled danger. It was Mrs. Fennelly's guess that the Major was somehow in need of protection and that it might be up to her to provide it. She had grossly misread his character at their first meeting and was therefore in debt to him. He was anything but the professional charmer she had taken him to be; his charm had a fear of failure in it —had, like his leg, suffered some irremediable injury, which had kept him from ever venturing as far afield as he may have wished to go. That could have been one of the reasons for his marrying his cousin—a course that Mrs. Fennelly regarded as always most unwise. The cases she could cite in Carolina! She saw that within a week Claire would be infatuated with Mrs. Merriot and would not rest until Mrs. Merriot was infatuated with her. For once, Claire's headlong ways left Mrs. Fennelly unperturbed. Those two could take care of themselves; she would have no quarrel with

Claire as long as the Major remained content. "I warn you, Major Merriot," Mrs. Fennelly said, "my daughter is an unscrupulous woman. It amuses her to get people drunk."

"People get themselves drunk, Mother, as you very well know. The Major looks as if he must be every bit as well disciplined as you." On her way to the bar, Claire had the temerity to clap the Major lightly on the shoulder. A sisterly gesture, though Mrs. Fennelly, observing it, feared otherwise. Well! she thought, but I, too, have my weapons; no one shall take advantage of him in my presence.

Mrs. Fennelly had no reason to worry; it struck Claire as inconceivable now that when she had begun corresponding with Major Merriot over the rental of Plumes she had speculated on whether the man who wrote such curious, crabbed replies to her inquiries might prove worthy of having an affair with. She stood beside Kate at the bar, pouring gin into one of the shakers. All that she had learned in life so far was that the world was full of wonders and that one was constantly tempted to underestimate their number. She had flung herself into dozens of affairs, fearing always, and always falsely, that her share of the world's wonders was just about to be used up. She had the feeling that the woman beside her knew more about the infinity of wonders in the world than she did, and more, too, about how capriciously they were distributed—Kate, buried here in the west of Ireland, while she, Claire, had the run of every city on earth! She permitted a tincture of vermouth to fall into the shaker and then filled it with ice. She could sense Kate's eyes studying her hands as she worked, and for a moment it appeared possible—no; certain: oh, Christ, make it certain—that Kate would bend over and kiss them. Claire's hands trembled, waiting. She picked up the shaker

65

and swung it slowly back and forth like a censer; the silvery surface grew fogged with cold. Four stemmed glasses, she thought, dismissing the fantasy of her kissed hands. Ice in the glasses. If indeed it had been a fantasy. Four strips of lemon peel. She emptied the ice from the glasses and poured out the Martinis. Their color was the palest white-gold. The leftover gin and vermouth went into the second shaker; it was the cardinal rule of Martini-making that there be no dilution. Knowing even that much, she was surely not the worst hostess in the world. She rubbed the rims of the glasses with the peelings, then squeezed them and dropped them into the drinks. Handing one to Kate: "You be mine." A beat. Two beats. "My official taster."

"Oh, God! Delicious!"

"You, Major." Claire handed him his drink, then carried a drink across the room to where Mrs. Fennelly sat stubbornly erect by the hearth. "And one for my dear old suspicious mother, who has never been drunk in her life."

"Sobriety is nothing to be ashamed of," said Mrs. Fennelly to the room at large. "I will not grovel to Claire because I have led a respectable life and she has not."

"Hear, hear," said the Major, then bit his tongue. He had been reckless again. Getting ready to applaud the first part of Mrs. Fennelly's statement, he had not anticipated the reference to Mrs. Gault's private life. "I beg your pardon," he said to Claire.

"No, no, Mother is perfectly right! I am a scandalous person." Those words were for the Major, but the rest were not: "You touch me at your peril."

"Moreover," Mrs. Fennelly said, determined to hold the Major's attention, "I intend to go on being respectable."

The Major thought it over—how likely was it that this

remarkable lady would be lowering standards at her age?—
and then risked a second "Hear, hear." He seated himself
with some difficulty on the narrow fireplace fender next to
Mrs. Fennelly's chair. "Ireland," he said, "is a good place.
To stay sober in. If you can stand it." He tasted his drink
for the first time. "Ah, Jesus, Mary, and Joseph!" he burst
out, in a cataract of speech. "Ah, that's a beautiful Martini,
that is."

Claire and Kate sank simultaneously into the cushions
of the disemboweled sofa, whose springs rang out sharply in
protest. Nicky and John tramped in from the kitchen bearing
trays: cheese and biscuits for the grownups, peanut butter
and jelly and brown bread for the growing boys. Claire lifted
her glass above her head, holding it in both hands as if it
were a chalice. "To ourselves!" she said, and the four
adults drank. A few moments later, she added, "To each
other!" and again they drank. For the second time that
afternoon she caught Kate's eye and would not let it go.
It was true that she liked to take chances, true that the
greater the risk of failure the greater the exhilaration of
success. There were emotions she had felt in childhood that
she would never outgrow with age, and that was one of
them. From the fireplace, unexpectedly, Claire heard her
mother chirping, "To each other!" and the Major replying,
"Hear, hear!"

Nicky and John had seated themselves cross-legged on
the floor, with a checkerboard between them. Checkers was
the one game at which Nicky could invariably defeat John.
It was distressing to Nicky not to play the fool and let John
win, but John could tell as if by instinct when an adversary
was not fighting his hardest; he would have despised Nicky
if Nicky had ever done less than his best. Their two heads
almost touched above the checkerboard; they had shut out

the murmur of adult voices, the sh-h-h of the rain on the French windows. Claire and Kate lay back in the sofa, hands almost touching. There was no need for them to speak; Mrs. Fennelly, that accomplished conversationalist (she who could hold her own in Venice and Bar Harbor), was drawing out the Major about local sights. She assured him that she was a born sight-seer, and so was Bailey. As soon as the weather cleared, she wished to organize a series of short daily excursions in the Rolls. Bailey liked castles best and, after them, ruins, but great houses would do very well; such natural wonders as waterfalls and caverns were of no interest to Bailey or herself. She was counting on the Major to help her make plans. He said he would be delighted to do so. She was also counting on his joining them on any expeditions that might prove of interest to him. That was most kind: in recent years he had missed such expeditions very much. Mrs. Merriot must come as well, of course. Alas, the Major feared that his wife did not share his enthusiasm for the West Country and its illustrious past—pirates, shipwrecked Spanish sailors, and the like of that. The fact was that his chief companion in the seeking out of local lore had always been old Horne. It was Horne who had fished with Yeats at the trout pool here at Plumes. Horne remembered Lady Gregory driving up in a wicker pony trap from Coole to fetch Yeats home; he did a capital imitation of Lady Gregory's vexation with Yeats for having fished so long when he had poems to write. Mrs. Fennelly was delighted to add Horne to their little band of explorers. There would be plenty of room for him on the front seat beside Bailey. They got on splendidly with each other. Perhaps Bailey would let Horne help him with the road maps, several of which, to Bailey's indignation, had turned out to be in Gaelic.

"Crown my king," Nicky cried, in a stricken voice, in the bearable misery of love.

Claire sprang up to pour another round of drinks. At first the Major protested that they mustn't outstay their welcome. Mrs. Fennelly said, "Nonsense! I won't hear of your leaving," and from the depths of the sofa Kate called out to him that there was no need to hurry away—as soon as Mrs. Begley had dinner ready, she would make sure that Horne announced the fact and they would take an immediate departure. "Mrs. Begley keeps us. All on schedule. A holy terror," Major Merriot said, and held out his glass. As Claire was filling her glass and Kate's, she noted a sudden change in the sound of the wind. She stood in the embrasure, feeling as eager and greedy as a child. She wanted to be out running barefoot in the storm; she wanted also to be indoors, among these people in this room, with the fire burning and the gin lovely inside her. And she was like a child, too, in her satisfaction with herself; she was glad she had green eyes and a slender body, glad to be desirable, glad to be falling in love. "Listen, my God! To the wind," she said.

The others joined Kate and Claire in the embrasure, peering out: six Noahs at six windows, waiting for a sign. Where the kitchen wing projected at an angle from the house, they could see Horne and Bailey at one window, Mrs. Begley and Agnes at another. The rain had almost stopped, but the wind was rushing in now at gale force off the sea. It screamed in the trees and tore at the ivy along the window frames. A gull was blown past the kitchen wing, struck a corner of the house outside the morning room, and fell onto the waterlogged terrace. Nicky was all for plunging out and rescuing it, but before he could do so the gull picked itself up and, evidently abandoning hope of flight, waddled off, head down, slowly inland, away from harm. Something cracked in the direction of the sea. One of the high, leafy poplars swayed violently to and fro, as if it were the only tree among so many that had been singled out for a particular lashing by the wind. Heavy with rooks' nests, its topmost branches bent, bent, and then could bend no more; the entire tree was lifted up, hurled sidelong, and uprooted, a ball of sticky, wet earth rising out of the turf at the base of the trunk as the upper trunk struck and shuddered along the ground. Another tree was leveled and then another, until within a few minutes some twenty or thirty trees lay scattered in a debris of leaves, branches, and hairy roots across the lawn. In the gap caused by the fallen trees, they saw for the first time what the builders of the house had intended them to see—the great gray spume-covered Atlantic, thrashing at the foot of the cliffs of Plumes. A thread of yellow light broke and widened and then vanished in the western sky. "Tomorrow," said the Major, "you will see the sun."

Claire raised her glass. "One last toast," she said.

"Mother!" Nicky said, from the floor. "Who cares?"

Claire was notorious for the frequency of her toasts; she proposed them on every possible occasion, public and private. Birthdays, holidays, picnics, weddings, christenings —it scarcely mattered so long as a glass was at hand. In the lemon-yellow dining room of the big house on Gramercy Park, she would have hurled her glass into the fireplace; here at Plumes, until she had had the opportunity to lay in her own supply of glassware, she would resist the temptation.

"Now, Nicky," Mrs. Fennelly said. "Let your mother have her little toys. As you have yours."

70

John said, "Here it comes—the beginning of the end! Damn it, Nick, I never learn."

"Johnnie, you do! You're getting better every day. Look at all the men you still have!"

John's words astonished Claire. For they were hers. She had uttered them silently just before he spoke: the beginning of the end. It was possible that the words had come into their minds at precisely the same moment, but it was likelier that she had put them into John's mind by thinking them—by charging the snug room with them, as it was charged with firelight and the sour odor of coal smoke and the sweet smell of their bodies. She had been thinking that this evening marked, for her mother and Nicky and her, the real beginning of their holiday; and then she had thought that it almost certainly marked the end of their holidays together. She had thought it coolly, without the least taint of melodrama (she who in the old days would have doted on a scene—would have uttered the dread words aloud in hopes of making their flesh creep); she would keep the thought to herself. Tomorrow, the Major had said, there would be sun. If he were right, the boys had a dozen projects ready to undertake. The Major would help them to rent a couple of likely horses. The gardener would help them to lay out a badminton court in the meadow beyond the stables. Even the sneezing groom had volunteered to assist them in rigging up a basketball court in the carriage shed. They would be sending off to Dublin for a basketball and a hoop and a backstop, and if the carriage shed should prove too small for their purposes, the Major had proposed that they mark out a court in the shuttered ballroom. Mrs. Fennelly and Bailey would be plotting the first of their excursions. Perhaps

Horne would take them to see the burial place of his old
fishing companion in Drumcliff churchyard—Bailey was
very keen on graves. If the weather was warm as well as
sunny, there would be bathing on the beaches that bounded
the southern portion of Plumes. Claire imagined herself
lying on the sand beside Kate, their bodies baking. Her
honey color would turn brown, then bronze. The skin of
Kate's body would be very white, and they would have to
take great care that she didn't burn. They would fix up a
makeshift shelter of parasols and lie beneath it, reading
and napping. She wanted her toast to embrace the promise
of all those shining days to come, and of course it could not,
and she said, "To the happiest summer of our lives!"

"Mother, how soppy!" Nicky said.

"On the contrary," said his grandmother, "I call that a
very nice toast."

"Hear, hear," said the Major. Kate was content to remain silent, tasting the gin, delicious on her tongue and
lips. Except for the boys, they were all a little drunk. They
were drawing close. They watched in wonder as, despite its
great weight, a twenty-foot-high sphere of broken green
branches bowled past the windows, driven uphill by the
gale. It was becoming a night of signs. After dinner, John
and Nicky wanted, they said, to go out and clamber about
on the rocky cliffs, feeling valiant and endangered. They
wanted to rescue from the murderous Atlantic who could
guess what—a gull? a wrack of seaweed and broken spars?
No matter, so long as they could risk being heroes together.

"Can we go, Mother?"

"We'll see."

"Johnnie and I have to know right now!"

"Imperious Nicky!" He was coming to have his father's
face, and tonight, for the first time, he pleaded with the

same ardor. Poor Nicholas Gault, he had got his way in the end; much good it had done him. Nicky would be wiser, in part because he was her son. Of course she liked him. Of course she admired him. Someday perhaps they would be friends. "Then, yes," she said.

"Take care," said the Major, "you don't drown. Give Plumes. A bloody bad name."

Horne stood in the doorway: "Madam, dinner is served."

"In a few minutes, Horne," said Mrs. Fennelly. She wore a mask of total sobriety; very convincing it was. She was making an effort. The façade would hold. They would have their summer. "We have our guests to say good-bye to."

For a moment they all stood about shaking hands and saying, "Good night! Good night!," unwilling to let the party end.

Claire had foreseen correctly that Plumes would be the last of the houses that the three of them would visit together. Throughout the fall and into the winter, for no reason that her doctors could agree on, Mrs. Fennelly began to fail. She became rickety, and in her pride she would not conceal from Claire and Nicky that the usual miseries of age were closing in on her. She noted the progress of her decay with interest and described it ably. She was certain she would not be leaving Carolina again. If Claire wished the European Rolls as a gift, she was welcome to it; otherwise, Mrs. Fennelly would put it up for sale. She was thinking of selling the American Rolls as well. Bailey, she wrote, had never been so disagreeable; she was retiring him to a cottage on the property—one that was at the farthest possible distance from the main house.

In the late winter, turning over in bed, Mrs. Fennelly

felt her hips crack, neatly and without pain. She spent several months in bed, wearing one or another of the pretty lace bed jackets that Claire kept sending down to her from New York. They spoke often on the phone, as they had always done, but curiously there was less and less to say. Having no future to make plans for and discuss, they bored each other with their small talk. As Mrs. Fennelly saw death approaching, she was surprised to discover that she had no urgent messages to impart. She was relieved that she would die before she had had time to grow dotty—one of her oldest friends had recently picked up a miniature Yorkshire terrier and placed it with care in a whirring Waring blender. She had a mild stroke and then a second and more severe one. She could remember the German word for "oak tree," taught her in childhood by her beloved Fräulein, but for hours at a stretch she could not remember her daughter's name. *Eichbaum,* but not . . . ? For a week or so there were nurses round the clock; bed trays, bed-pans. She phoned Nicky at school. He was tongue-tied, as he always was on long-distance. She spoke with a show of crispness and took care to say "Good night" to him and not "Good-bye." She was drowsy and abstracted; it was proving easier to let go than she had expected. The last thing she ever saw, through half-shut eyes, was one of her nurses stealing a bottle of perfume from her dressing table. And the last thing she thought was how remarkable it was that it didn't seem to matter; there, she thought, that's dying for you.

A private funeral ceremony of mumbled psalms and prayers was held in the big front room of the Larkin house, after which Claire and Bailey took Mrs. Fennelly's ashes out into the rose garden. Bailey scattered the ashes vigorously among the blood-red flowers: dust that the sprinkler at nightfall would flush from the petals. Nicky did not attend the funeral. It would have been foolish to snatch him out of school with the end-of-term examinations only a few days off, but the possibility of doing so never arose— Nicky said flatly that he would not go. "I don't believe in funerals," he said.

Claire said, "Neither do I. Skip this one and then skip mine."

"Did Grandma leave a lot of money?"

"The lawyers haven't told me yet, but the answer is sure to be yes."

"If she left some to me, I want to go to Indonesia this summer."

"Darling, whatever for?"

"There's a kind of salamander there I want to look for. Nobody's seen it for years. We might be the lucky ones who rediscovered it."

"We? Is this an invitation?"

"John said he'd come, if I could swing the money part."

"John's nice. You're lucky to have him for a friend."

"I know."

So Nicky's days as a traveler with her were ended. He was getting ready to become whatever he had it in him to be—a naturalist, a scamp, a nobody. It would be motherly in her to admire him and she wished to do so, but she found it difficult. Nicky's unformedness had given her nothing to get a grip on, and now that he was taking form at last he would not be held. How little she had learned about him over the years! That he liked snakes, that he liked horses. That he liked, so it now appeared, salamanders, if salamanders were different from snakes. Rummaging about in the

75

library at Plumes, Nicky had discovered in an old book on
the fauna of Ireland that the country had no woodpeckers,
voles, or common shrews, though it had an abundance of
smooth newts and natterjack toads. He had been so proud
of bringing them the news. No doubt it was important to
know such things, but wasn't a mother entitled to more
than a few bleak facts of nature on which to base her admiration of a son? Having so little gift for parenthood, Claire
and Mrs. Fennelly had been helpless not to do Nicky harm
("We know, do we not, that he is not a very happy child?
And we know why?"). Nevertheless, he had survived, as
Claire herself had survived, by a hundred ruses of ac-
commodation; the ignominy of his years of subjection was
at an end. With the help of John, and of all the other
Johns to come, this gloomy boy might grow up into quite
a happy stranger. In that case, Claire and he would find firm
ground for friendship; she had always sought out happy
people. Her luncheons and dinner parties were famous not
only for their food and wine but also for their merriment.
It was possible that Nicky and she might yet become friends;
though not probable. She hardened her heart against disappointment: in family life nothing fortunate was probable.
Then she caught herself, marveling that she dared to pass
judgment on something she had scarcely known. In all the
years of their bickering, how often had the three of them
ever risked drawing close? Wasn't it once only, in the green
fastness of Plumes? And now she was alone. The words had
a grim sound, but she was far from feeling grim. In the
drawing room of her house on the Park, under the great,
glimmering mirror, she said aloud in celebration, "I am
alone." People would be asking her how she could bear to
rattle around by herself in all those empty rooms and she

would answer that she looked forward to enjoying the emptiness for a while; there would be plenty of time later for her to fill the house with parties. She looked up at the golden mandarins, her household gods, whispering old secrets among themselves. She felt exalted. Her mother was dead. Her son was rushing away from her into the world. Long ago, she had predicted that she would be coming to the simplest things last. And so she was. And it was not too late.

The Mischievous Sinfulness of Mother Coakley

Even in old age, Mother Coakley was as round and smooth-skinned as an apple. In her billowing black habit, she had the air of being about to be caught up in a gust of mountain wind and carried aloft to the sunny corner of heaven that had long been set aside for her. Not that she was in any hurry to go. She loved God, but she also loved life. "He knows where to find me when the time comes," she said to Father Naylor, the chaplain of the convent school. "Sure, I haven't budged from this spot in fifty years."

Father Naylor had a weakness for drink, which was a problem especially serious for a priest. He had a second problem—one that, again because he was a priest, was scarcely less serious than the first. It was a horror of death. He was revolted to be in its presence. To touch a dying or dead person made him ill; on more than one occasion, performing the last rites, he had fallen unconscious beside the bed. As a parish priest out in the world, he could never avoid this horror. In his eyes, the best thing about the convent school was that it was filled with laughing, teen-age girls, who looked as if they would live a thousand years.

The Bishop's theory in placing Father Naylor in the school was that keeping him away from the one problem might keep him away from the other. The Bishop was a kind man, but a trifle simple-minded; his theory had yet to be verified.

Mother Coakley was well aware of Father Naylor's attitude toward death, and that may have been the reason that she chattered on about it—she was convinced that it was good for people to have their noses rubbed in things they didn't wish to face. Besides, there was a touch of malice in Mother Coakley, for all her virtue. The obvious misery of her friend gave her an ample measure of satisfaction. "There must be many and many He has to scour the world for," she said to Father Naylor, "but not me—the moment He whispers my name, I'll be up and away, leaving not a pin behind."

It was true that she was a quick little thing; if she moved in death as she had always moved in life, her guardian angel would be hard pressed to keep up with her in the race to heaven. On earth, her most notable manifestations of speed were on the tennis court. Despite the Mother Superior's hints of disapproval—hints that by anyone else would have been taken as commands—Mother Coakley liked playing tennis with the younger convent girls. The court was on the crest of a hill behind the ramshackle wooden buildings that made up the convent chapel and school, and what seemed in the Carolina town in the valley below an agreeable summer breeze approached, on that dusty oblong of root-ribbed and rocky court, the force and temperature of a winter gale. Mother Coakley paid no attention to temperatures, hot or cold. Gathering the full skirts of her habit into her left hand, she scampered about the court like a frantic chipmunk, letting her veil float out behind her in ghostly disarray and only just showing the tops of her high black shoes. She had learned to play tennis as a novice at the mother house in France, no one knew how many years ago, and she played it unexpectedly well. Like most people who learned the game in the early years of the century, she had little interest in rallying. She was prepared to lose point after point in order to attempt a ruthless high-bounding put-away or a cut shot that would drop ever so gently and venomously over the net; when she had done so, the ball being unreturnable, Mother Coakley would drop her racket and clap her hands in unaffected delight.

She had no use for the conventional courtesies of tennis. If she failed to return an opponent's serve, she never called, "Good shot," but, screwing up her face in an expression of extreme self-contempt, would say, "Drat it! A six-year-old couldn't miss a serve like that!" As she played, her cheeks grew more and more deeply suffused with blood; they went from pink to red to purple, and this was so alarming to her opponents that it impaired their game. They began to lose points out of fear of having to witness a massive cerebral hemorrhage right on the court. Mother Coakley took advantage of their fears by scorning them. She never heeded suggestions that it might be wise for her to rest for a few minutes between sets. "I always get to look like this," she would say, panting heartily. The French crispness of tone taught her at the mother house in Dijon would slur away into the soft Irish brogue of her earliest childhood. "Sure, I looked like this in the cradle. Didn't the doctors and all despair of me? Don't give it a thought. Come take your beating."

Sinful Mother Coakley—base taunts were among the

weapons she used to secure victory. Short of outright cheating, she was unscrupulous in her desire to win. Where words would help her, she used words; where delaying tactics were needed to confound an adversary, she would fall back upon one or another of a host of ignoble tricks. A favorite trick was the manipulation of her habit, with its numerous layers and mysterious fastenings. Luckily for her, she belonged to an ancient order, which felt no need to be in fashion; the Mother Superior in Dijon had affirmed that gear which had been à la mode in the saintly thirteenth century might well be judged worthy to outlast the licentious twentieth. *"Le genou, c'est le communisme,"* she had written to Rome, and Rome had yet to contradict her. At a moment of crisis, with the score at, say, forty-love, Mother Coakley would astonish the server by suddenly retreating to a point back of the baseline and plunging both hands deep inside her habit, to adjust some strap or placket that had presumably gone askew. It was hard to maintain control of one's service after an interruption of that kind. Mother Coakley also made cunning use of her rosary, which, stuffed carelessly inside her belt at the start of a set, would work itself loose and flail about her waist until, with tears of excitement streaming down her cheeks and wisps of clipped gray hair showing at the sides of her wimple, she would be obliged, with a shout, to stop playing. "If I didn't, Lord love us, I'd strangle myself on my own beads," she said. "But for them, I'd be happy to go on playing till dark." Perhaps so and perhaps not so—it was nearly always the case that Mother Coakley used her beads as an excuse to stop playing while she was still ahead but had plainly begun to lose ground.

———

Pride (wishing to be the best player in the convent), envy (wishing to possess another player's backhand), and greed (wishing to keep the court when her allotted time was up) were among the sins that Mother Coakley wrestled with in vain from year to year. In the months when frost and snow and the muddy rains of spring made the court unplayable, Mother Coakley was in and out of the confessional in a matter of seconds and was finished with her penance so fast that, by the calculations of other nuns in the chapel, it could have consisted of little more than a token "Hail, Mary" or two. But in high summer and in the long, golden days of the Carolina autumn, the length of her stay in the confessional and the amount of time it took her to say her penance were the subjects of much whispered comment. Some of the younger nuns would dare to tease her about this as they made their way at night up the steep, worn stairs to their cells. "What a temper Father Naylor must have been in today!" they would say. "To think of his making you suffer so because of his migraine."

"My penance is none of your business," Mother Coakley would say, with a great show of indignation. "Kindly respect the secrecy of the confessional. *Vous connaissez les règles.*" It happened that "migraine" was the nuns' word for Father Naylor's hangovers, which were prolonged and overlapping, and Mother Coakley took care to defend his good name as well as hers. "It strikes me as curious," she said, "that at the very moment when you are expected to be contemplating your own no doubt manifold sins, and bitterly regretting the anguish they have caused Almighty God, you can find time to speculate upon the imaginary failings of others!" She might be old, but her tongue was as sharp as her feet were nimble. The young nuns stared at her in love and admiration: she was who they would like to become in the course of the long journey leading to their promised bridegroom.

It was Father Naylor who was given the shock of his life when, late one windy October afternoon, he rounded a corner of the chapel and caught sight of a nun lying by the backboard of the tennis court. He lumbered up and knelt beside her. Even from a distance, something about the round shape of the body had let him know that it must be Mother Coakley. For once, her little face was as white as paper. Her racket lay where it had fallen; the two or three balls with which she had been practicing shots against the backboard had rolled this way and that, unregarded. Summoning all his courage, Father Naylor reached out and touched her forehead; it was cold. Awkwardly, he called her name, knowing there would be no answer. He took out the vial of holy water that he carried with him always and sprinkled a few drops over the body. If there was the least faint tick of life left in her anywhere, it would be worthwhile giving her conditional absolution, and he did so. He was trembling with hangover and still more with fright. He had squandered his strength in the act of touching her; now he was faced with the task of picking her up. No, it was impossible. He felt sure he would faint; then there would be two of them lying there on the court. He took out something else that he carried with him always: a flask of whiskey. He unscrewed the cap, tossed back an ounce or two above Mother Coakley's unmoving face, screwed the cap back firmly into place, and returned the flask to his pocket. She would not have liked him to be afraid of her. She would have given him a good scolding for his cowardice. She would have made him rub his nose in it. But she wouldn't have minded his taking strength from the whiskey.

Father Naylor worked one hand and arm under Mother Coakley's neck and his other hand and arm under her bent knees. Slowly he lifted her and then, finding the burden easy, got to his feet and started for the convent. To anyone who didn't know the nature of his burden, Father Naylor would have seemed a jaunty figure, striding across the lawn in the clear dusk. The wind was freshening; there was a taste of November in it. He cradled her in his arms as if against the cold. She didn't like winter to come, because it put an end to her tennis. She took the game seriously and seriously deplored her moral lapses in respect to it. She faced her sins—pride, envy, greed—head on and struggled to avoid them. Envy was the worst. Envy was her implacable foe. More than once in the confessional they had agreed that the best way for her to outwit her enemy would be for her to improve her skill. That was why she had been out at the backboard: she had been practicing for spring. He gave her a little toss in his arms; oh, but she was light! Like a bundle of feathers. And he was not afraid.

Too Late to Marry,
Too Soon to Die

They sat at a table in one corner of the bar. For almost a month now they had sat every night at the same table and ordered the same number of drinks and left the bar a few minutes before midnight. The man was something under fifty. He was getting fat and his thin blond hair had darkened to the color of tobacco stain. The girl was twenty-six or twenty-seven, tall, white-cheeked, and pretty. She had straight black hair and blue eyes, and when she and the man spoke together her voice seemed somehow lower than his, perhaps only because it was steadier.

"Want to hear the one about a man with a harelip trying to get fitted for a suit at Brooks Brothers?" he said. And when she shook her head: "Anything to keep you from sitting there looking so goddam solemn."

"I'm not solemn, I'm merry. I'm looking at all the merry people at the bar and thinking how merry they are."

"They're a bunch of old rummies."

"Five old rummies, one young sailor, and three middle-aged women with sagging bottoms."

They finished their drinks, and at a sign from the man

the waiter went to the bar and fetched them two more of the same. The waiter was an old man with gold-rimmed bifocals and a chin that hung ajar, easing his dentures, and his worn shoes went slap-slap over the sawdust-covered floor.

The girl's mouth was exquisite. She sipped her drink and shuddered and said, "I wish your china would break and your silver would be stolen and your house would burn down. I wish your wife and children would go on a five-year trip to the moon. And sometimes I wish you'd go with them."

"We're having one of our better evenings, aren't we?" the man asked.

The young sailor left the bar and entered the men's room, directly across from their table.

"A beautiful merry sailor," the girl said. "With such nice merry eyes."

"He's going to be sick."

"Poor lamb. I've been watching him. He's all alone in this rotten place."

"Why don't you ask him home with you? Tuck him into bed and give him a cup of your famous camomile tea?"

"I wish I could."

"For Christ's sake, why not?"

"For one thing, there's Ellen."

"You and that girl. People will talk."

"It was her apartment. She *found* it. I couldn't afford it alone."

"I'd pay her share."

"Oh, no, you wouldn't."

"Meaning you don't think I would, or you wouldn't let me?"

"Something like that."

They could hear the sailor being sick behind the thin pine door.

"Besides," the girl said, "he'd think I was a tramp. Quite an elderly one."

"Talking old age now, you'll be a number-one bore at thirty."

"Give me a quarter."

"Not if it's for that goddam song."

"Just once more."

"Number-one bore right now."

"Then I'll ask the waiter for money."

The man spilled some coins out onto the table, and the girl, picking up a quarter, walked to the jukebox beside the bar. She made her selection and drifted back across the room in a half dance, taking her time. She sat down, patting the man's hand. "Ah, but it's the lovely song," she said, in a false brogue. " 'Too late to marry, too soon to die.' "

The record was loud and brassy; it seemed to go on and on. The sailor came out of the men's room as the record ended. He looked pale under his tan, and surprised and offended by what had happened to him. The girl said, "Sit down a minute. Before you fall."

The sailor teetered over them, glancing uncertainly back and forth between the man and the girl. The man took a drink and then, looking not at the sailor but at the girl, said, "You're sick. Better get back to your ship."

"Hell, no, I got twenty-four hours." The sailor was still so young that he was willing to walk away without making trouble, but he was also eager to carry some memory of a risky and gallant shore incident to sea with him. "Listen, mister," he said, "it was her who started talking, not me.

If you want to make something out of it, I'll be right up there at the bar."

The man smiled and said, "O.K., sailor boy."

"And don't call me sailor boy, hear?"

"O.K., sailor." And then silently, for the girl to see: "Boy."

The sailor ducked his head, frowning with an almost imperceptible fuzz of brows. "Excuse me," he said to the girl and walked slowly, with a pallbearer's dignity, back to the bar.

The girl said, "God, what a shit you are."

The man finished his drink. "I let the little lambikins thumb his nose at me, didn't I?"

"Mean, mean, mean, mean. You wanted me to speak to him for your sake, didn't you? To set it up for you, so you could spit on him?"

He shook his head. "So I could see what you'll be doing here this time next month. When Carol and the children come back to town, and I can't sit holding your hand every night in the week."

"Please," the girl said. "Ah, please. You didn't have to tell me that." The mascara she had brushed onto her lashes earlier in the evening had begun to print itself in straight wet lines against her upper lids. "Time to go home."

"To your neat, narrow little bed?"

"Narrow it is, neat it isn't."

"It's early yet. Ellen will think we've had a row."

"Ellen doesn't know anything about you."

"Don't be a fool."

"She only knows there's someone. She thinks you're tall and lean and dark, and can bring a girl off by just looking at her." She took his hands. "There. Now we're even."

"Finish your drink," the man said.

"You're angry with me. Very well, then, I'm sorry."

"Now you're being childish."

"All right, fine, I'm being childish. I'm being anything you say. Only say you're not angry with me."

"I'm not angry with you."

"And you'll see me tomorrow?"

"I'll see you tomorrow."

The waiter came up to their table. His feet throbbed in his shoes, and his eyes looked dazed back of his gold-rimmed bifocals. "Want your check?" he asked, fumbling with a greasy pad, and it was as if he were saying, "Ah, for the love of God, why don't you two go home? Can't you quarrel in bed as well as here?"

The man said, "Bring us a couple of more drinks."

The waiter nodded and turned away, his shoes dragging in the soiled, two-day-old green sawdust.

"I wish it were over," the girl said, and that was the moment, though she wasn't to know it till later, when, between one drink and the next and without another word spoken, her wish came true.

The Triumph

To Mrs. Battle and her daughter Edith, the issuing of the invitations to the tea was in itself a considerable event. This annual party was the point on which their year and their world revolved. As soon as the forced gaiety of Christmas was over, they started looking forward to the great day. Edith was fifty, Mrs. Battle seventy-three. In the last ten years they had grown to look like sisters. Both had flat cheeks, large chins, and thin gray hair. And when either one of them spoke of the time of day or of the weather, it was in the same tones of courage and regret with which they spoke of their life in the city, so many years back now, or of the house they had later owned on the Torrington road, or the furniture and friends they had been forced to sacrifice.

Edith and Mrs. Battle always set aside one whole day of the first week of January to walk down to the drugstore in the village and buy paper, envelopes, and a fresh bottle of ink. It took an hour or more to make a choice among Mr. Crabtree's sleazy samples of stationery. Edith and Mrs. Battle sat down on the high stools at the soda fountain and took off their gloves to rub each sheet between their fingers. "If you'd only told me we were out of paper, dear," Mrs. Battle always said, "I could have written to Tiffany's for the usual. The dies are there." They tested two or three bottles of ink before they found the particular shade of light blue they wanted—the shade they never failed to purchase. By the end of the next week, when they could no longer bear to leave the paper untouched, Edith and Mrs. Battle would carry the telephone book up to their small, square room on the second floor of Mrs. O'Connor's boarding-house and copy from it a list of possible guests. This, to-gether with a list of their friends outside the village, totaled nearly a hundred persons. After twenty years, the Battles knew perfectly well whom they intended to invite, but it was a sacred custom to savor and reject the remainder, name by name.

"What about Mrs. Roger Shipstead?" Mrs. Battle would ask on the first day, her finger happening to rest against that name in the book.

Edith would say, "We'll write it down, in case."

On the following day, when they began to prune their list of the more obviously distant acquaintances, Edith would say, "I've Mrs. Roger Shipstead here." Mrs. Battle always pretended to waver—"Let's wait and see." On the third day, Mrs. Battle would cut Mrs. Shipstead from the list. "We've never had her, you know," she would say, and Mrs. Shipstead would drop from their thoughts for another year.

The list took shape finally as the Battles had known it would. They were always careful that, of the twenty-five invitations they sent out, eighteen would be to those acquaintances in New Haven and New York and Philadelphia and Washington who were certain not to attend but who bore uniformly distinguished names. One was a former governor of Connecticut; one was the president of Yale (whoever he happened to be—the Battles were an old Yale family); one an elderly gentleman who, in Hoover's time, had been minister to one of the Scandinavian countries. The remaining invitations were always sent to a handful of friends in the village, who never thought of refusing them, and to perhaps one new friend, by way of adding a sense of risk to the occasion. The risk this year was Mrs. Paraday. She was a stout, red-cheeked widow, new to the town, whose vigor appalled and attracted Edith. She said whatever she pleased and gave the impression that all her life long she had done whatever she pleased. Mrs. Battle asked, "Who are her people?" and Edith answered, "None living, I believe."

"That fails to answer my question."

"New York," Edith said, then risked adding, "Old New York."

"I don't believe it for a moment. What was her maiden name?"

"I can't recall her having mentioned it."

"And no wonder. Irish blood there, you mark my words." Mrs. Battle had a low opinion of the Irish. There was something the matter with their blood. In that respect they were very like the Poles and the Spanish and the blacks. "People who touch pitch—" Mrs. Battle said. "I warn you not to go running after Mrs. Paraday."

"I, who've never run after *any*one!"

"If we invite your Mrs. Paraday, it must be with the clear understanding that she is very much on probation."

"She's not *my* Mrs. Paraday, and if you're going to carry

on like this, I'd a thousand times rather not have her at all."

"Fiddlesticks!" said Mrs. Battle, her old heart afire with jealousy. "You've a crush on her, that's all. The sooner you get over it, the better."

Edith burst into tears, and for forty-eight hours, living in the same room, sleeping in the same bed, they spoke not a word to each other. The inconvenience of silence at such close quarters and the need to get on with the preparations for the tea party caused them at last to come to terms; and by then each felt that she was forgiving the other.

As usual, the writing of the invitations took scarcely an afternoon. "Mrs. Robert Gardiner Battle and Miss Edith Nevins Battle," Edith wrote down, again and again, in a straight, slender, unchanging script. "At home Monday, January twenty-seventh, four to six. R.S.V.P." Then, with Mrs. Battle sitting on the bed and calling out names in a voice charged with excitement, Edith addressed the twenty-five envelopes. The next morning they walked down to the post office to buy the proper number of stamps from the postmaster. This made it possible to show him some of the letters addressed to New Haven and New York and Philadelphia and Washington, since they always affixed the stamps at his window and even asked him to weigh one of the letters to make sure that it had sufficient postage. Together they dropped the invitations, with slow caution, into the brass-plated slot in the wall.

All through the next week they received at least two letters of regret a day. "Isn't it a shame?" Mrs. Battle said, reading one of them. "Mrs. Amory writes from Washington that she and the Senator have promised themselves for dinner on Monday." In the end they received, as they did each year, eighteen letters of regret from New Haven and

93

New York and Philadelphia and Washington, and seven letters of acceptance from their friends in the village.

On the morning of the tea, they dropped in at the bakery shop and purchased three dollars and fifty cents' worth of sandwiches and cakes. Then they hurried back to the house to make ready the front parlor. At noon, Mr. Atwood, a middle-aged bachelor who worked at the Brown Lumber Company and was the most presentable of Mrs. O'Connor's five other boarders, obligingly brought in wood for a fire and laid it with his own hands. Edith carried the canary down from upstairs to give the room a more homey look. They dared not remove Mrs. O'Connor's portrait of the late Pope from its place of honor above the mantel, but, as former members, during their New York days, of the Brick Presbyterian Church, they diminished his presence by setting a bowl of bittersweet before the picture. They went without lunch in order to give themselves time to bathe and dress. Mrs. Battle always wore a lavender dress with long sleeves and a pleated skirt touching the floor. She had bought it at Altman's fourteen or fifteen years before, but, as she often said, "The material's so much better than what you can get nowadays, it would be criminal to think of giving it away."

Edith wore a dress she had bought in Winsted some years back. With the changes she had made in it this year, it looked almost like new. At four o'clock, with a card table crammed with plates, cups, and Mrs. O'Connor's green porcelain teapot, and a cozy fire burning on the hearth, the Battles sat down and waited for their guests. They were so moved by the occasion that they could scarcely speak.

No one ever came before five.

The room clinked with china saucers and cups. The fire on the hearth cast skeins of smoke over the partly empty plates of sandwiches and cakes. Next to Mrs. Battle sat Miss Day. She, too, had lived in New York and knew many of the people Mrs. Battle had known in the old days. In spite of altered times, she still kept three servants in the green-and-lemon-colored house on the hill. Beyond Miss Day sat Mrs. Urbino, the nice Italian Dr. Urbino's wife, who showed by her silence how grateful she was for being asked to the Battles' tea. On the other side of the room, Edith, together with Mrs. Reuben Clark, who was eighty-four, and her granddaughter, and Edith's friend Mrs. Paraday, kept up a drumfire of whispers and giggles. Mrs. Battle felt that the annual tea was a great success.

"My parents could remember Brooklyn," Miss Day was saying, "before the Bridge. I hate to think what age that makes me, but they could. It was like the open country in those days, all woods and brooks and sandy shore. And the nicest people!"

"Why, in those days," Mrs. Battle said, sitting as straight and motionless on her little wooden chair as a queen on a velvet throne, "in those days, you know, Westchester and outer Long Island hadn't been dreamed of. They didn't exist. If anyone had dared to live in a village like this, a hundred miles from New York, they'd've been thought quite mad." Mrs. Battle lifted her teacup lightly in her mottled hands. The canary fluttered and scolded in a cage above her shoulder as she talked. "My mother was a Nevins—one of the oldest of the old Brooklyn families. When I was a little girl, we lived on Washington Park South, in the loveliest home, with a long green garden that I always think of as full of pompons and cosmos and nettles. We had a coach house covered with lattices at the end of the garden, and I remember the horses my father kept there—two black ones with white feet and white stars on their foreheads. He called them Gog and Magog."

"What a marvelous memory!" Mrs. Urbino said. It was almost the only remark she had made all afternoon.

"Later, the financial troubles came—I was much too young to know what it was about; money was as much a mystery to me then as it is today—and my father had to surrender everything he owned, but he refused to give up his horses." Mrs. Battle drew a slow breath, building a stage of silence under her voice. Each year she enjoyed this moment more. For this was how to live: tea, cakes, friends, a fire, a story. "He went down to the coach house the morning we had to move away. He said good-bye to the horses and lifted a pistol out of his pocket and shot them dead, just where they stood in their stalls. My mother and I were waiting for him on the front stoop and we heard the shots. He couldn't bear to do anything else."

"Imagine living in Brooklyn today and having such a memory! It would be horrible," Mrs. Paraday said, and burst into prolonged laughter. Wave on wave, the sound rose in the crowded room. The canary flattened his wings on the wire walls of his cage. Mrs. Battle lifted the lid of the teapot, studied the black tea, and replaced the lid. In all the times she had told that story of her father's horses no one had ever followed it with a less appropriate remark. She smiled, all courtesy. "Do have another cup of tea, Mrs. Paraday," she said. "Such a cold day."

Mrs. Battle pressed her hands to her eyes for a moment. The last of the guests had gone. Edith and she had repeated for the last time the words "Do drop in again very soon," which everyone knew better than to believe. They lifted the plates from the table and carried them down the dark hall to the kitchen. Mrs. O'Connor was there, preparing supper. "How was the party?" she asked. "Were you both the pride and joy of the day?"

"Everything was just as it should have been," Mrs. Battle said. It was best to keep the Mrs. O'Connors of this world at a distance. The Irish were nothing if not pushy. Nevertheless, today she could afford to unbend a little. "We have to thank you for the use of the room. And for your plates."

"Why shouldn't you have the use of the room whenever you want it?" Mrs. O'Connor asked. "The rest of the boarders only use it at night, the big tramps in their dirty shoes!"

Edith and her mother found the stairs exhausting. Mrs. Battle lay down on the big double bed. She did not wish to hear Edith launch out on a long chatter of distress over Mrs. Paraday. Edith could be remarkably obtuse at times. In ordinary circumstances, apologies would certainly have been called for and, after due consideration, accepted, but these were far from ordinary circumstances. Mrs. Paraday's gaucherie had made any further relationship between Edith and her an impossibility. She had proved herself, and not alone in the Battles' eyes, a total outsider. Word of the incident, Mrs. Battle thought with satisfaction, would be all over the village by nightfall: the clumsy grossness of the guest, the unfaltering magnanimity of the hostess. Surely Edith ought to see that apologies would open the door to discussions that no longer needed to take place. Mrs. Battle had played her trumps superbly. She had taken every trick. She was still a match for any of them. She heaved an artificially loud sigh, as a signal that she was falling asleep. That would keep Edith from bothering her. She lay there listening to her daughter as she fluttered nervously about the room. After so many years, the least sounds were easy to identify. A faint *chck!* was Edith hanging the canary's cage back on its accustomed hook. After a minute or two, finding himself at home between wardrobe and shoe rack, the bird would start singing. Just so, just so. Wrapped in glory, Mrs. Battle, pretending to fall asleep, fell asleep, and so never saw her daughter's tears.

Signs

Father Ryan opened the window of his study on the ground floor of the parish house. He blew a drift of coal dust from the sill, then set his palms against it and leaned into the night. The air was hot. Rain was falling noisily on the tin roof, silently on the almost invisible statue of Mary crowning the chapel. Between the house and the chapel, a bank of red Carolina clay had been cut to frothing gullies; now and then a sizable stone would be washed free by the scouring water and would set off down the valley. The first day of the downpour, Father Ryan had said to Buck, his altar boy, "Now the heat is bound to break. Winter's coming at last." But Buck had said, "Hit don't make no difference about the rain. Rain'll just gobble up the air."

And that was what the rain had done. Father Ryan felt as if he had been drowning minute after minute for five days. From the open window, he looked out across the town. Hundreds of dancing oblongs of light fell from the windows on the opposite hillside, in the white section of town. Here in the black section, about the new Franciscan school and chapel, a handful of yellow lights swam in the dark. Father

Ryan wondered, maybe for the thousandth time, how he was ever to learn what lay in the light of those lamps. This was missionary country—there were said to be fewer Catholics in Carolina than there were in China. With the rain falling and the roads growing impassable, he had had to dismiss classes two or three days before the proper time for Christmas vacation. The children had vanished without a trace into their sullen, unpainted, inscrutable shacks. Buck, who had been Father Ryan's first convert, had missed Mass this morning for the first time. Unless the rain stopped soon, it was plain to Father Ryan that his year's work might go for nothing—might go, he thought, unable to resist the grim joke, straight down the drain.

Buck was sixteen, which was two years beyond the age limit of the school, so Father Ryan had trained him as an altar boy. This had turned out to be such excellent strategy that it caused Father Ryan to suffer an occasional twinge of conscience. He was thirty-three, and he believed in conversion by reason rather than example. Still, it was a fact of life that if what Buck called "rollin" Catholicism was good enough for Buck, it would be good enough for scores of young people in the neighborhood; if it wasn't, it wouldn't be. Simple and sometimes shameful were the means by which souls could be won for God. So far, Father Ryan had achieved what his superiors regarded as an exceptional success in the community, but he knew better than they did that it was all in continuous jeopardy. Watching the rain stream from the overhang of the tin roof, trying to draw a breath of the sour night air, Father Ryan noted without self-pity that he had no clear proof of his success. He stood alone on Christmas Eve in an empty house, beside an empty chapel, and never had he felt so sure that the world that lay about him was not his world and that it might prove, in the end, impenetrable. Hadn't there been tens of thousands of black converts in Africa in the seventeenth century? Hadn't they built their own cathedrals in the jungle, and hadn't they been presided over by their own archbishops and cardinals, appointed by the Holy Father in Rome? And hadn't the continent reared back and swallowed up the whole enormous, prosperous enterprise, church, priests, and laymen, leaving not the least word of God behind? Father Ryan shook his head at his temerity—that was what living alone did for a man! He had just narrowly escaped comparing this dreary little pinpoint of a coal-mining town in the Smokies with all of West Africa. Still, if they had nothing else in common, they had this: that no one—especially no stranger—could ever hope to put a lasting mark on them.

Father Ryan tightened his grip on the sill. He was living alone, and that was a hardship; he was also lonely, and that was a greater hardship. There had been an old monk at the seminary who sometimes at night, after he had a drop taken, would sigh and say that he was lonely, lonesome, and alone. Father Ryan used to wonder how he distinguished between "lonely" and "lonesome." Perhaps there *was* a difference, and perhaps he was about to find out what it was. Tonight in the North, where Father Ryan had grown up, the snow would be lying deep in the yards or piled high beside the roads by the big plows. The air would be cold and sharp, the sky crowded with stars. Candles would be lighted in the windows of houses. Through the windows you could see trees covered with tinsel and ornaments, trees glittering with tiny bulbs. Father Ryan remembered seeing, a year or so earlier, a spruce higher than the house in front of which it grew, and every branch of the spruce had been covered with lights. In another front yard, someone had fashioned, out of snow, Mary and the Child, and the moonlight had fallen ice-blue, like satin, over Mary's head and cradling arms.

Up North, Father Ryan had seen Christmas in the faces passing him in the street. He had heard it in voices speaking while doors were opened and closed against the cold: "Come in, come in! How good of you to stop by!" "I can't stay. But I had to tell you merry Christmas." He had been actually shaken by the sounds of Christmas, standing under the brassy amplifiers in the city park: "Oh, little town of Bethlehem, how still we see thee lie!" In his room in that Northern parish house, Father Ryan had arranged, last year, his private Christmas celebration. He had set a shoe box on its side on the table beside his cot. He had covered it with pine twigs broken from shrubs growing around the house. He had placed inside the shoe box a plastic Jesus and Mary from the five-and-ten, a prayerful Joseph, and two placid cows. When he had gone shopping that morning, he had had money enough to buy either a set of shepherds or a set of Wise Men. He had weighed the decision with care, while the girl behind the counter tapped with her painted nails on a hill of sparkling snow. Father Ryan had chosen the shepherds. They had seemed closer to him than the Wise Men, with their proud names and gorgeous raiment. That night he had propped the shepherds upright by the infant Jesus. Then he had knelt in front of the shoe box to say his rosary.

For the moment, the rain appeared to be slackening. Father Ryan heard water foaming and chuckling in the gullies and circling the open foundations of the house. He heard a report that might have been a shot fired at a rat in a nearby shanty, or a car backfiring. Somewhere down the slope a tethered donkey began to bray. Then the rain came down once more, through the sieve of heat, on the slick banks and sodden road. Father Ryan turned from the window and glanced about his barren study. No wreaths, no crèche, no twinkling lights. So many hundreds of miles from home, he had lacked the will to improvise a Northern Christmas. Besides, he had promised himself that, coming among these people, he would follow their customs. They had outwitted him by apparently having none. Ah, damn them, he thought, for shutting their doors in my face! His supposed success among them wasn't worth a straw for as long as he didn't know what they were thinking and feeling. No doubt they were using him by letting him win an occasional trophy for the Church from among their children. This was as it should be, because he was there to be used— it was a part of his giving himself to God to be used and not to know at the time, or perhaps ever know, whether he had been used for good or ill. It was the bleak misery of the not-knowing that created a loneliness beyond aloneness. All those years ago, was it not-knowing that the drunken old monk had been hinting at and taking care to conceal from the young seminarian running full tilt at God? No wonder that people who gave themselves to God were constantly on their knees to Him, begging for a sign. It was among the gravest of temptations and among the hardest to resist.

Father Ryan heard a second report, followed by a sound of voices. Beyond the roof of the house and chapel, a faint glow colored the sky. It looked like a fire, which in that neighborhood was a commonplace. Nearly every week a faulty stove set ablaze one of the paper-roofed shanties that surrounded the chapel; within an hour or two nothing would remain but the brick piers on which the shanty had stood and the teetering chimney to which the stove had been attached. Leaning from the window, Father Ryan watched as the glow faded and then returned, closer to the chapel and much brighter than before. A yellow flare lighted the road in front of the house. He saw that the road was filled with boys, their black faces tilted up at him, and he called out, "What's happened? Is it a fire?"

Ankle-deep in mud, the boys surged under his window. He saw that Buck was in the lead, his bushy hair glittering with raindrops, a pine torch in his right hand. They shouted, "Merry Christmas, Father!" and a dozen firecrackers exploded in the darkness above their heads.

"Buck!" he said. "What *is* this?" His temper was short these days. He felt a wave of anger mounting in him. "What kind of crazy stunt are you kids staging?"

Buck's eyes gleamed with pleasure. He lighted a fuse with his torch and sent a firecracker looping off to explode beyond the crowd. Buck said, "Don't you all know how to celebrate Christmas up North?"

"You're damn right we do!" He glared down at Buck. It was as if in his anger he were bent on turning his first convert into his first victim. "This is the birth of our Saviour, not the Fourth of July!" The moment he uttered the words, he saw that he was being the biggest fool on earth and he bent down out of the window and said, "Buck! Quick! Give *me* one!"

Buck pulled a six-inch salute from his pocket and said, "We saved this little old baby just for you." He handed the salute up to Father Ryan, then lifted his pine torch to the sill. Father Ryan held the fuse against the torch. It sizzled for a moment from dampness, then began to hiss. He felt again, remembered from boyhood, the incomparable thrill of time running out, of one's having to act in haste and yet with perfect control. "Watch this!" he shouted, and with all his strength he hurled the salute toward the chapel roof. It climbed up, up, up through the streaming dark, its fuse faintly spiraling, and then burst in a sheet of white flame over Mary's head.

Country Fire

By the time the first townspeople reached the farm, five minutes after the siren in the town hall had begun its keening, the smallest of the four barns was a yellow kettle of flames. It was still possible to see in the midst of the fire the outline of a burning truck. It was surmised that the old Ford, on being driven into the barn, had backfired, kindling its load of hay. Now, with a roar, the fire was beginning to spread.

More and more volunteer firemen kept arriving. The chief of the department was said to be shopping in Lakeville, and old Dr. Harley, who was eighty-nine, had not yet reported; the rest of the men were happily sizing up the ground and looking for water. The pumper, which had been taking part in a parade in Canaan, arrived with flags and bunting and driven by a Pilgrim Father. Beside him, filling the valley with the clangor of the bell, sat a painted Indian.

The nearest water lay high on the hill behind the barns. The pumper started through a plowed field and could not make the grade. Francis Nolan, the plumber, took over the wheel. He was a black-haired Irishman, and he looked, as he sent the shining red-and-chromium chariot against the slope, like a god in armor, but the pumper remained unheroically mired. Francis swore. His curses echoed across the fields and among the trees. The firemen tugged and thrust against the wheels until the pumper began to rock; then slowly it slid back and down the hill.

Dick O'Brien, the grocer, still in his apron, with a pencil over his ear and a yellow pad in his pocket, began to pay out the hose. It would have to be carried up the hill by hand. In the meantime, as the crowd gathered, the smallest barn burned to its skeleton. Between the last of the flames and the charred timbers, the blue September sky opened in squares. Everyone was waiting for the gas in the truck to explode; the explosion, when it finally came, made very little sound, no more than a tree, heavy with leaves, crashing in a woods. Then the timbers fell, wall by wall, laying themselves out precisely across the scorched ground.

The owner of the farm, a man with one arm, did not seem concerned. He stood under a nearby tree, pointing out with seeming good humor to everyone who passed how clumsily the volunteers lifted the heavy hose. He held in his single hand a big silver watch, timing the destruction of the barns. The house was two hundred yards away, out of the direction of the wind, but, for double assurance, two farm hands were dousing the roof with water handed up to them in tin milking pails.

Another barn caught fire. The flames were so high and strong that they swallowed the barn, with its stored-up hay, in one immense burst of fire, making bright loops of light through the loft, orange and yellow and white. One minute the roof was solid black shingle; the next, it began to curl, and candles of fire were shining under it; then it was one wide, coppery blaze. The heat reached out to shred the leaves on branches twenty yards away. A rabbit darted from under the burning floor, his white tail bobbing. He wheeled, panting, at the feet of the crowd and stared at the burning barn, and then, as if he suddenly realized that home was where he wanted most to be, plunged back into the smoke.

Everyone in town had heard the siren or had caught sight of the smoke lifting above the hills. Mrs. Abley, an elderly paralytic, had been driven over in her Cadillac to occupy a place in the front rank. The volunteers had to circle her car with the hose to reach the barns. A dozen young girls, in halters and shorts and dark glasses in spite of late September, paraded before incurious boys. One mother had brought her baby, wrapped in blankets. Dr. Hill, the distinguished surgeon from New York, went about picking up the late apples from under the trees in the orchard.

The volunteers finally reached the little pond at the top of the hill. They straightened the hose into easy curves, set it free of kinks, and attached the wide nozzle. Twenty minutes had passed since the siren began. All three remaining barns were by now smothered in smoke. Mr. Degnan, the butcher, his apron spotted with hamburger, his straw cuffs at his elbows, brushed back the hair that no longer grew on his bald scalp and directed two of the youngest volunteers to carry the hose first to the third barn and then to the fourth. There was now no hope of saving the second, which was shaking in readiness to fall.

"It's coming!" The words, shouted from the top of the hill, fell in the clear air through the upland meadows, through the clover, through the orchard, and along the green plateau. And then the water, as it poured down, began to quicken the hose. The white case turned and quivered under the firemen's hands, and, finally, with a spurting kick, the foam shot forth into the blaze. There was a hiss, a black cloud that dirtied the sun, and the flames fell back.

Ladders of every size and kind were brought forward. The volunteers mixed in confusion with the crowd and the ladders were set up, lifted away, and set up again. Boys picked up rocks and tossed them against the windows of the biggest barn so that the firemen could send the water into the loft and against the roof, but the draft made by the broken panes served only to feed the fire.

This biggest barn was the pride of the town. It had been built in 1888, and the date was worked into the slate roof and carved into one of the stones of the immense granite foundation. It bore geometric designs in the shingles of the side walls. It also had a cupola with stained-glass windows and a gilt cow weathervane. It held quarters for the farm hands as well as a loft for hay, stables for horses, and a wide basement for the cows. The horses and the cows had been let out into the fields, the horses galloping off, snorting, into the orchard, the cows staring back reproachfully, without alarm. The firemen soaked the walls of the barn till the steam rose and glittered in the sun.

The third of the barns suddenly collapsed, the south wall falling outward over Tom O'Connell, the garageman. The square of timbers dropped about him, boxing the ground at his feet; he leaped out over the blackened grass without a word, without turning his head.

The crowd was beginning to get bored. The worst of the blaze seemed over and apparently the big barn was certain to be saved. The younger boys crawled up on the pumper, asking questions of Francis Nolan and hammering at the silver bell, and the girls in their halters began to shiver as the wind strengthened. Mrs. Abley was driven away. The mother carried her sleeping baby home to its crib. The owner of the farm stood alone, saying nothing, simply waiting.

As the firemen worked on and as the flames continued to fall back, rumors swept through the crowd. Mrs. Clennan, the real-estate dealer, was supposed to have said that she had only last week sold the farm to a couple from New York. That explained the calmness of the one-armed man. This couple was planning to move an old house from Winsted to a site by the pond at the top of the hill. According to Mrs. Clennan, the couple wouldn't have minded losing the present house, because it was such a fright—early twentieth century and in very bad taste; but their architect, who had been up to see the farm only yesterday, had fallen in love with the barns. He would be heartbroken. He had planned to make of them the most charming, the most delightful Early American group. Another rumor had it that the architect had intended to tear down the barns the very first thing, and now the couple from New York would be able to collect insurance on what they had wanted to get rid of. In these matters, the truth was always a long time in coming out.

The crowd drifted away; it was suppertime. At seven o'clock only the firemen were left, still stubbornly washing down the walls with water, stamping out the little tongues of flame that were constantly spreading across the grass. At eight o'clock they wound up their hose. The job was done. They were not hungry—the fire had taken their appetites away. They talked for a minute or two about the fire, and then Francis Nolan climbed into the driver's seat. The pumper churned, choked, and sputtered. Here in this meadow in the dark, with the ruins smoking behind them and their beds lying ten minutes ahead of them, they were out of gas. They walked in silence to the road to stop the first approaching car.

The Sunflower Kid

Justin Kelly stepped from the low doorway of the house into the yard. His wife called to him from the kitchen, "Where you going, Just?" and without turning his head he answered, "I got to give Jimmy his walking papers." The kerosene lantern in his hand threw a circle of yellow light around his boots. It was six o'clock on a cold October morning, and the grass through which Kelly walked was tipped with rime.

Kelly crossed the yard, rolled aside the barn door, and stood motionless for a moment, listening. He could hear the stock impatiently rattling their stanchions in the cellar under his feet. A rat scampered across the loft; dust sifted through a knothole. The loft was filled with hay, which gave heat and a sweet smell to the barn. Kelly walked through the harness room and knocked on a batten door in the far wall. "Jimmy!" he shouted, then kicked at the door. "Up, you big ape!"

When Kelly opened the door, his shadow, cast by the lantern in his left hand, blotted out much of the little room. Kelly raised the lantern over his head. The room held only an iron cot, a chair, and a chest of drawers. The single high square window in one wall was sealed with newspapers. A tall, slope-shouldered black man lay asleep on the cot. He lay curled with his legs almost touching his chin. The light of the lantern gleamed on his blue cheekbones and open mouth. On the bare floor beside the bed were scattered four or five brightly colored comic books: *Harry and Margie, The Goldnut Family, The King of Mars.*

Kelly yanked at the covers of the cot, and Jimmy opened his eyes, unseeing. He lay with his cropped head on the lumpy pillow. Gradually Kelly came into focus in the pools of Jimmy's eyes. "Boss," he said. Then his eyes widened, he was awake at last, and he swung his big feet onto the floor. He was dressed in long gray winter underwear and woolen socks. He got up and pulled on denim trousers and a soiled brown shirt. He shoved his feet into his shoes, not troubling to lace them. Whenever he got into trouble, his first ruse was to try playing the clown. He would be the dumb nigger who never did anything right. Now he made a terrible face and said, "You ain't saying it's past five?"

"Past six."

Towering over Kelly, Jimmy rolled his eyes and groaned. "After I went and promise to be careful!" He bent down and fumbled under the pillow. His hand cupped an old-fashioned alarm clock with a bell and ringer fastened to its top. "The clock Mis' Kelly give me. Set right for five."

Kelly said, "No use, Jimmy. I've warned you fifty times."

Still playing the clown, Jimmy spoke with exaggerated slowness, doling out the words: "I must have reach out in my sleep and shut it off. I must have dream I was up and tending the cows and chickens and building a nice coal fire in the kitchen for Mis' Kelly."

"I can't help that. Pack what's yours and clear out."

"I only doing what Mis' Kelly say. Like she say I got to read more. So I do." He made his voice rise to a squeak on "do." "I *do* read more."

Kelly stamped on the comic books. "Not her fault if you stay up all night reading junk like this. I've warned you twenty times in the last three years. This time I mean it. I want you out of this room and off the farm by ten."

Jimmy took note that the number of times that Mr. Kelly claimed to have warned him had dropped from fifty to twenty. The change might be a sign. He was quick to read signs. "I'm a good worker," he said. "You know you won't find no better worker'n me. I belong on this farm."

"Young Polsky down the road has been after me for work all fall. I'll drive over and pick him up before we leave for the fair. He knows the kind of work I expect. I'm not like Carter, over Riverton way, who plays at farming. Who has a showplace. I have to *work* this farm. I need a man I can trust."

"And you can't trust Jimmy?"

"You see I can't, goddam it! You're big and you're strong, but putting a head on you was a waste of time."

"I'm a lazy good-for-nothing nigger, and that's a fact." It cost Jimmy no more to condemn himself than to praise himself; the important thing was to keep Mr. Kelly talking. It had always worked before, but this time Kelly turned and walked through the harness room and out of the barn. The sun, not yet risen, was beginning to lighten the sky beyond the hills. It would be a fine day. Jimmy followed Kelly, carefully shutting the barn door behind him and picking up stray bits of paper as he crossed the yard.

"You and Mis' Kelly'll have an awful nice time at the

fair," Jimmy said, as if nothing had happened between Kelly and him.

Kelly stopped at the kitchen door. "Finish your chores, then get your breakfast. Mrs. Kelly's baking a cake, so keep your big hulk out of her way." Kelly lifted the chimney of the lantern and blew out the little butterfly-winged tongue of flame. "We'll be leaving the minute I get hold of Polsky."

"Mis' Kelly and her cakes!" Jimmy said. "She'll be winning first prize till she's a hundred! You got your basket of McIntoshes all shined up?"

"It's a wonder, Jimmy, you don't choke on all that crap."

"Sir?" A foot higher than Kelly, Jimmy seemed to hang there against the sky. His breath was whiter than smoke in the still air. He was waiting for a sign, and it didn't come.

"That hokum, that dumb-nigger crap. You're broke, I suppose?"

"Yes, sir."

"I'll pay you up to the end of the month, is that O.K.?"

"That'll do fine."

"Hold onto the money this time. Don't throw it away like every other cent you ever had." Then, in a voice less harsh but no less unforgiving: "Maybe you'll amount to something, maybe you'll do better somewhere else. Learn to stand up for yourself, once we stop coddling you."

"The thing is, Mr. Kelly, I been figuring to stay right here. I don't *want* to do better somewhere else." But Kelly had not heard him out. He had slammed the kitchen door shut without a word. There were times when it did no good to play the clown. Those were bad times, but the times afterward were worse: the times when there was nobody left to listen.

Jimmy was carrying feed to the chickens when he heard Mr. Kelly drive out of the yard. He crouched at one of the low windows of the coop and watched the little red pickup truck raising a cloud of dust along the lane. When the truck reached the state highway, it turned left down the hill; that was the way to the Polsky place. Jimmy shook his head. He was beginning to feel sick to his stomach. He was hungry, and when he was hungry he felt sick, but this was a different feeling—it had more pain in it, and less ache. He had to milk the cows and turn them out to pasture, he had to put down fresh bedding for the horses, he had the stinking coop to clean. The feeling in his stomach was like the one he used to feel when he was a child, walking alone on a road at night, under big trees. They were trees full of goblins, and you could see the goblins' faces grinning at you through the scary undersides of the leaves. Even when you didn't see them, the goblins were there.

Someone was calling his name. It was Mrs. Kelly, and maybe she was bringing good news. She was nearly always on his side, and she might have talked Mr. Kelly out of firing him. She had done it before, a dozen times. He clambered out of the coop and up a narrow flight of stairs to the first floor of the barn. Mrs. Kelly was waiting for him outside his bedroom door. She smiled and brushed back her thinning gray hair with one hand; in the other hand was a bundle, neatly wrapped in brown paper.

"Well, I heard, Jimmy," she said, and went on smiling and fussing with her hair.

"That's all right, ma'am."

"I'm sorry."

"Now, don't go getting yourself upset." A big—no, an enormous—idea had just entered his mind, and it pleased him very much. "People, they keep saying, 'Jimmy, I want you to come and work for me,' and all along I been saying, 'I like it fine just where I am.' But lately it seems like the pestering's been getting worse than ever." He felt a moment of panic; the stream of invention threatened to run dry, but a name leapt up out of nowhere into his head and again the stream rushed and tumbled forward. "You know Mr. Carter over in Riverton? Nicest farm around *that* town! Well, he sweet-talk me into it. 'You be happier with a change, Jimmy,' he said. 'You never stay in one place so long before. Time you made something of yourself. Time you got ahead in the world.' "

Mrs. Kelly said, "Time to get ahead in the world—that always sounds so lovely!" She dipped her hand into a pocket in her apron and brought out a roll of bills. "This is your month's pay, Jimmy. Mr. Kelly left it for you in five-dollar bills. He thought you'd think twice before spending them if they were all in fives. Dollar bills, they just slip through your fingers." She handed him the roll. "That's a lot of money, Jimmy," she said.

"I'll stick as tight to it, ma'am, as a duck's foot in the mud."

Mrs. Kelly handed him the bundle, glancing as she did so at Jimmy's soiled shirt. "A couple of old shirts of Mr. Kelly's," she said. "You'd better put one on before you go to your new job. I've packed two or three pairs of socks and a suit of long underwear, practically brand-new, that shrank too small in the waist for Mr. Kelly. And I wrapped up some cookies and a nice piece of store cheese in a wax paper inside the underwear. In case you get hungry."

"No more hungry for Jimmy, ma'am. I'm on my way."

" 'Hungry' reminds me—come along in and have your

breakfast. There's a cake in the oven that I have to keep an eye on."

"I sure hope it wins you first prize, Mis' Kelly."

"Jimmy, I declare!" They both saw that the difficulty of saying a formal good-bye would be too much for them. It was lucky that she could feed him and lucky that he liked to be fed. Mrs. Kelly turned and started for the house and Jimmy followed her. Mrs. Kelly's eggs and bacon—the Kellys' own eggs, the Kellys' own bacon—couldn't be matched by any eggs and bacon in the whole wide world.

After breakfast, cleaning out his room in the barn didn't take Jimmy long. He threw his old shirts and socks into the rusty wire incinerator behind the barn and put on his lumber jacket and fleece-lined leather cap. Sorting out on the cot his collection of comic books, he found that he had thirty-seven in all. He wrapped them up in a bundle and tied them with a stout length of string. The weight of the bundle would be a nuisance, and yet it made him proud. There was an awful lot of reading in that bundle. He drew on a pair of heavy gloves and feinted a few hard blows with them, like a boxer feinting as he waits for the bell.

Mr. Kelly had expected him to finish all his chores before he left, but Jimmy saw now that there wouldn't be time. What if Mr. Kelly were to come back with young Polsky when he, Jimmy, was still at work on the chicken coop? Jimmy had no intention of encountering Polsky. He wanted the boy to think he had gone off in his own car, with a couple of big suitcases on the back seat. Besides, why wouldn't cleaning out the chicken coop be a fine job for Polsky to start on? If he wasn't used to the smell, it would make him good and sick. Jimmy grinned to think of Polsky scraping the chicken droppings off the wooden perches and shoveling them up off the concrete floor. All that greeny-gray shit! Glory be! The kid was in for a surprise.

Jimmy had just started down the lane with a bundle under each arm when he saw the red truck turning in from the state highway. He ran back into the apple orchard and lay down in the soft, high grass. As the truck went by, Jimmy could see the Polsky boy sitting very straight on the seat beside Mr. Kelly. He was short, with yellowy hair and a pug nose. "Little old puny," Jimmy said aloud. When the truck swung around in back of the house, Jimmy got up and ran along the lane to the highway. The sun was over the tops of the highest trees by now. Jimmy figured that it must be nearly eight o'clock. His shoes crunched in the soft gravel of the highway shoulders. He felt he could walk a thousand miles.

No need to walk more than a few—the moment he told Mrs. Kelly the lie about Mr. Carter wanting him on his farm in Riverton, the proposition began to seem a reasonable one. It was as if he wouldn't have been able to think of it if it hadn't been capable of being true. No two ways about it, the Carter farm was the place for him. A showplace, Mr. Kelly had called it. Most of the harvesting was over, but even in winter there was always room on a farm for a good worker. Besides caring for the stock, he could mend walls, pour concrete, whitewash cellars, shingle roofs. He was as strong as any man he had ever met; once, on a bet, he had lifted four eighty-pound sacks of cement, feeling his guts churn in his belly as he did so. Well! He would ask Mr. Carter for a job, and Mr. Carter would say, "Jimmy, it's a deal."

The sun was hot for October. After he had walked four or five miles along the Riverton road, Jimmy wanted to take off his lumber jacket, but because of the two bundles there was no way to carry it. He decided instead to walk more slowly. He counted his steps all the way up to a hundred, then started over again. He kept a finger bent for each hundred steps he walked. Once he had used up his ten fingers, he stopped counting. He turned his head whenever he heard a car or truck coming along the road behind him, but he knew that there wasn't much chance of his being picked up, unless it was by somebody who thought he was still working for the Kellys. The cars that shot past him were driven by strangers. Even the farmers' trucks looked as if they had come from a long ways off. Jimmy noticed that most of the trucks had a lot of children packed in among calves, chickens, and baskets of fruit, and finally it dawned on him—they were on their way to the fair! He grinned and waved to them as they went by; some of the children waved back and some of them thumbed their noses at him.

At every step, Jimmy could feel rubbing against his leg the roll of bills in his trousers pocket. All fives! Maybe after he got his job from Mr. Carter he would go on to the fair. He would give himself that little treat. He had never been able to go, since, when the Kellys went off to it, they would have to leave Jimmy behind in charge of things. Jimmy imagined himself going into Riverton and buying himself a new suit of clothes for the fair. Then he imagined how he would stroll into the fairgrounds as free and easy as if he were the first selectman of Riverton, nodding right and left and saying a pleasant hello to all those strangers. He would make his way up to the front row in the tent where the judges were taking a bite or two out of Mrs. Kelly's cake, or rolling a bit of crumb between their fingers, or even sticking their noses into the cake and sniffing it (for Mrs. Kelly had told him that the smell of a cake was mighty important to judges), and Mrs. Kelly would see him there and her eyes would pop. She wouldn't be able to say much of anything because of the judges and the people watching, but she would be thinking that he had made a million dollars, all in one day. And then he would go into another tent and watch the judges looking over Mr. Kelly's apples. Mr. Kelly had told him that the judges used a magnifying glass—a magnifying glass!—to look for the least little blemish on those shiny McIntoshes. Pretty soon Mr. Kelly would see him there among the judges, and then *his* eyes would pop. "What on earth are you doing here, Jimmy?" Mr. Kelly would ask, and Jimmy would answer, "Happen I find myself free, Mr. Kelly. I thought I'd just drop in and see how our little old apples is making out." The expression that would come over Mr. Kelly's face when Jimmy spoke of "our" little old apples! Jimmy was delighted with the image he had conjured up. He thought hard about it in order to make himself forget the heat of the sun and the way his feet were beginning to hurt inside his shoes.

When Jimmy reached the bridge that stood on the outskirts of Riverton, he turned right, off the highway. He followed a path down through some willow trees to the sandy bank of the river. Seating himself on a dead log, he took off his gloves, lumber jacket, shoes, and socks. He wiggled his toes, then dipped them into the water. The water was much colder than he had expected and made his feet sting. Jimmy lifted his feet and rubbed them to bring the blood back to the surface. He glanced back and forth between his lumber jacket and the two bundles. If he was going to carry the lumber jacket, he would have to get rid of one of the bundles. Jimmy stared at the comic books tied with string and shook his head. He couldn't let them go. He had been a couple of years collecting that much reading. They were old friends by now—Maizie Spinach, Shultzie, and Emerina, blonde vixen daughter of the King of Mars.

Jimmy opened the bundle that Mrs. Kelly had given him. In it were two white shirts, three pairs of socks, and a suit of long underwear. Wrapped in wax paper inside the underwear, as Mrs. Kelly had promised, were a dozen cookies and a hunk of yellow cheese. That part of his problem was quickly solved. Jimmy swallowed the cookies and cheese in alternate bites. In five minutes the food was gone. He scooped up some river water in his hands and drank, to take away the heavy taste of the cheese. Then he sat down on the sand with his back against the log and thought. He felt sleepy, but he knew that there wasn't time for sleep. By the end of half an hour, he had made a plan. He stood up and stripped off his trousers, soiled shirt, and old gray underwear. He would have liked to give himself a nice bath in the river, but the water was too cold. He was glad now that Mrs. Kelly had made him take a bath the week before. He drew on the long underwear that Mrs. Kelly had said was practically new. It felt prickly, the way new woolen underwear always did. If it had been too small for Mr. Kelly, it was bound to be even smaller for Jimmy. Where it hurt him most was across his broad shoulders, so Jimmy picked up a sharp piece of stone and scratched a hole in the shoulder seams of the underwear. He tugged at the hole until he had widened it into a rip. That made the underwear a lot more comfortable. Jimmy put on the three pairs of socks, one on top of the other. He put on both of the white shirts, leaving the collars unbuttoned. He had to wear his old denim trousers for the time being, but as soon as he got into Riverton he would be able to buy new ones.

With the three pairs of socks on his feet, it was impossible to lace his shoes. He made up his mind to buy some new shoes in Riverton—shiny black ones with long pointed toes, of the sort that Mrs. Kelly had never let him buy. Jimmy piled his old shirt, socks, and underwear into Mrs. Kelly's paper bundle and threw the bundle into the river. The current swept it—a jaunty little canoelike object— downstream under the bridge and out of sight.

Jimmy knew better than to try buying a suit in the best part of town. He avoided the main street of Riverton and followed the only other important street block after block until, where the town petered out into open fields, he came on a shop with a weather-beaten black-and-gold sign reading, GENTLE-MEN'S FURNISHINGS. Over much of this sign had been hung a cheap canvas makeshift sign, which read, THRIFT SHOP. BUY HERE AND SAVE. To one corner of the canvas had recently been affixed a sheet of cardpaper, on which someone had crudely hand-lettered the words WELCOME, FAIRGOERS! PRICES SLASHED. In the open air on either side of the doorway to the shop, scores of suits and overcoats hung on galvanized-iron racks. As Jimmy walked up and down in front of the racks, hoping to attract attention without demanding it, an old man shuffled into the doorway. He seemed dazed by the sun. He raised both hands to screen his eyes from it; his skinny old arms were very white, and he held a cigar between the fingers of one hand. *"Just looking or looking?"* he asked.

"Looking," Jimmy said.

"You're outsize," the old man said, in an accusing voice. This remark was followed by a spell of coughing and spitting, through all of which he took pains not to lose the long ash of his cigar. "Outsize," he said at last, catching his breath, "is not so easy." The old man riffled along the cuffs of the jackets of the suits, reading the price tags. He hoisted from among its fellows on the rack a suit of bright-green tweed. "A lovely," the man said, turning it about in the sun. The suit seemed to blaze there, like green fire. "Boston cut. You like it?"

Jimmy nodded. Of course he liked it; he had never seen such a beautiful suit. Within fifteen minutes, after little bargaining, Jimmy had bought the suit and changed into it in a closet at the rear of the shop. He had also bought a silk necktie and a pair of shoes that were every bit as black and sharp of toe as he had longed to have them be. His roll of bills might be terribly reduced—when the old man totted up the cost of the three items, Jimmy felt his heart contract—but the results were worth it. Staring at his reflection in the triple full-length mirror inside the shop, Jimmy reasoned that he had not thrown away a penny of his precious money. On the contrary, he had made a good investment. He took off one of Mr. Kelly's shirts and, buttoning up the collar of the remaining one, put on his new necktie. He could not get enough of staring at himself; he flexed his elbows and knees, he bowed and smiled at his three selves. He felt transformed. There would be no more clowning Jimmy now. He was a big man in a green suit and black shoes, and he wouldn't be playing the fool for anyone. "Outsize" was what the old man had called him, and outsize was what he planned to be.

The old man fitted Jimmy's extra clothing and his bundle

of comic books into a neat cardboard box. This was perhaps to be the old man's one transaction of the day. He had put out a sign welcoming fairgoers, but none were likely to come by—the direct route to the fairgrounds lay on the other side of town. The sale had put the old man in a good mood. He was sorry that the suit was too small and would give poor wear, but his conscience was clear: it was the largest size he had in stock. "On your way to the fair?" he asked Jimmy.

"Yeah, but first I got to see a Mr. Carter about my new job."

"Carter that owns the big farm out east?"

"That's him. Where I'm going to be." He was too proud— oh, especially in his new suit, tie, and shoes he was too proud!—to seek directions. "Coming into town, seems I got myself turned round," he said. "The Carter place . . ." He stood hesitating on the threshold, ready to turn either left or right; it was like him in his transformation to be able to learn things without having to ask.

"Straight out of town a good four miles. Last place on your left before you get to the fair. Fairgrounds is one of the old Carter meadows. In this town it's all in the family, and the family it's all in is Carter." The old man coughed and spat and drew happily on his cigar. That was one of his favorite jokes; it had lasted him a lifetime. "See you later," he said to Jimmy, waving him good-bye. "Haven't missed a fair since I was ten. Danbury isn't a patch on what we got up here."

Jimmy stopped to rest at the top of a hill a couple of miles beyond Riverton. At the end of the valley that lay in front of him were scattered five or six farms. Beyond the last of the white farmhouses, through the blue haze that hung over the valley, Jimmy could make out a Ferris wheel slowly turning, turning. The sun winked and glinted on its swaying gondolas. A crazy quilt of colored tents and sheds lay all round the base of the wheel. The road along the valley was filling up with cars and trucks. Jimmy lay back against the trunk of an oak tree and caught his breath. It was hard work walking in a new suit and new shoes, but it was worth it. Almost everyone who had driven by him had turned and stared, and some of them had waved. The Kellys in their little red truck had driven past him without recognizing him, and that had pleased him more than anything.

A car pulled off the road onto the green knoll where Jimmy was resting. For several minutes after the driver had turned off the motor, it went on puffing and coughing, like an old horse clearing its head and chest after a long uphill pull. The car was evidently very old; it was much higher than an ordinary car, and above the open back seat rose a ten-foot-high plastic figure of a woman. Or, rather, it was a figure of two women, one inside the other; the bigger woman was outlined by red neon tubes, and the smaller one by blue, and the face of the woman in red was frowning, while the face of the woman in blue wore a sultry smile not unlike that of Emerina, daughter of the King of Mars. Jimmy picked up his jacket and cardboard box and strolled across to the car. Seated behind the wheel, the driver had just started eating his lunch out of a paper bag. He was wearing a large white sombrero, a white leather vest, and high white leather boots. He had a white beard and the brightest blue eyes that Jimmy had ever seen.

"Hi, there, cowboy!" the man said.

With his new confidence, Jimmy said, "Cowboy! What you use for eyes?"

"Don't get your Dutch up, cowboy. I'm not a cowboy either." Adroitly, he kicked open the right front door of the car with the heel of his boot. "Like a lift to the fair?"

"I got to stop off first at a farm down there. But I could use a lift. My feet's burned up."

"Climb in, cowboy. Dump it right there. The name's Buckley."

"Sir?"

"William H. K. Buckley, D.M.M."

Jimmy had never heard anyone speak so fast; the words sputtered and popped. "Sir?" he asked again.

"Doctor of Medical Mineralogy. A little specialty of mine."

Jimmy scrambled up onto the high front seat of the car, placing his jacket and the cardboard box carefully beside him. "Split a sandwich with me," Buckley said, reaching into the bag, fetching up a sandwich, and at once pulling it into two parts, paper wrapping and all. "Tuna fish," he said. "Nothing like the natural oils of the tuna to keep the lower bowels well lubricated." He bit heartily into the sandwich, and, with his mouth full, urged Jimmy by repeated nudges and winks of the eye to do likewise. Buckley was ready to talk again when his mouth was scarcely half-empty; bits of bread and tuna flew through the air as he spoke. "I sell a product," Buckley said, "that is guaranteed to take ten pounds of blubber a week off any man, woman, or child in the country. That's where mineralogy comes in. Mineralogy means stone, or the next thing to it, and my product is ninety-five per cent water and five per cent crushed lime-stone. You drink my product, cowboy, you're drinking stone! No wonder the fat falls off!"

Buckley reached into the paper bag and brought out an orange, which, like the sandwich, he split in two with a deft motion of his fingers, giving a half to Jimmy and plunging the other half into his mouth. A few moments later, he was ready to continue; flecks of orange dotted the windshield. "Before I got into calories, I used to be in oils. That's how I learned about tuna and the like of that. Christ, I used to scare people half to death, talking about their lower bowel. Diet is the big pitch nowadays. I sell this little product here"—he handed Jimmy a bottle out of the glove compartment of the car—"that costs a dollar a pint. Deadliest appetite killer known to medical science. One spoonful of this and you want to spit on your food! Take a look at the rig over the back seat." Jimmy turned his head as Buckley flipped a switch on the dashboard. The bigger of the two female forms was outlined in flaming neon. "I call her Fatty," Buckley said. He flipped a second switch, and Fatty faded; in her place, in brilliant blue neon, appeared the smaller form. "I call her Slim," Buckley said. A third switch, and an electric sign over Fatty and Slim began to blink the message, FAT-OFF, FAT-OFF, FAT-OFF.

"Before and after," Buckley said. "Testimonials from coast to coast. Potbellies pour off the fatties like grease off a skillet. Not that you need it, but would you care to try a bottle?"

Jimmy said he would be glad to. It was the least he could do by way of thanking Dr. Buckley for his share of the lunch. Lifting his jacket from the seat, he took care that Dr. Buckley should catch sight of the roll that he drew from the pocket of the jacket. He had only twelve dollars left, but the amount was in one-dollar bills, and he fluffed them out as much as he could. Without haste, he peeled a dollar bill from the top of the roll, then slipped the roll back into the pocket of his jacket. Maybe he could make a present of the bottle of Fat-Off to somebody at the Carter place; he certainly didn't want to take any medicine that would kill *his* appetite.

"Why, good Lord, I meant to let you have it as a gift," Buckley said, tucking the dollar into his vest. He started the engine and swung the big old car back toward the road. Jimmy could hear the plastic figures of Fatty and Slim squeaking above the back seat as the car cleared the ditch at the edge of the shoulder. "You got quite a roll there, cowboy," Buckley said, keeping his eyes on the road.

Jimmy leaned back against the seat, grinning. If there was anything he was sure of, it was that this was the happiest day of his life. Here he was, in his new green suit and black shoes, riding along in a big open car with a doctor who would give you the shirt off his back. You could tell by the expression in the doctor's bright-blue eyes that he was used to having a good time, and why not? Driving around the countryside, heading from one fair to the next, maybe going South in winter— Glory be! Some people had all the fun! Jimmy wished that Mr. and Mrs. Kelly had not already gone on ahead to the fair. He would have liked to have them drive up alongside Dr. Buckley's wonderful car so he could wave to them. "Yeah, I got me a pocketful," Jimmy said. He could not resist adding, in a casual voice, "They mostly fives."

The road had begun to level out along the valley floor. Jimmy could make out the top of a bandstand in the fairgrounds; it vanished at a bend in the road, and Jimmy sat forward to catch his first glimpse of Mr. Carter's farm. At that moment, Dr. Buckley swung the car over onto the shoulder, angrily hammering the steering wheel with his fist. "Now, goddam it to hell!" he said, thrusting the sombrero back off his forehead. "If that isn't the luck of the Irish! I could feel it jumping right out of my hands."

"You got yourself a flat?"

"Take a look at that left rear tire, will you, cowboy?"

Jimmy jumped down from the car and examined the left rear tire. It looked sufficiently full of air to him, and it felt hard to the pointed toe of his shoe. Jimmy crouched to look under the car, and a blast of hot, suffocating air shot without warning from the rusty exhaust pipe. Jimmy choked, trying not to swallow. The tires of the old car spun savagely on the shoulder, throwing gravel up into his eyes. He fell back on his hands, shouting. By the time he had scrambled to his feet, the big car was two or three hundred yards down the road, weaving wildly in and out of traffic. A few seconds later, it had vanished behind a grove of maples. Jimmy shouted, "You got my coat! You got my box!" His voice rose and broke. "You got my money! You got my money!" Though he knew it was hopeless, he started running after the vanished car. What else was there to do but run? Shouting was hopeless, too, but he would have kept on shouting if he could. He had no breath left for it; after the first five minutes, he was too exhausted to run. His heart was hammering not in his chest alone, but, so it seemed, everywhere in his body. He could feel it hammering in his ears, his mouth, the back of his head. His new green trousers had cut welts across his thighs; his feet were afire inside the new shoes. He stood as close as he dared to the stream of traffic, trying to make one among all those cars stop and pick him up. He called out to them, but they could not hear his words; nor could he hear theirs when they called back, though by their gestures he could tell that many of them were jeering at him. Goblin-faces! He was unable to run, he was scarcely able to walk. He felt his eyes stinging with dust and sweat. The once cold October-morning air had turned unexpectedly hot and close. It was like midsummer. Jimmy noticed an ample white farmhouse standing on a rise across the road. Before he could read the name lettered on the tin mailbox, he knew whose house it would prove to be. Carter's place, where he had been going to get his lovely job. Jimmy blinked, only half seeing the big house, the long red barns, the blue metal silos. The showplace. The truth was that there would never have been a job for him there, never in a million years, but he would have asked. Now it was no matter. The job—any job—would have to wait. He had to reach the fairgrounds and get back his money and jacket and bundle of comic books.

Jimmy walked on in pain past the Carter farm. He could hear the band playing clearly now, march after march. The music seemed to come out of the trees in front of him. Jimmy bent down and took off his shoes. There was blood on his socks, blood smeared on the inner lining of his shoes. The soles of his feet were too sore to touch. The people in the cars and trucks that sped past, catching sight of him in socks and holding his shiny new shoes in his hand, laughed and pointed him out to others. He rounded a fringe of woods and there, filling a thirty-acre meadow, was the fair.

The crowd at the fair was much bigger than Jimmy had anticipated. It was going to be a hard job finding anyone in such a mob. He would have to look for Dr. Buckley's car and for FAT-OFF winking on and off above it. A high wire fence surrounded the fairgrounds. Scores of cattle and sheep were lined up inside the fence, waiting to be judged. He saw their owners standing watch over them, polishing the brass tips of the cows' horns, waxing the hoofs of the sheep. Each of the six big tents in the fairgrounds had a sign hanging over the entrance flap; he could see one that said CHICKENS, another that said PRODUCE. Jimmy followed the line of the fence until he reached the entrance gate. There were wooden booths on each side of the gate, and signs in the barred windows of the booths said ADMISSION FIFTY CENTS. EXHIBITORS ADMITTED FREE. A tall man with a badge was standing between the booths, watching the double line of people edging slowly through the gate. Jimmy felt uselessly in his pockets for money. He stood there without moving, letting people brush against him or try to jostle him out of their way. He walked up to the man with the badge, holding his shoes behind him; that way, the man might not notice that he was in his stockinged feet. "Excuse me, Officer," he said. "I just been robbed."

The man with the badge kept his eyes on the crowd. "Sure you didn't leave your money home? People do."

"No, sir."

"You mean you're not sure?"

"No, I *am* sure."

"Happen to know the name of the fellow you claim robbed you?"

"Buckley."

"Doc Buckley?"

"Yeah, him, that's the one! He pick me up in his car and then he rob me. Took my money and my new coat and a bundle of reading I got."

"Doc's been coming here for years." For the first time, the man looked straight into Jimmy's eyes. "Very well liked around here, Doc is. If you don't want those pretty white teeth of yours knocked down your throat, better not tell anyone else what you told me."

"He took everything I got. And just drove off."

"On your way, sonny-boy. I got a job to do."

"*I want my money.*"

The man with the badge glanced down then at Jimmy's stockinged feet and smiled. He fixed his gaze on the crowd and brought the heel of a shoe down on top of one of Jimmy's feet and twisted the heel back and forth and, still smiling, said, "Now, beat it. I've had just about enough from you."

Jimmy turned and limped up the road beyond the gate. He felt pain flooding up and down the length of his leg —new pain raging all round and through the old. Inside the fence stood a long canvas booth with netting down each side and across the back. A man in dirty chinos and a checkered cap was standing behind the booth, pouring himself a drink. He caught sight of Jimmy as he threw back his head to swallow. Holding the bottle in one hand, he walked over to the fence. "Want to see the fair?" he said. "Want to get in without spending four bits?"

Jimmy nodded.

"I'll give you a job," the man said. "Two bucks an hour. Five hours, ten bucks. The nigger I had ran off last night. A nice, easy nigger job. All you got to do is use your head."

"Meaning what?"

"Meaning ask me no questions and I'll tell you no lies. If you can use the money, I'll pass you in."

The man was smiling, and his smile meant something that Jimmy couldn't understand. He said, "No, thanks. There's something else I got to do."

Jimmy followed the fence along the road to where it

turned at right angles and ran across the narrow end of the meadow. The fence led him through a tangle of mountain laurel and hardhack, but he was still in sight of the gate; he could see the head and shoulders of the man with the badge. Finally, he reached the river. The fence paralleled the bank of the river for several hundred yards. It was useless to try and climb it there, because a number of picnickers were seated at tables just inside the fence. A gate in the fence had been opened where the river broadened and grew shallow, but farmers were standing there watering their oxen and horses; there was no hope of sneaking past them unnoticed into the fairgrounds. Jimmy fastened the laces of his shoes together and hung them around his neck. He rolled up his green tweed trouser legs and started wading across the shallow part of the river. The water was icy. Twice he slipped over boulders, bruising his fingers as he caught himself. He sat down on a boulder in the middle of the river to get back his strength. Floating on a water-logged branch below him was a pair of faded denim trousers. Jimmy rubbed his palms against his thighs. He knew the feeling of those old pants well enough. Caught in the twigs of the branch were the soaked, many-colored pages of a comic book. As Jimmy watched, the branch turned over in the current and was swept away. Another comic book lay in the black mud along the riverbank. Jimmy swallowed. He climbed out of the river and up the bank, drawing himself close to the fence with both hands. He saw a few feet beyond him a place where the bank dropped away under the wire mesh of the fence. Dogs had made a hard, regular track there, and the track led on into waist-high laurel on the far side of the fence. Jimmy crawled to the opening and squeezed himself on his belly between the bank and the fence. He had always been so proud of how strong he was, and now he felt so weak, so weak. Once he had got inside the fence, he lay face down on his hands and caught his breath. In a minute or two, he sat up and put on his shoes and rolled down his trousers. He got to his feet and walked quickly out of the laurel into the crowd. Anyone seeing him might have supposed that he had been relieving himself in the bushes; no harm in that. But no one had seen him. He was safe.

Jimmy walked through the fairgrounds, keeping in the thick of the crowd. A weight-pulling contest for oxen was taking place in a wide dirt pit beyond the bandstand. A yoke of oxen was tugging at a wooden boat filled with roughly squared-off chunks of granite. A sign at one side of the pit said PRESENT LOAD, 4450 POUNDS. A farmer was cutting the oxen across the flanks with a long thin whip and cursing them. Farther on, a man and a woman in silver tights were roller-skating on a platform high above the crowd.

Jimmy had almost reached the gate when he caught sight of Buckley. He was standing on a little stage in front of his car, with bright-red Fatty shining behind him. Jimmy stopped on the outer edge of the crowd that had gathered around Buckley. "I ask you," he was saying, "who would be Fatty if she could be Slim?" He pressed a switch in his hand and Fatty went dark as Slim came flickering on in saucy blue neon curves. "You ask what makes you fat, ladies and gentlemen? Simple enough—eating! And what causes eating? Appetite! And what kills appetite? Fat-Off! A harmless product of Mother Nature. Successfully recommended by this physician a thousand times, in a practice extending from coast to coast. Never lost a thin patient! Never kept a fat one! Try your sample bottle of Fat-Off today! Thank you, ma'am! Thank you, sir!" The crowd shifted and began to move away as Buckley hopped down off his little stage and began a lively bottle-by-bottle sale to the latest group of Fat-Off converts. Jimmy edged closer and closer. Buckley looked up from making a sale and saw Jimmy standing there. His bright-blue eyes went blank. "That'll be one dollar," he said, holding out a bottle.

Jimmy said, "I got to have my money."

"Get lost, cowboy," Buckley said.

"You thought I had a big roll," Jimmy said, "and they wasn't anything but ones. Twelve bucks, Mister! You just can't steal that little from a nigger!"

Buckley leapt up onto the stage and whistled twice, sharply. Jimmy saw the man at the gate turn and look toward Buckley, who jerked a thumb in Jimmy's direction. The man started away from the gate, and now he, too, was whistling. Jimmy ducked his head between his shoulders and ran. He tried making a zigzag half circle through the fairgrounds—with his blistered feet, he knew he could never outdistance them running in a straight line. Besides, he was in a cage, so straight lines were dangerous; the meadow was fenced, and there was only the entrance gate and that one break in the fence by the river, too far away for him to reach undiscovered. Running head down, he found himself in front of the long canvas booth with the netting down the sides. He had almost stumbled over the legs of the man with the checkered cap, who was sitting sprawled in front of the booth with his eyes closed. An empty bottle lay on the counter. Jimmy could smell fear coming out of his body along with the sweat, and he shook the man by the shoulder and said, "Mister! I want that job!"

The man opened his eyes. He was drunk and content

and no longer in a hurry to make a deal. "You got your-self in trouble, black boy?" he asked.

"I got to get out of this crowd. Give me the job."

"Getting so late, wouldn't be worth more than a dollar an hour to me now."

"You say," Jimmy said.

The man stood up, steadying himself against the counter, and led Jimmy down the side of the booth. A narrow flap hung open at the end of the booth. Jimmy and the man stepped under the flap. In front of Jimmy was a wall of padded canvas with a round hole in the middle. There were two worn leather grips on each side of the hole. The man said, "All you got to do is stick your head through the hole. You can grab those two handles if you start getting tired. Nobody'll look for you here. These hicks'll try to bounce some imitation baseballs off your head. Most of the time they'll miss. The balls are a little tough, but they won't kill you."

Jimmy hesitated, and the man started to turn away. "It's you who're in trouble, smart ass, not me."

"All right."

Jimmy stuck his head through the hole in the padded canvas. The front of the canvas was painted with broad yellow petals radiating from the hole. Jimmy took the two leather grips and stared straight ahead. It was hard to keep his head up; the starchy canvas at the top of the hole cut into the back of his neck. The man in the checkered cap was setting out rows of balls on the counter at the front of the booth. When he finished setting out the balls, he picked up a megaphone and in a high flat voice started shouting, "Hurry! Hurry! Hurry! Take a crack at the Sun-flower Kid! Hit the Sunflower Kid smack on the old bean!

Three balls for a quarter! Test your aim! Test your skill! Try
out that old baseball arm! Hurry! Hurry! Hurry!"

Jimmy felt the sweat pouring down his face. He could
taste the salt of it on his lips. A couple of men sidled up
and dropped quarters onto the counter. The bigger of the
two men threw the first ball. It struck the padded canvas a
yard over Jimmy's head. Then the big man threw two more.
They both missed Jimmy's head. "Goddam!" the big man
said. "But I'm gaining on it." The other man threw his three
balls easily, taking careful aim. The third ball hit Jimmy
on the forehead. Jimmy flinched, feeling the sting of the
leather against his skin.

The big man dropped another quarter on the counter.
"By God, if it takes me all day," he said.

The man with the cap shouted, "Look at the old high-
school pitcher, folks! Thinks he's pretty good! Can't even
clip the Sunflower Kid! Can't even get close! Can't throw
'em hard enough! Step right up and test your skill! Three
for a quarter!"

The big man threw the first two balls very hard and fast.
The man beside him said, "Take it easy, Carter. Don't try
to kill the guy."

Carter, Jimmy thought. He saw the big man throw the
third ball, and he saw the ball coming at him. He ducked
his head. No use. The ball smacked against the side of his
head, along his cheek. The skin was cut. Jimmy could
feel the blood against his cheek, and the air cooling his
blood.

Jimmy could hear Carter saying, "By God, I hit him!
I really got the son of a bitch!"

The two men walked away, laughing. Jimmy shook his
head, trying to keep the sweat out of his eyes. He saw

Buckley and the man with the badge crossing the field in front of the booth. They glanced at him for a moment, then glanced away. They were swallowed up in the crowd. Jimmy ducked as three boys started throwing balls at him. The balls thudded into the canvas all round him. Two of them struck him on the top of his head. His hands gripped the worn handles. His knees were shaking so hard that he couldn't stand. He slumped against the canvas. A lot of people were coming out of the exhibition tents beyond the booth. The judging was over, Jimmy guessed; the people would be wanting to have some fun. The faces in the crowd grew blurred. Out of the blur emerged a face he recognized; it was the face of the old man at the store in Riverton. He was running a skinny white hand over his face and smiling. He placed his cigar carefully on the edge of the counter and picked up a ball. Jimmy tried to keep his eyes focused on the man, but his eyelids faltered and he dropped his head. Two balls struck him in succession. Jimmy hung against the canvas.

A voice he knew cried, "Just!"

Jimmy tried to call to Mrs. Kelly, but his voice was gone. Besides, the canvas was pressed against his throat; he could scarcely breathe. Then he heard two voices outside the back of the booth. One of the voices belonged to the man with the checkered cap, and the other voice was Mr. Kelly's, and they were arguing about money. Then the talking stopped. Jimmy hung against the canvas and waited. There were so many things to ask, if only everything didn't hurt so much. He had to be sure to ask Mrs. Kelly about her cake. That was one thing. And there was something else, if he could remember it. He felt somebody lifting him under the arms, and he stumbled across the field with someone's

arm across his back. At first he could see only the trampled
grass under his feet; then he saw the back of the Kellys'
red truck. He heard the tailgate rattling down. The bed of
the truck held a few inches of hay, covered by a tarpaulin.
He lay on the tarpaulin, drawing his legs up close to his
chin. He could hear the Kellys talking on the front seat
of the truck. "If we drop him off at the hospital," Mr. Kelly
said, "they'll patch him up, and in a day or two he can be
on his way. If we take him home, we'll never get rid of him."

"But, Just—"

"I know. Goddam it, I *know!* I'm taking him home."

They were wrong. He was too weak to tell them, but
they were wrong. He wasn't that Jimmy—their Jimmy—
any more. He would rather have gone to the hospital than
back to the farm. As soon as he was well enough, he'd light
out so fast they'd think he flew. They hadn't seen what he
had seen: the big man in the mirror in the store at Riverton,
bowing and smiling. The truck started out of the fairgrounds, and at every bump his body hurt anew. A smell
of apples came up out of the hay. That was the other
thing he would have to remember to speak of. Mr. Kelly's
apples. He felt himself slipping into space. He felt a darkness closing over him. Nobody had to worry about him any
more. He was so full of pain and so content. For a while
there, he had thought it the happiest day of his life, and
maybe it would be, maybe it was.

The Other Side

My earliest memory is of my father becoming an old man. He and I are in a room I have never seen before. It has varnished matchwood walls and a wooden ceiling, and from a pole in a doorway hangs a portiere of iridescent sea shells. The room is cold and smells of damp. My father goes about opening windows to let in the fresh summer air. The sashes are hard to raise after being stuck fast all winter, and he strikes the frames again and again with his plump fists. Once the windows are up, a breeze from the Sound makes the shells on their knotted cords rustle dryly together, and I run to part them. I want to be first to see what is on the other side. But it is a jumble of shadows, and for a moment I hold back, my fingers among the shells.

"Go ahead, Tim," says my father. "There's nothing there."

His saying it has put something there, and I choose a shell and spin it round and round on its cord, as if that were what I had run across the room to do. My father stands at one of the windows, the sky behind him, his face a blur. I make out the top of his pink bald scalp and the fringe of curling gray hair above his ears.

"Go on," he says. "It's just a room."

"Don't want to."

"You did a second ago. What are you afraid of?"

Round and round goes the pearly shell. "Not afraid."

"A big boy like you!"

It is still daylight outside, but the room is darkening. My father's body seems to swell and swell against the window. Kate and my mother are unpacking the car and piling luggage by the locked back door. Because I am younger than Kate and have behaved so well on the long trip from home, I have been given the treat of entering the house alone with my father.

"There's something there."

"Now, Tim," says my father. "We won't have any of that, will we?"

"There is. I saw it."

"Don't lie."

"I'm not. I really did see something."

"A bear? A witch? A goblin?"

"Something."

"Cowards and liars," says my father, "are the two worst things in the world, and the sooner you learn that, the better."

I remember how he came smiling across the room at me then, getting bigger and bigger until everything else in the room was blotted out. He picked me up under the arms and thrust me face forward through the shells. My back was pressed against his fat belly and I tried to hit him across the face, but my arms wouldn't bend right. I kept hitting air, and he kept laughing and lifting me higher and higher into the shadows and saying, "Nothing, see? Nothing! Nothing!"

At last I hit him, and he stumbled and let me go. I fell

sidewise into a shadow that was more than a shadow. It was a table, and I struck the edge of it above my eye and burst out crying. My father bent down in the dark, groping for me with outstretched hands, then picked me up and carried me into the other room. He sat in a wicker rocker and bounced me on his knees, so bony compared to the rest of him, and said in a loud voice, "No, boy, no! It's all right. Don't yell."

But I went on yelling, partly because my forehead hurt and I was uncomfortable in his lap, and partly because I wanted Mother and Kate to find me there, with him to blame for my misery. Sure enough, in a moment they hurried up the front steps and into the dusky room. Mother took me away from him, and as soon as she had tucked my head into the safe place between her neck and shoulder, I stopped yelling. "Poor baby!" she said, marching up and down the room and swaying under the weight of me. "What happened to my baby?"

"An accident, but he'll live," said my father. "He knocked his head against something in the dining room."

Mother held me away from her. "Look at that bump!" she cried. "It's a wonder the skin isn't broken! I never saw such a bump!" Then she hugged me closer than before, and the thought of how my skin might have broken and the blood gushed over everything made more tears come. I squeezed them out against her soft white neck.

Kate danced about Mother and him and me and said, "What do you mean, accident? What kind of accident? How come?"

"Now, now! Water over the dam," said my father. "Let's finish opening the house before dark. Those windows were the devil."

"Only, it wasn't an accident," I said.

143

Kate could always guess when I had more to say. She tugged at my feet in the folds of Mother's skirt and said, "What wasn't, Timmy? Tell me what!"

They were waiting for me to speak. I held the words in for as long as I could, and when I couldn't hold them in any longer, I said, "He dropped me."

"Phil!" Mother said. She was ready to be angry with him then and there. It took her no time at all to get angry, or to get over being angry. "What on earth were you doing with my Bumpo?"

He was hoping to catch my eye, but I wouldn't look at him. "We needed some light in there," he said, ducking his head toward the portiere of shells. "God knows where the lights are in this old dump."

"There's only gas," Mother said. "The agent told us that in March. They haven't run the electric wires to this end of the beach yet. We thought it wouldn't matter." I didn't want Mother drifting off onto that subject, and I moaned a little into her neck and brought her round. She crossed to the doorway and, parting strands of amber shells, peered into the room. "You sent poor Tim in there alone?" she asked him. "Into that cave? Knowing how he hates the dark?"

"It's you who've taught him to hate it, if he does," my father said. "You're worse than any child about the dark." He was still trying to catch my eye, but I wouldn't let him, and he said, "We both went in there. I was holding him up to see if he could find a light, and he fell."

"He said you dropped him."

"I say he fell."

"Phil, Phil! You're always so hard on them."

"Hard!" he said. "They're spoiled from morning to night, and you know it."

He hadn't told Mother the truth, and I wasn't going to tell her the truth either. I wanted her out of it, so that whatever was going to happen would be only his and mine. I said to Mother, "Let me down." She would have held me, but I had had enough of that, and I squirmed against her body and said, "No! Let me down!" She opened her arms and I slid out of them to the floor. I said to Kate, "Look at Daddy's hands. What he did to them."

"Poor Daddy!" Kate said. She ran to him and patted his reddened hands. He stared at me over Kate's head, wondering what I would say next, and I stared back.

"Poor Phil!" Mother said, her voice like Kate's. My leaving her had made her give up being angry with him. "You do rush into things so! We'll be here all summer. There's no need to kill yourself."

"The windows had to be opened," he said. "The house was a grave."

"Darling, how awful you make it sound! I think it's a very nice house."

"I love it," Kate said. "Love it, love it, love it!"

He saw then that Mother and Kate had forgiven him, but he couldn't make out whether I had forgiven him. "Tim," he said, "what about helping me get the back door unlocked? And a fire going in the kitchen stove?"

If I agreed to help him, I would seem to be forgiving him, but if I didn't agree to help him, he might ask Kate instead. I said, "All right," thinking of "All right" as weaker than "Yes."

He reached out to touch me, and for a moment I let his hand rest on my head. Then I asked him, "Which way's the kitchen?"

He nodded toward the portiere. "That way."

"All right," I said again, and plunged through the shells.

The shadows on the other side were deeper now than ever. From their darkness, I looked out through the rocking and rustling shells into the twilight of the room I had left. I could see the three of them standing there, but they could not see me. My father called to me to be careful, and when I failed to answer, he said sharply, his voice rising, "Tim! Where are you?" I called back to him out of the shadows, "Here! What are you waiting for? Come on!," and at last he came toward me, but how slowly, holding one hand before his face, like an old man afraid of getting hurt.

The Loser

In any organization above a certain size, whether it be a pension-planning company of the sort I work for here on Fifth Avenue, or a law firm down on the Street, or an architects' collaborative out in Westchester, if the sample contains a minimum of from fifty to a hundred people, it is safe to predict that among that number will be found at least one specimen of what I call the classic loser. Now, the proportion of classic losers to be found in the population as a whole is, of course, much larger; the organizations I've cited will have taken pains to screen out every loser, classic or otherwise, so the presence of even a single specimen is a cause for wonder to the other employees and a greater cause for chagrin to management. Nevertheless, in my experience no organization has ever succeeded in reaching the statistical goal of what we may call zero losers. Why should this baffling situation arise and why does it remain an insoluble problem? The question is well worth asking in the light of the fact that the classic loser will stand out with such a vividness of unsuitability that one would expect him—or, though far more rarely, her—to be rejected by Personnel the very moment he steps across the threshold. What are the powers-that-be thinking of when they hire such an obvious misfit? Or are they simply not thinking?

The answer, I believe, is that they are indeed thinking, but that the classic loser has the power to alter people's thought *against their will.* His sorry demeanor and the evidence, readily vouchsafed by him, of a past crowded with disastrous episodes become, in an uncanny fashion, his credentials; he is accepted not because he is desirable, but because he is, for the time being, irresistible. He parades his naked weakness as if it were a kind of armed strength. The display of old wounds amounts to a method of hypnosis, in the presence of which the skills acquired in a lifetime of coolly assessing one's fellows are suddenly rendered trifling. Personnel, so quick to expose the hidden places in the lives of ordinary candidates for jobs, stares with fascination upon the sad man without secrets. I mentioned that the classic loser is irresistible for the time being, and this is because it is in the nature of the hypnotic state that it cannot continue indefinitely; still, for as long as it does so, what a menace it represents to any well-knit group! For the role of the loser is precisely the reverse of the ancient role of the scapegoat, upon whom once a year the sins of the tribe were ritually heaped and the scapegoat then sacrificed for the common good; in the case of the loser, it is not the sins of the many that are concentrated upon him, but his sins that are scattered among the many. He poisons the once healthy air and diminishes the energies of the entire establishment. He will move on at last—the classic loser always moves on at last, in effect choosing to sacrifice the tribe he has adopted before the tribe has found any adequate means of sacrificing him—but the infection he leaves behind will in nearly every instance require many years to purge.

Of the handful of losers I have encountered in the course of my long career with this organization, most have moved in and out of our highly efficient little whirlpool with a merciful speed, vanishing after a while as if they had been so much mere soiled and ineffectual foam. But they were not foam, or not altogether, and it is sometimes the case that long after their departure an obituary of one or another of them will appear in the New York *Times*—an obituary whose importance the *Times* evidently will have judged according to the dead man's connection with our firm. It may turn out that few of us who read the obituary will be able to remember a word that the dead man spoke, or even perhaps what he looked like: was he the hawk-faced little man who used to flatten himself like the crushed corpse of a crow against the wall of a corridor when anyone passed him, though the corridor was wide enough for two big men to pass in comfort? Or was he the sour blond boy who spent much of the day in a nearby bar, writing his calculations in cramped wheels of equations along the circumference of innumerable cardboard beer coasters, which he would gather up at nightfall and deposit in the catch basin at the corner of Fifty-seventh Street and Fifth Avenue? (We had assumed of the blond boy that he was out interviewing clients; his stay with us was, for a loser, unusually brief.) Scores and hundreds of faces pass in an office and blur in memory, and the names affixed to them are blotted out; if I remember one particular loser more vividly than any other, it is because it was a portion of the only genius he possessed to make me feel guilty for disliking him. It was a guilt I had no reason to feel—had I not the right to dislike a dis-likable man?—and yet I go on unreasonably feeling it to this day. I perceive that even writing about him now, so long after his death, will not lessen my guilt. He has me locked in an embrace that nothing as simple as his death or the passage of time can release me from. It was his gift to gather a person in against the person's will and then never let go; I will try to tell the truth about the Loser, but not in the hope that I can slough him off at last.

He was lame. One had to feel sympathy for him because of that inescapable burden, and it didn't occur to any of us in the organization not to feel it, at least for a time. (A good many of us are actuaries, and actuaries are commonly thought to be cold fish; I can only protest that it is not so.) I have always assumed that the head of Personnel hired the Loser in part because of his disability; I have assumed, too, that the Loser was well aware that this was one of the reasons he had been hired. For it became plain early in his sojourn with us that, whether consciously or unconsciously, he trafficked in his lameness. His limp was much more pronounced on the days when he was in need of encouragement than it was on the days when he was not. I would see him approaching a colleague's door for help, and his gait would be almost literally tumble-down; leaving the colleague's door, his gait would be close to normal. Moreover, with a cunning that one couldn't fail to admire, he managed to make the low quality of his work a function of his lameness. He was a careless handler of statistics, who sought constantly to borrow the other statisticians' work notes and mathematical tables, but his professional failings had nothing to do with the condition of his legs; how, then, did he contrive to trick us into feeling that if we didn't admire his work we were despising him as a cripple? It was a blackmail that he practiced with mastery in half a dozen forms. One of the most contemptible of these forms was the device of praising a colleague above his worth, at the same time flagrantly abasing himself. One would cringe at the extravagance of his compliments—an analysis of a retirement plan for a bottled-gas handlers' union cannot be dealt with as if it were a canvas by Matisse—and one would cringe equally at the intimacy of his confession of self-loathing. He would come up to me, I remember (*very* close up to me, for it was among his disagreeable mannerisms to make every encounter an eyeball-to-eyeball affair), and assure me that never in a thousand years would he be able to write a presentation as excellent as one of mine. It was a remark that presented difficulties. On the one hand, what he said was true: any piece of work that reached a certain level of competence was far beyond the Loser. On the other hand, for this very reason the compliment, despite its immense thousand-year scale, was a tiny one. To make matters worse, the Loser, though he happened to be speaking the truth, was the last man on earth by whom one wished to be judged. Even less did one want to be warmly congratulated by him. I would feel his valueless praise fastening itself to me like some odious poultice, but any protest on my part would be in vain. He would hail it as demonstrating that my modesty was a match for my great gifts; more slovenly glop of commendation would come flooding in on me. Worst of all was the fact that he really did admire me and really did deplore his ineradicable second-rateness. He saw plainly enough that he was not fit to succeed, but to insist that the rest of us see this, and then that our seeing it be a means of his making good—! That was but one of his forms of blackmail, and so was his indirectly conveying to the rest of us that if we didn't consent to his becoming a peer, we would be forcing him to become a pariah. All or nothing, said the silent, outrageous threat: there was to be no middle ground. That is not how offices of our high reputation are run—the middle ground is where the greater part of our work is accomplished, and it is a perfectly honorable place to be—but none of us could bear to pronounce anathema upon him; he was, alas, a member of the human race, and we were still mesmerized by his past miseries. (So much for our being cold fish!) And so he trapped us one by one into a seeming friendship with him. We became unwilling accomplices of his mediocrity. He linked arms with ours and smiled his classic loser's smile and said how great it was that we were all toilers together in such a wonderful institution.

If how losers get hired by companies normally as discriminating as we are has an element of mystery in it, how losers get fired is also curious and worth examination. In our shop, the word "fired" is nearly always too strong a term for the actual event, which in most cases consists of having reached the last, negligible step in a series—of facing that point of dissatisfaction at which both the company and the employee are equally grateful for a parting of the ways. In the case of the Loser, however, there was an abrupt and identifiable proximate cause, which was an injudicious act of hubris on his part. It appeared that his private life, about which I knew very little, was every bit as ramshackle as his professional one, about which I was getting to know more than I wished to. In the brief time that he worked for the company, the Loser was, as he put it, between marriages, and the moment came when, deciding to cut corners for financial and perhaps other reasons, he simply moved into the office and began to live there. Hard as I find it to believe in retrospect, he actually set up a form of light housekeeping on the premises. The gall of the man! His cubicle was too small to contain a couch, and there must have been many a night when, with some of the partners working late, he couldn't avail himself of the couch in the reception room. Perhaps he slept at his desk, or perhaps he stretched out on the linoleum-covered floor; nor am I beyond supposing that from time to time some poor loser of a girl took pity on him and let him share the sweaty dishevelment of her bed. His desk, as I was later to learn from the office manager, was transformed into a sort of chiffonier—odds and ends of ill-pressed clothing filled the drawers, and an overcoat and a pair of galoshes were kept wrapped in a plastic shopping bag in the knee space of the desk. He brought in an electric hot plate, which he kept concealed in a large orange cardboard letter file. Other files held cans of instant coffee, boxes of biscuits, jars of marmalade and peanut butter. The blotter on his desk grew soggy; it became a Sargasso Sea of cookie crumbs and specks of cheese. For the first time, the office had a mouse. No doubt the Loser had brought it in with his groceries, in a brown paper bag from the nearest deli. The mouse throve on the Loser's leavings and, for all I know, became his pet.

These distasteful domestic arrangements were to be revealed only after the Loser, true to the temperament of all losers, went too far and by choice became the agent of his doom; which is to say that he expanded his territory to include the men's room. We might never have noticed that he brushed his teeth and shaved there and —I trust—treated himself to an occasional early-morning sponge bath; what attracted the attention of no less a person than the chairman of the board and gave us a sufficient reason for discharging the Loser was an incident that resulted from his having the nerve to do his laundry there. He would improvise a cat's cradle of strings from the mirror above the sinks to the stanchions supporting the toilet-booth doors and suspend from these strings an assortment of newly washed hose, boxer shorts, shirts, and handkerchiefs. Doing his laundry early on Saturday night, before setting out on his weekly spree (we do not spy on our employees, but there are people about whom it is difficult *not* to acquire information), he would take care to have the laundry down and out of the way before anyone turned up on Monday morning. Unfortunately, his schedule did not allow for chance visits to the office—especially not a chance visit by the chairman, who, on his way home late one Saturday evening from a supper party at "21," had his driver stop off at our building; it had occurred to him that he might as well pick up some papers that he would be needing to study in preparation for a conference being held the following week. The chairman located the papers in his office and then, passing the men's room on his way out and being not only elderly but also the most efficient of men, thought to take advantage of his opportunity. He pushed open the door, perhaps a trifle vehemently—for all his age, he is a man impulsive to the point of brusqueness—and the door struck the outer reaches of the Loser's cat's cradle of strings. Down on the chairman's carefully barbered head as he stood in the dark and fumbled for the light switch fell the great soft web of the Loser's dripping-wet underclothes. It cannot have been pleasant, pulling the clammy, unknown things off one's face and shoulders; nor can the wetness seeping from the papers into the chairman's Weatherill evening jacket have improved matters. Worst of all must have been the discovery, once the light had been turned on, of what those clammy things were. I have heard that the chairman spent a sleepless night and a raging Sunday; be that as it may, the gravely hung-over Loser had left our employ by Monday noon. Two office boys filled several paper cartons with his household effects and left them for him on the sidewalk outside the building. It was a week before the mouse was caught, and by then it was half-dead of hunger.

Remembrance

Rosemary brought the news home at noon, as proudly as if it had been an *A* in arithmetic. "Want to know something?" she asked, sitting down to lunch, and when her mother said, "What is it, dear?," she answered, between mouthfuls, "Mr. Hubbard's dead."

"Oh, no!" Mrs. Lawrence said. "*Our* Mr. Hubbard?"

Rosemary nodded. "I saw one of those funny-looking flower things on the door and Katie was just closing the door and I asked her. He's dead, all right."

"Poor man, I didn't even know he was sick."

Rosemary, who was ten, had not often possessed information of value. She paid it out little by little as she ate. "He wasn't sick, he just died," she said. Then, with a knowing shake of the head, "He was awful old."

"He must have been eighty. I can't imagine the neighborhood without him."

"Eighty-six. Katie said he went to sleep and never woke up."

"Poor Mrs. Hubbard! What on earth will she do without him?"

"She still has Katie and Jox." Katie was the Hubbards' housemaid, and Jox was the Hubbards' dog.

"That's true. But she and Mr. Hubbard—they've lived in that house so long. They've never *not* been there together."

"Maybe I better write her a letter."

"That would be nice, dear."

"Now."

"No, no, finish your lunch first."

"I want to write it now."

"You sure you know what you want to say?"

With shining eyes, scornfully, Rosemary said, "Of course! Writing's easy." In three or four minutes, she was back in the dining room with a sheet of note paper boldly scrawled over from top to bottom. "You can look at it if you want to," she said to her mother, neither holding the letter out to her nor withdrawing it.

Mrs. Lawrence took the letter, which read:

Dear Mrs. Hubbard:

So sorry to hear about Mr. Hubbard. We all loved him and you so much. I even overherd some people say you were the wonders of this whole town. And you are. And even now, when one sunbeam has gone from the sky, there are fifty of yours left up there to shine for us. Remember I am thinking of you.

Your friend,
Rosemary Lawrence

Mrs. Lawrence gathered Rosemary in against her. "Darling, it's beautiful," she said.

"Oh, pooh!" Rosemary said. She adored praise.

"I think you must be the lovingest child that ever was," her mother said. "I'm glad we named you just what we did."

"Whatever that means," Rosemary said.

"My mother was dying when I started to have you," Mrs. Lawrence said. "In a famous play that you'll see someday is a girl who's very sad and is scattering flowers over the stage, and she says, 'There's rosemary, that's for remembrance.' And I named you for remembrance, and you are."

"Oh, pooh!" Rosemary said again, this time without pleasure. She didn't understand about the play, but she saw that her mother's eyes were full of tears, and she hated that. Taking back the letter, she folded it and stuffed it into an envelope. "I'll leave it under their front door on the way to school," she said. "We got a big test this afternoon. All about the stupid colonies."

The test wasn't really until the next day; she had told the fib to distract her mother, but, for once, fibs didn't work. "I wish she could have known you," her mother said. "She'd have been so proud."

Rosemary thrust herself away from her mother. "I'd never have told you about Mr. Hubbard if I'd known you were going to be such a *cry*baby about it," she said, and ran straight out of the house to keep her mother from kissing her good-bye.

Something
You Just Don't Do
in a Club

It will be telling you more about a club I belong to than about me when I say that, as a lawyer, I'm apt to be looked down on by the other members. Artist members of the club are particularly skeptical of giving us lawyers the run of the place, but they're by no means alone in their prejudice—even the architects appear to consider themselves better than we are, though it beats me how a follower of that dog-eat-dog profession could possibly stick up his nose at anyone outside it. Such distinction as we lawyers may have acquired in the world is beside the point in the Parnassus; there we are simply people who are not "creative," whatever that anomalous word may mean, and our supposed uncreativeness makes us the butt of innumerable not very witty jokes. Still, there are times when, far from being looked down on, we come close to being looked up to. These occasions are familiar enough in any club: some nasty little mess, usually involving both money and an infraction of club rules, arises and must be dealt with as quickly and quietly as possible. Oh, then how eagerly we're sought out and begged—with many a flattering word about our special competence in manipulating people and keeping confidences—to clean up the mess, report its cleaning up in a discreet whisper to the powers that be, and leave not a trace of the mess or our secret labors behind!

More than once in my twenty-odd years in the club, I've been called on to do such a job. The last time was only a couple of weeks ago, and, to put it far more temperately than it deserves, I'm still of two minds about it. As a lawyer, I like to stand well back from a situation. I haven't been able to do it in this case, and the sensation is novel and unpleasant. No doubt the affair has troubled me more than it should have, because it marks one of my rare failures. (I risk sounding vainglorious when I use the word "rare," but the truth is that my failures, both at the bar and away from it, have been exactly that. After all, the record has been piling up for a good many years now, and can be examined.) I notice among the younger men in the club a tendency to belittle the competitive spirit, but I was brought up believing in it, and I still do. I like to succeed at things; what's more important, I hate failing at them. Frankly, it irks me to have failed so conspicuously in respect to Johnny Pinkham. I gather that I am not—or not yet—a laughingstock in the club, but I *feel* like one. I feel outwitted. A certain small sum of money has been lost to me, probably forever, but the money doesn't matter. My annoyance springs from my having been exposed to ridicule in an episode that I strongly preferred to play no part in. It will be a long while before I can be forced to play such a part again.

I say "forced," and the term is not too strong, for, in my opinion, the board of governors, of which I am myself a member, did wrong to drag me into the very middle of the affair. To make an Irish bull, I oughtn't to have been dragged into it, because I was already there. Pinkham was an old friend of mine—I had, indeed, put him up for the club. To the board, this fact and the fact of my having dealt successfully with similar club matters were reason enough for placing the whole burden of Pinkham's case on my shoulders; to me, however, these facts were precisely the reason for *not* having the burden placed there. As Pinkham's proposer, I was, after all, an interested party, potentially subject to two thoroughly contrary temptations; one threatened injury to the club, and the other threatened injury to Pinkham. Either I might be tempted to whitewash him in order to protect my reputation as a judge of men, or I might be tempted to blacken his name unduly in order to punish him for having implicated me in a club mess. Needless to say, to a man of honor both of these temptations were bound to remain potential, but, knowing human nature, the law has seen fit to remove all such temptations from the ordinary processes of adjudication, and even in private matters they ought not to be lightly disregarded. Moreover, as a lawyer I had already rendered the Parnassus a sufficient number of unrecorded services; in my modest, "uncreative" way, I had done my share to keep the club the fine institution it is. I tried to beg off on these grounds, and the president said, affecting to speak to the board at large but staring at me across the table, "*Some*body is going to have to do the dirty work, and it is a tradition in the club that, wherever possible, this particular dirty work be done by a friend."

Having given in to the president—for all his jokes and stories, there is iron in the man, and few people manage to refuse him what he really wants—I rang up Pinkham in the country and arranged to meet him at the club in the following week, on the occasion of his next visit to town. It appeared that he would be taking a late-afternoon train back to Connecticut that same day, so, at some inconvenience to myself, I agreed to come up to Gramercy Park a little before three. It meant leaving Wall Street a couple of hours early and throwing away the best part of the afternoon, but I had no choice; as far as I'd let Pinkham know, our meeting was to be entirely social, and I was afraid that if I made difficulties about the time, he would suggest, in his amiable way, postponing it.

I'd asked Pinkham to meet me in the so-called Red Room of the club ("so-called" because it was long ago painted white and gold; the clubhouse was once a private mansion and is old enough to be full of such booby traps for new members). It is a rather forbidding room, and few members of the club ever go into it, so it was an admirable place for our encounter. I expected Pinkham to be late and had armed myself with a copy of *Country Life* and, though it was by no means my usual hour for having a drink, a long Scotch, but he surprised me by being on time. This made me more uneasy than ever about my task. His punctuality was, I thought, a pretty good sign that he suspected why I'd invited him to stop by. We often saw each other in general gatherings at the club, but it had been a couple of years since we had had a private drink together.

Catching sight of me at the windows, Pinkham rushed across the room in his usual boy-athlete fashion——I half expected him to vault the couch that lay between the door and me. Would he never slow down, I wondered, never act his age, which was surely past fifty by now? The curious thing was his being all of a piece in his youthfulness. Some of us, as we grow older, contrive to remain youthful in

one or two respects, but rarely in many; Pinkham was remarkable for the fact that his body, his manner, his
interests, his very way of thinking were all those of a playful, intelligent undergraduate. Furthermore, it apparently
cost him no effort to keep these diverse aspects of himself up to the same bouncy mark. I would have liked to
think that his legs ached from running up to the club's
third-floor dining room two steps at a time, as he always
did, but I was sure they didn't suffer the slightest twinge.
Instead, it was *my* legs that ached as I rode up in the elevator
and thought of how his legs ought to.

I was sure, too, that Pinkham's enthusiasm for new
people, new books, new works of art was as spontaneous
now as it had been at twenty. Pinkham was a sculptor,
and it's been my experience of sculptors that they tend
to go sour a lot earlier than the rest of us. For all I know,
this is a hazard of the profession—maybe there aren't
enough juicy commissions to go around these days, or
maybe the gaps between the different schools of sculpture
have become so great that they're no longer schools but
armed camps. (I owe that witticism to our president; it is
one of his good things.) Whatever the reason may be,
it strikes me that sculptors speak more disagreeably about
the new men coming up than painters and writers do, and a
thousand times more disagreeably than lawyers do. But
I except Pinkham. I don't know whether he was a first-
rate or second-rate sculptor, but I know he was a generous
one. There was what can only be called a sweetness about
the way he welcomed younger men—a sweetness that was
itself intrinsically young. I had yet to see in him a trace
of that tired miserliness of feeling that people have in
mind when they call somebody patronizing.

But that, of course, is my point: Pinkham never *was*

tired, never had to fake a freshness he didn't feel. Even in respect to his memory (my own began to decay in my twenties and is now a daily embarrassment to me, not only professionally but at home), Pinkham remained a marvel of undiminished alertness. The impressions he took in might have been each of them a first impression, they were so clear and ineradicable. It was unheard-of for him to repeat a story or fail to recall the name of a person to whom he had been even casually introduced. In the nature of things, this made him a very desirable member of the club, and I had often been congratulated on having proposed him. It was unnatural for a man to be as pleased with simply being alive as Pinkham appeared to be, but, far from striking a false note, his pleasure in life seemed to all of us in the club the truest thing about him. We may not have understood what made him tick—I, for all our years of friendship, certainly didn't—but we were grateful for his joyous presence amongst us; though he had been a member for only five or six years, which is a very short time indeed as time inside the club is measured, he was well on his way to serving as our model of a perfect Parnassian.

Yet here I was in the Red Room, waiting, at the request of the other members of the board of governors, to ask him to resign.

"You're looking very well, Edward," he said, and the formality of this—for I am nearly always addressed as Eddie—I took for a clue to how much he suspected.

"I'm fine," I said. "A little overweight but fighting it. What'll you drink?"

"Maybe I should wait awhile. I had a couple at lunch."

I knew *I* would feel better if he had a drink in his hand. I said, "You can't let me drink alone."

"Is that a Scotch? All right, I'll have one, too."

I banged a bell and ordered a Scotch for Pinkham. (Bells are another booby trap in the club. Though they all look pretty much alike, some must be banged and others twisted to make them ring, and it takes a man years to distinguish bangers from twisters.) It seemed wise to keep off the reason for our meeting until after his drink had arrived, but Pinkham would have none of it. He was always so open and offhand that it was impossible to build any polite constructions between oneself and him. Ordinarily, one didn't want to, though as a lawyer I may note that I've a higher opinion of such constructions than most people appear to have nowadays.

"Never been in this embalming room before," Pinkham said. "I wouldn't call it exactly friendly-feeling."

"Oh, I like it," I said, thinking that if Pinkham had felt an air of unfriendliness, it must be mine and not the room's. We can never be sure how much of even our most carefully disguised emotions we emanate; it was certainly true that I was feeling unfriendly, and it was possible that he detected it but mistook the source. Unfriendly, and with good reason, for hadn't he let me down in the shabbiest possible way? I was justified in my irritation, no doubt of that; yet I didn't want him to become aware of it. The interview promised to be painful enough as it was. "I come in here a lot," I said. "Especially when I've some heavy reading to do."

Pinkham ducked his head at the *Country Life* in my lap. "Don't let me stop you."

That was his way of being droll.

165

" 'Heavy,' I said. I only look at the pictures in this."

"You buying a place in England? I pick about three a week out of those front pages. Usually in the Cotswolds. And always with a walled garden."

"Aren't they beautiful? But England must be getting very rich—the prices have been going up at a terrible rate. Even in my imagination, I can't afford anything but old rectories."

"Oh, I never worry about the money part!" Pinkham exclaimed, taking his drink from the waiter. "That'd spoil the fun."

Over Pinkham's conventional, not very strong protest, I signed the chit for his drink. He had given me the perfect opening, but I couldn't make out whether it had been given to me on purpose; his face was a merry, boyish blank. "Now that you've brought up the subject," I said.

Still blankly and merrily, he asked, "What subject is that? Houses? England?"

"Money."

"Oh, Lord, did I? How dull."

"Johnny, listen. This is serious. I'm sore as hell at you *because* of money."

Maybe I'd been wrong in thinking he knew why I'd asked him to the club. His ingenuous protest sounded entirely real. "Eddie! What on earth have I done?"

"For one thing, you've been extremely rude to my friend John Stanley."

"Stanley? I don't even know him, so how can I have been rude to him?"

"Stanley is the club treasurer."

"Oh, my God! You're talking about my bills."

"I'm talking about the fact that you've been in arrears on your dues for a solid year and in arrears on various house charges for at least eighteen months. And haven't had the courtesy to answer a single one of the three perfectly nice, polite letters that John Stanley sent you, asking you either to pay up *in toto* or, if you couldn't afford that, to talk over with him some arrangement for paying up little by little."

"Where the hell did *you* get all this inside poop?"

"I'm on the board of governors. At our regular meetings, matters of this sort come up. Last time, you came up."

"Oh-oh. Very embarrassing for poor Eddie."

"Well, damn it, it was! And all the more so because you were not a routine case. Nearly always it is a question of some poor old boy who's been retired on a diminished income and can't make ends meet but who hates to give up coming to the club for a drink now and then. When those old boys get in too deep, Stanley babies them along as best he can, sometimes in open defiance of the club rules. He's a kind man, Stanley; he truly is. But in all my time on the board, there's never been a case like yours, where a person has not only run up a big bill but has deliberately failed to answer the treasurer's letters—has deliberately refused to give any explanation of his conduct."

"So your kind Stanley's turning ugly?"

"You're damn right he is. We all are. Who the hell do you think you are, anyhow?"

I had begun to lose my temper, or, rather, I was making no effort to control it. I was trying to shock Pinkham into perceiving the enormity of what he had done, and I calculated that with him, as with a certain kind of flippant but vulnerable witness in court, my own obvious emotional involvement would produce such a shock.

"John Pinkham, Esquire, who was, is, and ever shall be your old friend, till debt us do part."

Just for a second, I'd forgotten the question to which he

was replying, and the thought flashed through my mind that he had gone insane; then I remembered, and said, "Spare me your rotten jokes."

"All right," he said, with perfect good humor, grinning and turning his glass of Scotch round and round in his hands. "No jokes."

It was surely up to him to speak, but he appeared to feel no obligation to. He sat there unabashed, forcing me by his silence to move on into the unpleasant country ahead. "Talking about you at the meeting, Stanley was a lot nicer than you deserved," I said. "He said that for all he knew you were traveling about on different jobs and hadn't received your mail. He said we were all aware of how scatterbrained about money matters our artist members were apt to be."

"But you were able to assure him that, in fact, I hadn't been anywhere."

"Somebody asked me that, and of course I had to tell the truth. Not that Stanley didn't already know. He had the dates of all the chits you'd signed—he could see for himself you were still running up bills at the club. Why the devil didn't you answer him?"

Still smiling, he said, "Honestly, I tried. I just couldn't think of a thing to say."

"Nonsense! You could have apologized and paid up."

"That's where you're wrong, Eddie boy. That's precisely what I couldn't do."

"Why not?"

"Oh, how pleasant it must be to be married to a rich wife and never, never have to learn the score."

Once on the defensive, a certain kind of witness always resorts to personalities. Still, it was a curious remark for

Pinkham to make. He had himself been married at one time to a rich wife, and since I had handled his end of the divorce, he must have realized, even as he was speaking, that his words would bring his past into my mind. If my wife was rich, his wife had been far richer, and he had not been above accepting a considerable settlement from her, disguised as a fair division of properties they had held in common. "If that remark is addressed to me," I said, "I assure you I've always been able to earn a very good living on my own."

"Yes, but you've had Barbara's big, fat income behind you. You've never *had* to make a buck in your life. Never not had a buck."

"All this is neither here nor there."

"No? It's by way of saying I didn't have a dime and therefore couldn't write to your friend Stanley."

"That was the thing to write. It was what he was waiting for, in order to help you."

"You think it's all that easy to say to a perfect stranger? If that's how much you know, don't get riled when I mention Barbara's dough."

"Other people have had to write him."

"Other people aren't me."

Now I was controlling my temper and not finding it easy. "If what it comes down to is your being so goddam special—"

In his maddening, cheerful way, he said, "It comes down to just that."

"I don't believe you mean it—no sensible man believes that about himself. Nor do I believe it about your being broke. After all, I used to know something about your affairs."

"That was a long time ago. I've never been very good at hanging on to things."

"I wouldn't have asked you to join the club if I'd thought you couldn't afford it."

"I could at the time. I'm hoping I can again. You know what sculptors' commissions are—it's a hell of a long time between the big ones. Uncle Sam seems to have run out of military cemeteries that need a couple of hundred thousand bucks' worth of bronze and marble. As soon as I can, I'll pay up here, as I'll pay up at all the other places in town—Brooks Brothers, Abercrombie—that carry you forever when things go bad."

I shook my head. It was extraordinary how much he didn't know, and yet it was he who had accused me of being ignorant of life—of never learning the score! "Owing Abercrombie is one thing, owing this place is another," I said. "Not paying your bills is something you just don't do in a club. Now it's too late."

For the first time, I felt I had got inside that youthful, smiling surface. "What do you mean, too late? I never said I wouldn't pay. I *want* to pay, for God's sake!"

"Johnny, I told you this was serious. You wouldn't answer Stanley, and he was obliged, under the club rules, to report your case to the board of governors. Now they've asked me to speak to you."

"O.K., so you've spoken to me. Many thanks. And you can report back, if that's what they want, that I'm turning over a nice shiny new leaf."

"If you haven't any money, I don't see how you can turn over any kind of leaf."

"Goddam it, I'll go to a bank right now and borrow enough of the lousy stuff to pay off the club. Will that satisfy you Scrooges?"

"New debts for old?"

"That's my lookout, isn't it?"

"You keep refusing to listen to what I say. Of course I want you to pay off your debt to the club, and of course it's none of my business how you get the money to do it, but even though you pay up, it's still too late. This isn't prep school, you know. What the club is asking for isn't an improvement in your conduct, it's your resignation."

Then, at last, he stopped smiling. The smooth surface had begun to break up. His face was that of any middle-aged man, and when he tried to reconstruct a smile and failed, his mouth, in its trembling, seemed not merely middle-aged, but old. This sort of sudden change isn't as rare as many people think. I've often seen it happen in court, when a jury brings in an unfavorable verdict. The uttering of a single word is enough to transform a man, and why not, if the word happens to be one that will alter his whole life?

At the start of my interview with Pinkham, the uneasiness had been on my side; now it was on his. Those blazing blue eyes had, I thought, a distinct flicker of panic in them. He said, "Now you're the one that's telling jokes."

"On the contrary, I'm in deadly earnest. I have been all along. Can't you be clear about the situation? You've been acting like a spoiled ten-year-old, you've been an irresponsible brat, but God knows I'm still your friend and would rather a thousand times not be telling you this—" I broke off. "I hope you understand that much?"

"Oh, for Christ's sake, Eddie!"

"But the board has requested me to tell you you've no choice except to resign."

He put down his glass and said, "Let's have another round." He twisted the bell, but nothing happened. "Damn these fool things!" he said. "If I live to be a thousand, I'll never learn." Then he banged the bell and, as the waiter approached, gestured to him that we would like two more of the same. "Tell me, do I write this famous letter before or after paying up?" he asked. "I'm sure you know the etiquette."

"The best arrangement would be to write the letter and enclose with it a check in payment of your total indebtedness to the club. Then the board can vote to accept your resignation at the next meeting and the incident will be closed."

" 'Incident,' Eddie?"

"I was trying to use a kind word, not a harsh one."

"You keep saying 'kind.' Stanley's kind, you're kind, I suppose the whole board is kind. And discreet, as well?"

"As to that, nobody in the club will ever know anything."

"Except that I've resigned. I can't help hoping that somebody will notice that."

"I was about to say how much you will be missed here, Johnny. You were certainly one of the most popular members of the club."

" 'Were.' I see what you mean by 'kind.' "

"Don't make this any more difficult for me than it is already. You know how much I personally will miss you in the club. And how proud I've always been of your popularity among the members. If I'd been a different sort of person, I'd have been bound to be quite openly jealous of you. In my twenty years here, I've made nothing like the mark you've made in five."

"Thank you for them words."

How he spoiled things! But I kept on. For his sake, I wanted to leave nothing unsaid. "If I'd known about your troubles earlier, if you'd dropped me the slightest hint, I might have been able to straighten the whole thing out. The business of your being broke—I'd have been glad to help you over that hurdle."

"Thank you for that, too."

I couldn't resist adding, "With my money, I may say, not Barbara's."

"I'm sorry I said that."

"No matter."

"You say you might have helped me. I don't suppose you could help me now?"

"Financially? I'm certainly willing to talk it over and see what we—"

"Nothing that simple. It just occurred to me that you might be kind enough, generous enough, to practice a little hanky-panky for my sake."

I didn't like it—there was something unpleasantly crafty in his tone. A trifle grimly, I said, "Go on."

"Suppose I borrow some money today and pay off my debt here, then drop out of sight for a week or two, and at the next meeting of the board you explain that you haven't been able to get in touch with me and therefore haven't been able to ask me to resign. Then Stanley pops up and says, 'Well, anyhow, the little so-and-so is all paid up.' And you say—couldn't you say?—'In that case, since Pinkham doesn't know of the action we took at our last meeting and has had the decency to clean up this mess on his own, is there any possibility of our forgetting the whole thing, of not asking the poor fellow to resign, after all?' Adding, if you felt up to it, 'I think I can promise on his behalf that the problem will never come up again'?"

It was I who had tried to shock Pinkham, but it was Pinkham who had succeeded in shocking me. I felt now that I had seriously misread as much of his character as had been open to my observation. It struck me that back of the boyish openness, the generous high spirits, there must lie a distinct talent for duplicity. That gift was far from being merely youthful; the only word I could find to apply to it was "feminine." Women tend to solve problems in what they call a sensible or practical fashion, which is to say without regard to morality, sailing past all abstract questions of right and wrong as if they were the sheerest irrelevancies. I hadn't expected to find that tendency in Pinkham, and I said, "Do you honestly think I could do such a thing?"

"Now, Eddie!" he said. "Don't go climbing up on your high horse!"

"The governors made a certain decision, which I was requested to carry out. That's what I'm doing now, as justly as I can."

As if it were the most natural thing in the world to say such a thing, Pinkham said, "I'm not asking for justice, Eddie. I'm asking you to do me a favor."

"Which I tell you I can't do."

"Won't do."

"Mustn't do—is that any clearer?"

"I should think it would be pretty awkward sometimes having such goddam high principles."

"It's awkward right now, but the principles are still there."

"Poor Eddie. I've put you through a lot, haven't I?"

The waiter set down our drinks, and Pinkham reached for the chits, and, with a show of lightness but intending a warning (for I know how even the most loyal of club servants gossip belowstairs), I said, "Johnny! The drinks are on me."

"No, no, this time they're mine," he said, and reached up to take a pencil from the waiter.

I intercepted the pencil. "I don't want to pick a public fight with you," I said, indicating the waiter as best I could with a raising of my eyebrows, "but the fact is *you can't sign for anything here any more.*"

He had crouched forward to scribble his name on the bits of paper the waiter had put on the table between us. Now, as he watched the waiter pick them up and carry them away, he maintained the awkward posture, intent and yet helpless-seeming, of a paralytic waiting to be shifted from one chair to another. Slumped forward like that, he looked a hundred years old. It was a hard moment for both of us, and, to hurry us past it as tactfully as possible, I raised my glass and said the first thing that came into my head: *"Votre santé!"*

"Santé," he mumbled, with a sidelong glance of surprise, then, "Thanks for the libation. Much obliged."

"Don't be silly."

He emptied his glass in two or three long swallows. Our club drinks are notoriously strong, and tossing them down like that, no matter what the provocation, is always a fool thing to do. Pinkham got slowly to his feet. "So long, Eddie," he said. "I'm off to the bloody bank."

As he stood there, two things—my own evocation of the happiness he had once brought us and the look of him slumped in the chair and sloshing down that far too powerful drink—prompted me to wonder if there was any as yet unconsidered way out of the mess. In my experience, this sort of question reaches the surface of the mind only when an answer to it has already been prepared somewhere in the depths. No sooner did I begin to consider the problem afresh than a possible solution occurred to me. It was one that couldn't have occurred to me before the start of our interview, because it was the interview itself that had provided the necessary ingredients. What if Pinkham were to pay up before the next meeting of the board and if, at that meeting, I were able to make a statement, disturbing but not too specific, about the condition I had found him in? A statement that would make the other members of the board sympathetic to rejecting his resignation? I would have to say something that wasn't a lie, and therefore wouldn't betray the board's confidence in me, but that would nevertheless rehabilitate Pinkham in their eyes. What would such a something be? Plainly, something to do with health. I could tell them, and not with a bad conscience, that I had reason to believe he had undergone some kind of obscure emotional breakdown in the course of the past year, evidence of which I had detected in his speech, his manner, his very eyes; that this breakdown had led to his deplorable irresponsibility in respect to money and his still more deplorable rudeness in respect to John Stanley; but that I felt sure (here I could mildly hint at having received a medical opinion) that, if he was by no means cured, the worst was over and that the board would have nothing to fear in future from our brilliant and high-spirited friend. . . . Yes, I thought, I might just bring it off. It would be worth trying, and, as a born advocate, I would be interested to try it.

On several grounds, I couldn't let Pinkham in on my plans. Circumstances might make it impossible for me to attempt it, or I might attempt it and fail, in either case causing him bitter disappointment. A worse hazard was Pinkham's taking offense at my belief—the honorable basis for my solution to the problem—that, by George, there *was* something a little odd about him. Pride is a curious emotion, flaring up at the most inappropriate moments, and Pinkham might flatly refuse to let me plead his oddness before the board. Though I was thus prevented from offering him any reason to hope for a reprieve, much less a full pardon, I had to make certain that he sent in his check to Stanley as quickly as possible. Our interview was on a Wednesday, and the board was to meet on the following Tuesday. Stanley, that naturally forgiving man, would need a day or two in which to begin to forget Pinkham's offense before his case came up. It seemed obvious that the fastest way to get the money to Stanley would be for me to lend it to Pinkham.

Breaking the awkward silence, I said, "Don't tell me if you don't want to, but how much will you be needing?"

"I must owe three or four hundred here—"

"Three hundred and seventy-six fifty, to be exact."

He stared, then went on. "So maybe I'd better ask the bank for five. They'll think I'm good for that, won't they?"

"Of course. But let me handle it instead. I'll give you a lot better terms than any bank. They pretend to be charging six per cent, but it's closer to twelve. I'll let you have whatever you need for as long as you need it, and at no interest."

Then he said something that fitted very nicely into my plans. I grant it was the sort of teasing remark with which any sensitive person might reject an offer that he was nevertheless grateful to have heard a friend voice; still, it could also be cited as establishing a certain emotional imbalance on the part of the speaker. "I'd much rather stick a bank with a bad debt than you," he said. "I wouldn't feel free to step in front of a bus or fall off a bridge or have any fun at all if I owed money to a friend."

I noted, for my own purposes, this sufficiently clear threat of suicide, then brushed it aside. "I'd really like to do it, Johnny."

"I don't know when I could pay it back."

"I've said it doesn't matter."

"You don't think five sounds like too much?"

"I'd just as soon make it six."

He shrugged then, as if on an unexpected impulse of surrender. I suppose I'll never know whether this had been his intention from the start. At the time, I felt sure I had prevailed on him to accept the money against his better judgment. Perhaps a little inflated by this victory, I reached for my wallet, fished a blank check from it, and made it out to Pinkham in the sum of seven hundred and fifty dollars. "Somehow, that always seems a rounder sum to me than six," I said.

"No, no! It's too much!"

"I want it that way."

"This is more money than I've seen in ages. You're tempting me to run amuck."

"Nonsense," I said. "I'm not worried about that."

Pinkham took the check, folded it, and put it away in a trousers pocket. I understood that it would have been impossible for him to thank me. He turned and walked carefully across the room—the Scotch couldn't have begun to take effect that soon, but he walked as if it had. In the doorway, he swung about, and, poor as the light in the Red Room always is, I was able to make out the look of incredulity on his face. "My God, Eddie!" he said.

"What on earth's the matter?"

"I've forgotten his name."

"Whose name is that?"

"Your kind friend. The one I've been so rude to."

"Stanley. John Stanley."

Then he smiled and said the last thing I was ever to hear him say in the club: "So this is what it feels like to forget things."

I brought with me to the meeting of the board on Tuesday evening a sheet of foolscap bearing some notes for the talk I planned to give on Pinkham. My assumption was that John Stanley would first report to us that Pinkham had paid his debt to the club and had submitted his resignation, and then suggest that before putting the matter of this resignation to a motion the board might wish to hear a word or two from me. This was the usual practice in these affairs and would provide me with an ideal opportunity to save Pinkham's life in the club. I knew pretty well what I was going to tell them, and I think—though again this may sound vainglorious—that I would have swept them off their feet. My rough notes will indicate the nature of the proposed oration better and more fairly than I, in my disillusionment, can now do; they go as follows, verbatim:

Such episodes always painful.
This episode especially painful to me.
Pinkham a most charming fellow.
Soul of clubbability.
Our twenty years of friendship.
Proud to put him up for the club.
Bask in reflected glory.
No doubt of his standing in the arts.
Still, sculpture an uncertain gamble financially.
Unbeknownst to me, Pinkham falling on hard times.
Running up large bills here.
Our beloved treasurer's tactful promptings.

All in vain.

Inexcusable rudeness.

Nevertheless, if any excuse, this was it.

Pinkham emotionally unwell.

That lively, sunny person we saw in the club a
      mere mask of the real person.

His brightness all for us.

Darkness and despair within.

Too proud to reveal this darkness.

Easy perhaps for doctor to detect.

Discovered by me after long probing.

Terrible look in Pinkham's eyes.

Air almost of madness.

Threat of suicide.

Horror at having to leave club.

Shame at having offended Stanley.

My question.

Admittedly most irregular, but my judgment perhaps
      worth something in these matters.

Couldn't we find it in our hearts, one way or another,
      to table poor Pinkham's resignation?

Give him a second chance?

Make all the difference in the world to him.

Fresh start.

New career.

I personally to vouch for him.

Best tribute to values of club life.

Values of the Parnassus in particular.

So precious to all of us.

As I say, I'm sure my talk, presented with an adequate
amount of feeling, would have sufficed to restore Pinkham
to the good graces of the board, but, of course, it was never

given. John Stanley was late getting to the dinner, and I had no chance to consult with him beforehand. When the president called on him for his report, he got up and mentioned, in his matter-of-fact way, among half a dozen items of no particular importance, that he had heard nothing from John Pinkham since our last meeting, that Pinkham's debt was still outstanding, and that, unless I had something to suggest to the contrary, he would like to hear a motion to the effect that Pinkham be dropped from the club roster therewith. The president said that his recollection had been refreshed by the treasurer's remarks and that he now remembered having asked me to solicit Pinkham's resignation at the last meeting; would I care to speak on that point? I wouldn't. The fact was that I was too astonished to speak. I could only shake my head and throw up my hands in a gesture of helplessness. Under the circumstances, this was the wisest thing I could have done; heaven knows what I might have said about Pinkham then if I had been able to say anything. The president called for a motion, which was made, seconded, and carried—unanimously, I may add.

The next morning, I received a letter from Pinkham, which I append. You will note from it that he had managed almost overnight to regain his accustomed bouncy high spirits. How he can have written the letter after what passed between us in the Red Room I don't hope to understand. I've said that I feel outwitted, and the letter will show why.

EDDIE, OLD COCK!

Well, I cashed your fat check and then couldn't resist paying off a lot of nasty little debts up here in Connecticut, including the local grocery store and the water company and the phone company and the light company, and after that I ordered a lot of clay from a place that doesn't grant me credit any more and that took a big dollop of cash, and before you could say Jack Robinson, I had gone straight through all of your lovely money and there wasn't a penny left over for the poor old club. Kiss its brownstone walls good-bye for me. I'll miss those dear old coots and I hope they miss me. I realize, though, that I got out in the nick of time. I was actually growing old in there! Clubs do that, I guess. You seemed such a damnably serious old-maid fussbudget sitting there lecturing me the other day. I thought, my God, my poor Eddie! Is *that* what the club can do to a man? I know I'm a wretch to have pulled this fast one on you, but if you had any idea how merry I am this morning, setting to work here—! As the fellow said, if I felt any better, I'd be dangerous.

Your wicked but not very contrite,

J. P., Esq.

P.S. Apologize most profusely to the treasurer on my behalf. I swear I'll pay him *some*time.

P.P.S. Stanley his name is. John Stanley.

The Sacrifice

In the early years of his widowerhood, Connor and his only child, an impassive little girl named Harriet, took all their meals in the big, formal dining room of the Connor place on Prospect Hill. They were waited on by one or another of a series of couples—Axel and Olga, Peter and Della, George and Daisy—all of whom appeared ideally unselfish and hard-working during the early months of their tenure and who then lurched unsteadily downward into shiftlessness and debauchery. Or, rather, one member of the couple always did so, for by some fixed law of complementary opposites, if the woman were capable and sedulous, the man was a drunk; if the man liked nothing better than to sit up until midnight polishing silver or transforming a portion of the cellar into a playroom for Harriet, the woman would be whoring away downtown, in some steamy hotel bedroom available by the hour.

The only perfect couple that Connor and Harriet ever encountered were Jack and Larry, who gave them five years of impeccable, cheerful service. Though Connor wouldn't have thought twice about hiring two women, and if he had done so would certainly never have thought of them as lovers, he was wary of hiring two men; he subsequently took care to speculate as little as possible upon the nature of their private lives. It turned out that they were very quiet up there on the third floor, which they had to themselves. Connor knew so little about homosexuality, including even the appropriate descriptive terms, that he always referred to his perfect couple behind their backs as effeminate. As to that, he was half-right. Jack was a sweet-faced little nest builder and thus a natural consort for the virile bully-boy, Larry, who, foaming with curls from head to foot, was often to be found serving breakfast with half a dozen bloody Band-Aids affixed to his face. His explanation was always the same: he had been set upon by a gang of black drug addicts from the North End. "But I gave as good as I got," he would say, with a ghastly smile. The chances were that he was telling the truth, for he relished violence. Jack eventually provided him with the opportunity of manifesting this bent at home by falling in love and threatening to leave Larry. After the first noisy fight that they had ever inflicted upon Connor and Harriet, it was discovered in the morning that Larry had strangled Jack to death with the silk cord of his dressing gown. The event was a terrible shock to the Connors. Neither father nor daughter had ever been so close to the consequences of raw emotion before; Connor at sixty and Harriet at twenty-one were like untutored children, and this evidence of what lust and jealousy could lead to made them sick to their stomachs. The crime was a three-day wonder in the town. Connor's personal misery was scarcely diminished by the degree to which he had been made conspicuous as the employer of a murdered, to say nothing of a murderee—was he as prudent a man as bankers are supposed to be? Not to mince words, was Connor soft on fairies? Was it possible that he himself—? Oh, dear, no, but for a few weeks the suffering local celebrity felt sure that everyone he met on the street or in the bank was thinking, Oh, dear, yes.

The murder was by far the greatest melodrama in which the Connors had taken part. The second-greatest came ten years later, but the world would have been far from considering it in a class with a celebrated crime—it was simply a few moments of minor domestic crisis, and when those moments had passed, there was no outward sign that nothing would ever be the same in that house again. The circumstances in which the crisis arose had at least an indirect connection with Jack's death. For in the distress engendered by the murder and its attendant publicity, Connor and Harriet had shrunk from the ordeal of selecting successors to Jack and Larry (who, tried and sentenced, was reported to be having a good time in state prison: it was his sort of place). Connor and Harriet had acquired more than enough evidence that satisfactory couples were impossible to find and that even adequate single servants were in short supply. Moreover, Harriet was newly out of college and not much interested in being pinned down to a job. She certainly didn't need the money, and her volunteer work at the hospital and elsewhere gave her a sufficient sense of keeping busy. She proposed that she assume the task of running the house, calling on such daily outside help as might prove necessary. Big as the house was, there were only two of them, after all. They pictured their servantless status as a pleasing, if perhaps only temporary, adventure. They would be like babes in the wood, with no one but themselves to answer to.

Very early in the experiment, they gave up taking their meals in the dining room, which was at an irritating distance from the kitchen and was, in any event, a gloomy cave, paneled in mahogany and hung with large paintings of dead fish and animals. They enjoyed exploring the unfamiliar territory of the kitchen and its appendages. It was a lark for them to learn where pots and frying pans were hung and where the crocks of raisins and brown sugar rested at the pantry window, and they mastered, little by little, the eccentricities of the ancient gas range. After a few months, the playful feeling of camping out gave way to a sense of the drudgery of preparing meals and serving them; they began to cut corners, omitting butter plates and unnecessary knives and forks and pretending that, for their health's sake, they no longer had any interest in desserts. Connor failed to notice the extent to which they had altered their arrangements. Whenever Harriet happened to make some reference to what had begun to seem their former grandeur, he would look up in astonishment from the chipped enameled-iron kitchen table and say, "Oh, come, this isn't so bad! It's nice and snug, and it saves time."

Though Harriet had never done so, she might have replied that they had little reason to save time. Connor was a vice-president of the local First National Bank, and, as such, he had scarcely enough work to occupy a full day. He was always home by four-thirty, and the few outside household chores that it amused him to perform—rolling the trash cans from the kitchen door to the street, or returning them from the street to the kitchen door, and, in season, fussing over his small rose garden and the shrubbery surrounding the house—never used up more than an hour. By six he had read the evening paper, washed his hands, and was waiting to eat supper. Afterward, when the dishes had been dried and put away, he went upstairs to his bedroom and turned on the television. There, with a blanket over his knees, a sports magazine in his lap, he sat until midnight, dozing and waking, waiting until it should be late enough to undress, take out his teeth, and go to bed.

Harriet's day was hardly more eventful. Since they had shut off the third floor, and only two of the five bedrooms on the second floor were ever in use, she finished cleaning the house by noon. Having warded off the plumpness with which no Connor had ever been threatened by eating a lunch of lettuce and cottage cheese, she went downtown to do some shopping. One or two afternoons a week she went to a movie. Her father regarded going to movies while the sun was shining as a species of crime, and unless it happened to be raining, Harriet never told him of her debauch. Every Friday she had her hair washed and set at the most expensive of the local beauty parlors. Though she experimented from time to time, she was so conscious of being over thirty that she invariably ended with a neat bun of hair at the base of her skull. Once a month she had a manicure, but since her father referred to other women's red-enameled fingernails as claws, she was careful to ask for a colorless polish.

Friday was the most rewarding day of the week, not because of her visit to the beauty parlor, but because of the reason for that visit. Every Friday night Harriet had her date. It was always with the same man, Roger Andrews, a teller at her father's bank. Andrews was a year or so past forty and had never been married. It was understood that he had heavy expenses, not alone because he had to support his widowed mother but also because there was a shadowy defective aunt or uncle to be supported in an institution somewhere. He was exceptionally tall and exceptionally thin and he looked as if, tapped sharply on the belly button, he would buckle like a bridge in a high wind. His face seemed to have more features than were absolutely necessary; this was an optical illusion, based on the fact that his eyes, ears, nose, and mouth had been gathered into the lower portion of his face, on the foundation of an inassertive chin. He was full of small talk, not in the least malicious, and it pleased him to be able to make Harriet laugh.

Andrews's visits followed a precise schedule, perhaps natural in a teller. He would arrive at the house at eight o'clock, dressed in a blue suit and wearing the polka-dot tie that Harriet had given him two or three Christmases before. Andrews would ring the doorbell once, very gently; Harriet's father, having stayed downstairs in order to perform his once-a-week function as host, would be waiting for him just inside the door. The door would fly open in Andrews's face. "Why, hello, young man!" Connor would say, in a tone of friendly surprise. Andrews would say, "Good evening, sir," and then, "Is Harriet in, sir?" and Connor would say, "I think so, Roger. Just a minute and I'll go up and see."

Harriet would be waiting in the doorway of her room, fully prepared for the evening. Conventional in everything, she always had it in mind to follow the principle that a man should be kept waiting for at least ten minutes, but within five minutes she would be running down the stairs to greet him, feeling her freshly washed hair with her fingertips and smiling her still-girlish smile. For she was glad to see him, as he was to see her. He would say, "Hello, Harriet," and she would say, "Hello, Roger," and then her father would call down to them from the head of the stairs, "Now, don't stay out too late, you two" or "Don't be coming in at all hours. And don't forget to turn off the porch lights." Harriet and Roger had been going out every Friday for a couple years now, and they had never returned to the house later than half past eleven, but her father always repeated this advice in the same half-mocking, half-admonishing tone.

As soon as Harriet got home, she took off her dress and hung it in her bedroom closet, which smelled of sachet and naphthalene. Then, in a bathrobe and slippers, she would go downstairs and prepare for her father a second supper of sandwiches and hot chocolate to make up for his having had to spend the evening alone. She arranged everything daintily on the tray, and her father never failed to protest that she shouldn't have gone to all that bother for him; he wasn't a bit hungry. Harriet would answer that it wasn't any bother and that she hoped it would help him to have a good night's sleep. The fact was that the chocolate gave Connor a restless night, but he was too grateful for Harriet's thoughtfulness to put an end to the custom.

One Friday evening Connor was seated in the big wing chair in his bedroom, listening to the news he had heard four or five times over, when at eleven twenty-five Harriet opened the front door. She locked the door behind her, snapped off the porch lights, and came upstairs. Hearing her footsteps, he busied himself with a magazine. When she stopped at his door, he asked her, "Have a nice time with Roger, dear?" With his teeth out, "nice" tended to become a drunken-sounding "nyshe."

"Fine."

"Go to a movie?"

"M-m-m."

"That's good. Go anywhere afterward?"

"Just for a Coke."

Something in his daughter's voice caused Connor to glance up at her. Living at close quarters, they had long since given up seeing each other clearly—it was a mercy not to be burdened from day to day with the intimate topography of a face. Riffling the pages of the magazine with a show of alertness, he said, "I wonder if you haven't been trying to do too much lately? I mean with the housework and all?"

"Nonsense."

Alert, *alert!* The threat of trouble always made him sleepy. He could scarcely hold his head up. "Well, but you don't *look* well. Maybe we ought to try getting hold of some servants again."

"It isn't that."

Then something else, which was either to be explored or it was not. He would much rather it was not. "Shades of Axel and Olga!" he said. "And Peter and Della—remember them?"

"Of course."

"Nothing would do but Peter keep a flock of chickens in the back yard. He cared a damn sight more for those chickens than he did for Della."

"I'm sure."

"And Jack and Larry—oh, Lord!" But he mustn't begin on them. Though they had provided Harriet and him with so many delightful occasions, it was impossible to describe the means by which they had brought those occasions about. There was a mystery for Connor in their capacity to make themselves and other people happy, out of ingredients that didn't bear examination. Weren't they lustful, jealous, depraved? Yet they had made stolid little Harriet clap her hands with joy; they had made Connor feel half his age and only half a Puritan. To think that the pleasant times for the four of them had had to end with the cord of a dressing gown, a face bulging blue-purple over the foot of a bed!

"Now, if there's anything between you and Roger," Connor said, hearing in his voice a note of bantering camaraderie that Harriet would be as quick as he to perceive the falseness of, "and I wouldn't be surprised if there was, after all these years, why, out with it! If you've been thinking of me instead of him, if Roger wants you to marry him and you've been afraid of leaving me alone in this big old house, you can dismiss that thought from your mind this very minute." He stood up, the magazine slipping off his knees, and crossed the room to her, moved by his words, by the immensity of the sacrifice he was prepared to make. "I'll get along fine," he said. "You don't have to worry about me."

Harriet stared at him, wetting her lips. She tried to laugh again, but the sound broke in her throat, with the sullen unbecomingness of a burp. She said, "He hasn't asked me. Isn't that ridiculous? Isn't that the funniest thing you ever heard? He hasn't even asked me!" Then she turned and hurried down the hall to her room.

Connor started to follow Harriet, then heard her bedroom door slam shut behind her. After a moment or two he walked down the long, curving flight of stairs to the front hall. He snapped on the lights in the hall, the dining room, the butler's pantry, and the kitchen. He opened the breadbox and gathered up a handful of crackers, took a bottle of milk and some cottage cheese from the icebox, poured the milk into a glass, spread the cheese on the crackers, returned the milk bottle and the cheese to the icebox, and set the glass and crackers on a tray. He would have liked to prepare some sandwiches and hot chocolate, but it was literally the case that he didn't know how. He was unable to cover the tray with a doily because he didn't recall where the doilies were kept. Balancing the tray with care, he stopped to snap off the lights in the kitchen, pantry, dining room, and hall. As he climbed the stairs, the milk spilled from time to time over the top of the glass and one of the crackers fell from the tray to the floor. He carried the tray to Harriet's door and knocked with the back of one hand. He could hear Harriet crying inside the room, and he felt himself beginning to cry as he stood there rapping on the closed door, the discolored tray in his hands. "Harriet!" he said. "Now, Harriet! Let your old dad in!"

The Toast

When John Lawrence was a new father, twenty-odd years
ago, he was fairly good at making up stories, but somewhere along the line he lost the knack. At forty-six, he was
a full forty-two years older than his son Charles, and his
powers of invention weren't what they had been in the days
when he used to hold Charles's older brother and sisters
spellbound. As a last child, Charles was, of course, especially
doted on. Every moment with him was precious to John
Lawrence, who was eager to cut a distinguished figure in
his son's eyes. He certainly didn't fail him out of impatience
or laziness, as, in his youth, he occasionally may have
failed some of the other children. If he failed Charles in
respect to storytelling, it was because he simply couldn't
help it.

Charles slept late, while John Lawrence left the house
early and was away all day. Charles's bedtime was therefore Lawrence's only opportunity to make a good impression on him. Nightly, Mrs. Lawrence scrubbed Charles
to a high pink shine and got him into pajamas and tucked
him between the sheets and told him a story or two (*her*

powers never failed) and sang to him and kissed him a dozen times on ear and chin and nose and foot and neck and back of neck. His enormous eyes were heavy with sleep. He lay on the outermost verge of slipping off; all that was required was that his father ease him along with a rousing tale, as any ordinary father could and would. But alas! Poor Lawrence was no longer an ordinary father. For him, the stories refused to flow. The gift had gone.

For almost a year, Lawrence floundered his way through this tiny hell of parental failure. Night after night, he would be summoned upstairs, and Charles would pat the place on his bed where Lawrence was to lie. "Tell me a story," Charles would command, and Lawrence would begin, "Once upon a time . . ." Instantly, he would feel his throat constricting, his tongue growing dry, and a terrible lassitude sweeping in over him. Every start was a false start; the castles he conjured up proved all too easy to storm, and the giants inside them had nothing horrible to say. No sooner had the portcullises rattled up on their great chains than John Lawrence would yawn and ask, "And then what do you suppose happened?" A moment later, he would lift himself on one elbow and stare blindly down through the dark at the ardent creature beside him, hoping to discover, by means of his silence, that he had fallen asleep. But Charles was never asleep; irritation with his father would have goaded him into nervous wakefulness. "Go *on!*" he would say. "Can't you see I'm waiting?"

In the end, it was Lawrence who would wind up drugged with sleep, while Charles would have regained the energetic brightness of midday. Mrs. Lawrence would have to be called on to stir up her husband and soothe her son, and she didn't know which was the harder task. Surely, the Lawrences told each other, there must be some solution to the problem that hung so forbiddingly over them, but as things turned out, it was Charles and not his parents who found it. One night he broke into his father's first "And then . . . and then" to ask, "What if I tell *you* a story?"

Already sleepily: "That would be great."

"Which do you want to hear about—Christopher Robin or Robin Hood?"

"Let's make it Robin Hood."

"Well, once upon a time, in a deep, deep forest, there lived a man named Robin Hood. And he loved to kill people."

Suddenly wakeful, John Lawrence said, "That doesn't sound like the Robin Hood I know."

"This is a made-up story. One day Robin Hood took his bow and arrow and—zing—he shot the sheriff and then —zing!—he shot Friar Tuck and then—zing!—he shot Little John." In a voice blurred with pleasure, Charles said, "He shot everybody in the whole forest, isn't that a good story?" and at once fell fast asleep.

The next night, Charles again volunteered to tell his father a story, and John Lawrence chose to hear about Christopher Robin instead of Robin Hood. "Well, once upon a time, in a deep, deep forest, there lived a boy named Christopher Robin," Charles said. "And he loved to kill people. He took a gun and shot his nurse—bang!—and his bear—bang!—and his mother—bang!—and his father— bang!" The bangs grew softer as the story went on, and at the last bang, Charles sighed deeply and fell asleep. John Lawrence kissed the unmoving child and ran downstairs to make a drink for his wife and himself before dinner. "Charles's piling up the corpses that way," he said, tossing ice cubes into a silver pitcher. "I suppose there must be something very much the matter with him?"

"What else can you expect," asked his wife, "when a four-year-old child has to tell his father bedtime stories to put himself to sleep?"

John Lawrence mixed and poured their drinks. "In any event," he said, "it would be silly for us to worry about it for another five or ten years." He handed a glass to his wife and held up his own. "To all the dead in the deep, deep forest," he said.

The Cemetery

The Doctor was over seventy, but he still had a big practice.
Whenever Kevin came up from New York for the weekend,
he found the office filled with patients waiting to see his
father. They would be sitting in the wrinkled leather chairs
that Kevin remembered from childhood or standing at the
windows, looking down at the cemetery across the street.
That cemetery had been part of the Doctor's office equipment for fifty years. The humor of its location was inescapable. "That where you bury your mistakes, is it,
Doctor?" a patient would ask, and the Doctor would nod
his head, his silvered reflector catching the light. He always
smiled, as if he hadn't heard the question a thousand times
before—hadn't heard it, indeed, a dozen times from that
very patient. As a rule, the patients who asked the question
were the ones who were most afraid of being examined.
With them the Doctor worked the conversation around to
the point where they could spring the stale joke. "As long
as you don't bury *me* there," they would add, "that's all I
care." Then they would throw back their heads and laugh,
never seeing the contempt and solicitude that mingled in
the shadow of the old man's glasses.

The walls of the Doctor's waiting room were so thoroughly covered with pictures that there was but little space left to dust between the frames. Shutting his eyes in his law office in New York (dark burlap-covered walls, with a single brightly colored Hokusai behind his desk), or riding in the train to New Haven, Kevin could recall his favorite pictures out of all that clutter. On the north wall of the waiting room hung immense dark-brown etchings of the Castle of Chillon, the bell tower in Seville, and St. Peter's in Rome. The east wall was largely blotted out by some lithographs that the Doctor had bought on a Mediterranean cruise in the thirties. On the south and west walls, scattered between the windows and doors, hung a series of photographs of the Doctor at the various clinics he had attended fifty years earlier in London, Vienna, and Prague. The photographs showed him standing, smiling and self-confident, in the midst of bearded foreign professors two or three times his age. Except for the fact that his name was lettered in white ink under the Doctor's feet, none of the Doctor's patients would have been likely to recognize him. He was a stranger, a young Irishman with small, handsome features and a hint of the paunch that used to serve as an outward symbol of a physician's success. "Oh, I was cocky enough!" the Doctor would say. "I had the world in my pocket in those days, or thought I had."

On a bookcase filled with early twentieth-century medical annuals stood a framed and faded photograph of Kevin's mother, who had died when he was seven. Once, from the privacy of a newspaper he was reading, he heard a woman patient explain to her husband, "That's the Doctor's wife. She's been dead for ages. Think what a catch he was, but he never remarried. The love of his life—they say he can scarcely speak of her even now." Kevin was angry at the woman for imposing her sentimental thoughts on him. Every word she had spoken was true, but she had managed to turn them into trash. He hated having to see his father through someone else's eyes. As for pitying his father, nobody had the right to come as close to him as pity implied. He kept his distance from others; they invaded the outer kingdom of his person at their peril. Even Kevin took care to see his father chiefly on his father's terms: an august, tireless, expensively tailored man, who was not only the best eye specialist in town but also a citizen of importance—a director of banks and insurance companies, a sitter on committees doing public good.

Kevin and his father had always been careful to keep their conversation centered on the office. They had never been able to talk as Kevin and his mother might have been able to talk, for the reason that they were too much alike to risk it. Whenever Kevin came up for a weekend, they shared their few meals in silence, walked through a nearby park at night if the weather was fair, and went to bed early in the big, empty-seeming house. As Kevin had done since childhood, he remembered to say, "Good night, Dad. Pleasant dreams," and his father, from the adjoining room, would call out, "Good night, boy. Pleasant dreams." That was as close to intimacy as they ever came, and it was close enough.

Before his marriage, Kevin had spent every weekend with his father. During the past few years, however, he had come up to New Haven more and more infrequently. Libby disliked trains and they had no car and, besides, the children were too young to travel—it was exhausting for her to keep them out of mischief. And if they *were* to visit his father's house, what on earth was there to do? The house, which to Kevin was still a citadel of unexplored and unexplorable wonders, was to Libby "that old barn." On their rare visits, the children kissed their grandfather and listened to his stories of hunting and fishing in the Connecticut of his youth or, if they grew restless, of his encounters with murderous Indians, but Libby felt that these occasions were a great strain on everyone. Without having spoken a word, Kevin found that his agreement with this point of view was taken for granted. If, glancing up from a book or some legal homework after dinner, he would wonder idly how his father was, Libby would say at once, "For goodness' sake, why don't you run up and spend the weekend with him?"

Kevin would say, "Maybe I will, at that. Why don't you and the children come along as well? Dad'd be awfully glad to see you."

Shaking her dark head, Libby would say, "You know that's out of the question, darling. Give him our love. Tell him we think about him all the time."

Kevin had not sent word to his father that he would be spending this weekend with him. He had been summoned to New Haven unexpectedly, to deal with a legal problem facing one of the firm's most important clients; by the time the conference in the client's office was over, it was nearly six o'clock and it seemed easier to walk the few blocks to his father's office than to bother telephoning him. At that hour, Dr. Downing, his father's assistant, and Miss Miles, his secretary, had already left for the day. The waiting room was empty. From the faint seesaw buzz of voices in the room beyond, Kevin guessed that his father was treating a tardy patient or someone who had insisted on being seen without an appointment. Kevin picked up a magazine and began to thumb through its pages. Unlike the doctors of legend, his father subscribed to ten or twelve magazines, none of them medical, and kept only the latest issues on the square oak table between the windows. After a few minutes his father walked to the waiting-room door with his patient, a woman with a black patch over one eye. The Doctor was making his usual speech. Its humor must have been somewhat twisted for both of them, Kevin thought, by the fact of their common old age. "Now, you've nothing to worry about," the Doctor was saying. "Come back and see me in twenty years."

As he shut the door to the hall, the Doctor caught sight of Kevin sitting in the worn leather rocker. The room was darkening, and the Doctor, cocking his head, asked uncertainly, "Kevin? Is that you?" Kevin stood up and they shook hands. He noted with pride how the Doctor's pleasure at seeing him had lightened his face, erasing the network of lines around the small, firmly compressed mouth. With a show of briskness, Kevin said, "Had a bad day?"

"Pretty bad. Come in and sit down."

They walked together into the Doctor's consulting room, which was filled, as it had always been, with the latest, most costly equipment—exquisite devices with rounded corners that glowed softly under fluorescent lights. ("I like to keep up to date," the Doctor said. "A good rule for old fogies.") The Doctor leaned back in his swivel chair, the toe of one shoe steadying him against the bottom drawer of his desk. Kevin sat on a small, straight chair beside the desk. On the wall behind him hung his college-graduation photograph, taken in a rented cap and gown. On the opposite wall hung a snapshot of him taken when he was a baby playing on the lawn at home. A hand was holding him upright, and he had hoped once that it was his mother's; his father had told him curtly that the hand belonged to Anna, his nurse—he would not yield, even to his beloved child, the least particle of his possession of his dead wife. Kevin said, "I thought you'd promised to take things easy."

"Can't be done." It was what his father had been saying for as long as Kevin could remember. "Can't refuse them if they're really in need of help."

Kevin nodded toward a couple of stout black filing cabinets. "Miss Miles told me once how many thousands of names are in those files. Fantastic. You must have the biggest practice in the state."

"Maybe. In the old days I used to love the rush. Now I hope they'll get well by themselves. I hope they'll go to the wrong office. I hope they'll forget my name."

No doubt Kevin was mistaken in thinking so, but the Doctor sounded as if he were asking for sympathy. Well, he must not. It wasn't in his character. Kevin was astonished to discover that this first sign of possible weakness in his father irritated him. He said impatiently, "You're still miles ahead of everybody else in town. As far as income goes, you make me look like a nobody."

His father glanced at him without answering. He appeared not to have heard anything Kevin said. After a moment, he asked, "How are Libby and the children?"

"Just fine. They send their love."

"And mine to them."

"The kids loved the toys you sent them."

"Silly toys. At my age, how would I know?"

Weakness again! With an asperity that he recognized

as very like Libby's and perhaps learned from Libby, Kevin said, "No, they were just right. You couldn't have done better."

"They're fine children. You have a fine family." The Doctor stood up and squared his shoulders. He had always been proud of his erect posture, but now he was growing down, so he said, like a cow's tail. "Come in and let me take a look at your throat. Lots of colds around this time of year."

Kevin followed his father into a small space set off from the consulting room by frosted glass panels. In the early days, the Doctor had specialized in what was called "eyes, ears, nose, and throat," and for patients who were also old friends, he continued to fiddle with noses and throats on the trivial level of colds and laryngitis. Some of these friends were sure that the Doctor could cure colds, which he could not; but he made them feel better simply because they had been in his presence. For them he was the ideal combination of witch-doctor and priest. Kevin sat down on the familiar enameled chair and held back his head. This submission to treatment was a sacred ritual between them. It had nothing to do with his health, or the time of year. It was the Doctor's way of saying, "I'm glad you're here."

The Doctor adjusted his reflector. He pressed down Kevin's tongue with a spatula. "Looks good. You've been feeling pretty well?"

"First rate."

"I'll paint it just to make sure. A little creosote won't do you any harm."

The Doctor wrapped a bit of cotton on the end of a long probe, tipped it into a dark-green glass bottle, then rubbed the cotton vigorously against the sides of Kevin's throat. Kevin gagged, as he had been gagging for thirty years. The damned probe felt as if it were halfway down into his chest.

"Fine," said his father, and handed him a piece of tissue with which to wipe the spit off his mouth.

Kevin had never seen his father perform an operation, but he had seen at the hospital the room in which they were performed—a tiled, high-domed room with batteries of lights on brackets. The Doctor had given the room in memory of his wife, and her name was engraved on a brass plate on the operating-room door. Somewhere in the hospital Kevin had been born, and somewhere in the hospital his mother had died. Ever since childhood, Kevin had been meeting people who told him, simply and abruptly, that his father had saved their lives. The fact was important to them and so was the statement; it was not alone that their lives had been saved but that the Doctor had been the one who saved them. Learning who Kevin was, a stranger would say with something like truculence, defying Kevin to contradict him, "I'd be dead this minute if it wasn't for your dad." Kevin would answer, "I guess he must be pretty good." If, as was often the case, it was some middle-aged derelict whose life had been saved, Kevin's answer called for a protest. "Pretty good? He's the best there is. Why, all the other doctors give me up. Wrote me off. Just walked away! And I'll tell you something else. I was a bit on my uppers at the time, and he never asked a penny from me. Never a penny. That's your dad." Then came the inevitable, triumphant lie: "I was able to pay him back later, thanks be to God." To Kevin's delight, his father never remembered the names of any of the men and women whose lives he had saved. He said only, "It's nice once in a while to get a boost instead of a knock. But maybe they weren't dying at all. Maybe they only had wax in their ears."

Kevin got up from the chair. Tasting the bitter creosote, he always made the same objection. He said, "I feel a lot worse now than I did when I came in." He walked across the office to the narrow, old-fashioned windows. It was impossible by now to recall how many people had told him the same story about his father and their saved lives—the number must run into scores. But surely some of the Doctor's patients had died on the operating table or shortly afterward; surely there had been hopeless cases, of which Kevin had never heard. He wondered, feeling half-unwilling to wonder, whether the Doctor had ever lost a patient through—well, through some fault of his own. Some misjudgment, some slip of a scalpel, or however it was that a surgeon lost a patient. There must have been difficult moments for the Doctor when he was trying out a new technique; there must have been even more difficult moments during those months after his wife had died and, unable to sleep, he had walked the streets all night. Had his hand shaken next morning, had his eyes blurred, his mind gone blank?

Kevin said, "Who was the old lady you just saw? Someone who sneaked in without an appointment?"

The Doctor nodded. He was getting ready to shut the office for the weekend. He switched off the overhead lights and the gleaming stainless-steel sterilizer. "Time to go home," he said.

"What was the matter with her?"

The Doctor shut the instrument cabinet, took a handful of ten-dollar bills from a drawer of his desk (though he kept up with the younger doctors in everything else, with his old friends he maintained the custom of being paid in cash), and walked out into the waiting room. Following him, Kevin repeated the question: "What was troubling the old lady? I saw the patch."

"Nothing of importance. I cut out a cataract a couple of weeks ago. Now the eye's inflamed. Of course it's inflamed. That could happen to anybody."

"You told her she had nothing to worry about."

"Quite right. She has nothing to worry about."

Kevin turned to look out over the city; the sky was filled now with a lemony dusk. It was April. The air would be sweet in the park when they took their walk that night. In the cemetery across the street, a few gray stones made light patches in the shadows. Kevin was about to say, "That where you bury your mistakes, is it, Doctor?" He had asked the question many times before, mocking the Doctor's timid patients. He glanced across the room in anticipation of the smile with which his father always acknowledged the poor little joke. His father was staring at him with his lips drawn together, head cocked to one side. In that grim darkness he looked oddly shrunken and helpless. Kevin said, "Let's go. I'm getting hungry."

The Doctor held out a fistful of bills. "Take them. Buy something for the children."

"No, no. They don't need anything."

"Neither do I."

"I won't take it," Kevin said. "Goddam it, I mean it." He had never spoken so sharply to his father, and to beg forgiveness he reached out and touched his shoulder. It was the first time in years that he had touched him. Under the cloth of his suit, his father's shoulder bone felt as thin as a pencil and as quick to break.

And Holy Ghost

Usually, Rocco pretended to be asleep when Sister Louise entered his room. It was one of a number of tricks he had worked out during his stay at the hospital, and he repeated it day after day. The idea was to make her seem a nuisance. He would stir at the sound of her moving about in the room, and say, "Oh, hell! You woke me out of the greatest dream. Want to hear it, the dream you woke me out of?" And she would say, "I certainly do not. The less I learn about your dreams, the better." But today he had not troubled to pretend. He lay with his eyes open, his brown hands motionless on the sheet that covered him. The early-afternoon sun was moving across the bed toward his hands, and a fly was walking steadfastly along the sharp edge of the sunlight. Rocco was waiting to see whether, when the light reached his fingertips, the fly would walk up over his fingers or would choose to go around them. He had been in the hospital so long that this was as good a thing to think about as any other. Sister Louise lifted the sheet, glanced at the raw, rose-colored texture of his burns, and said, "They're better. They look fine."

Rocco said, "I had a nice thing going with a fly. And now you blew it. Why can't I be left alone? Why is somebody always snooping around?"

"Don't be such a crosspatch," said Sister Louise. "Did you have a nice lunch?"

"At eleven in the morning? Are you kidding? How's a guy supposed to work up an appetite at that jerky hour?"

"We always have lunch at eleven here. Besides, Sister Margaret said you ate everything on your plate."

"She must have finished the glop herself. She looks big enough."

"Goodness," Sister Louise said, taking his pulse with her cool fingers. "Somebody certainly got out of the wrong side of bed this morning."

"Yeah, sure, got out of bed and went down to the Midway Grill for a nice whiskey sour. Think nothing of it." As she lifted her fingers from his wrist, he said, "You're late."

"So that's it! What a spoiled brat you are! You'd think I had nothing better to do than run in and see you every two minutes." Nevertheless, she was flattered. Rocco was such a beautiful boy. She loved to look at him, with his black lashes and brown skin. The boys she had grown up with were Irish; they had pale-white freckly skin and short, sandy lashes, and she had never troubled to think what their bodies looked like under their clothes. She patted Rocco's hand and said, "I'm only a tiny bit late. Old Mrs. Kenney across the hall had one of her crying jags. She was afraid she'd die before she got to confession. Father Regan's in with her now. He must have confessed her every day for a month."

"What's an old bag like her got to confess? I don't get it, the goddam confessing." Then, always seeking to move in upon her, to discover by jostling and crowding who it was that she might be, this Sister Louise: "You go to confession, too?"

"Of course. We all do."

"Confessing what?"

"Things one did. Or didn't do. That's sometimes worse."

"Big deal! I want some facts. Gimme, gimme, gimme."

"You can ask Father Regan."

"That tub of lard!"

"Rocco, I'll wash your mouth out with soap if you're not careful."

Rocco began to feel better. "Go ahead and try. Jesus, you've done everything else to me. Almost."

" 'Thou shalt not take the name of the Lord in vain.' You know better than to use such language, Rocco, a nice Catholic boy like you."

"I'm not a nice Catholic boy, I'm not anything." Striving to wound her, he said, "What did the Lord my God ever do for me, I'd like to know? I get a job at the plant, I start earning some real dough for the first time in my life, and bang—some dumb shit sets fire to a bin of aluminum shavings. So I damn near burn to death." Rocco's eyes filled with tears. "Jesus Christ," he said, "that's a laugh." Whenever he told the story of his misfortune, it made him cry.

"I could do more good for you on my knees in chapel than I can here," Sister Louise said. "No use wasting my day on the likes of you, with your dirty mouth." It cost her a pang to say that—his mouth was lovely; it was only the words that came out of it that she couldn't bear listening to. With a show of efficiency, she checked the items on the night table beside his bed. The bottle of holy water and the cheap wooden rosary that she had left there days ago were still in place. She couldn't tell whether this was a good sign, because Rocco might simply have failed to notice them. Or he might have ignored them in order to keep her in suspense. He was twenty, but he was also six. As she was twenty-five, but also eighty. She had done more favors for Rocco than for any patient she had ever had under her supervision, and he had seemed to be totally unaware of them. She had moved him out of a room for four patients into a room for two; once his roommate had been discharged, by fiddling with the records in the nurses' bay she had given the admitting desk downstairs the impression that the empty bed was still occupied. Sooner or later, these would be matters for confession. Meanwhile, Rocco had what amounted to a private room, but never a word of thanks had he uttered. She could spank his round, hard bottom. She said, "Is there anything you need?"

"Lot of good it does asking for things around here."

"Tell me what you need."

"Some fresh water, and I don't mean that damn holy water there."

So he had seen it and had not ordered anyone to take it away. "Your thermos was filled after lunch."

"And I want an orange or an apple—something like that."

"I thought you weren't hungry."

"I wasn't hungry at *lunch*. I'm hungry *now*."

"You'll have to wait till supper. It'll do you good."

"Well, then, I have to take a leak."

"Now, Rocco."

"Go to the bathroom, then."

"You can ring for the floor nurse. She'll be here in two minutes."

"I have to go now." He made a grab for his crotch. "I'll pee all over the place."

"Do so. Then lie in it. I'm leaving."

Rocco groaned and drew the sheet up over his face. "I'm dead. Send for Father Regan."

Sister Louise turned back from the doorway. "More tricks?"

"You said you were sending him in to see me. O.K., where is he?"

"You claimed you'd throw him out the window."

Rocco pulled the sheet slowly down off his face. "I'll take a chance this once. For your sake. Because you're so pretty."

Whatever Rocco might be up to, Sister Louise was aware of one mighty fact: his immortal soul was at stake. "I'll have him look in as soon as he finishes giving Mrs. Kenney her penance."

"I suppose you've told him a lot of lies about me? Laid it on with a trowel?"

"You think you're pretty important, don't you? What if I haven't told him anything at all?"

" 'That nice Catholic boy lying there' is what you must have told him. I can just hear you." Rocco imitated the high sweetness of Sister Louise's voice. She had the best voice he had ever heard in his life. He came from a household of screaming women, three generations of them going at one another night and day, in voices that would cut through steel. " 'He's never been baptized, Father,' " Rocco said, " 'so he isn't really a Catholic, but he ought to be a Catholic, because all dagos are Catholics.' "

"I never called anybody a dago in my life," Sister Louise said. "I don't think you're being a bit funny."

" 'Baptize him, Father, before anything happens to him, because what if he died and went straight down to hell?' " Rocco was carried away by his own mimicry; his voice shook and his eyes again filled with tears. " 'Straight down to hell to burn forever and ever, and he's burned enough already, Father. He's all but burned to a cinder now.' "

"That's enough of such nonsense," Sister Louise said. She ought to be angry with him for mocking her and Father Regan and the Church; she was puzzled by the fact that she felt no anger at all. She felt no need even to forgive him. "Your burns are coming along fine," she said. "Nobody ever healed so nicely."

"You always tell me the same thing. For all I know, I might pass out tomorrow." Two large tears rolled off his lashes and down his cheeks.

"Stop crying," she said. "You're the worst patient on the floor."

"That's because I'm a dago. Dagos like to cry."

She picked up a towel that lay folded on the rack extending across the back of the night table and began to wipe Rocco's cheeks. "I want you to look nice for Father Regan," she said. "It's all right to play tricks with me, but no tricks with Father Regan. He's not young and quick like you." She pushed his hair back off his forehead with the towel. "And don't get him excited. If you swear or say any silly things, you'll get him excited. Have you brushed your teeth today?"

"Yes, ma'am."

"Make me a nice smile."

He grinned idiotically, rolling his eyes up into his head.

"I want you to make me so proud."

"I won't see him."

"Rocco, dear. You just promised."

"I don't want to go to confession."

"Don't be silly. Nobody's talking about confession. We'll be lucky if we get you baptized."

"Lucky?" Rocco asked. In spite of the pain of his burns, he sat up abruptly. "You mean I'm worse? Is that what you're getting at? You mean I'm not doing so good?"

"I don't mean anything of the kind." She put her hands lightly on his shoulders, urging him back against the mattress.

"You called me 'dear.' "

"Did I?"

"Jesus, I hope that's not a bad sign. That I'm going to die or something."

"No, silly, I must have called you that because you're going to live."

Rocco lay without protest as Sister Louise, in her stiff habit, rustled out of the room. Mostly, he was convinced that he was going to get well, but there were times when he felt certain that he was about to die, and then he would cry helplessly until the last wave of his fear had spent itself and was replaced, in his exhaustion, by an odd, dreamlike pity for the fact of his own death, for all the good times he had missed and all the wonderful things he had never seen. No matter how hard he tried, he found it impossible then to believe that Sister Louise's desire to see him baptized was only that—had nothing to do with some secret knowledge she possessed about the nature of his burns. At night, when she retired with the other nuns to the mother house across the street and only a frowzy, blondined old nurse remained on duty in the shadowy corridor beyond his room, Rocco suspected that Sister Louise had deceived him and that his burns would never heal. Something awful was happening to them, or to the blood under them, or to the bones under the blood. His whole body was rotting away, was full of pus and maggots eating the pus, and she wouldn't tell him. All she cared about was getting his goddam bodyless soul into heaven. That was because she was a nun, and nuns didn't give a shit for bodies. On the nights when he thought he was going to die, he lay staring up into the darkness and wanting to shout her name. He wanted to get out of bed and go across the street and find her, wherever she was, and make her hold his hands. No use: he couldn't walk and he wouldn't be able to find her and she wouldn't want to hold his hands.

Those were the times when he wished that his father, who called himself a freethinker, had let him be baptized like all the other kids in the neighborhood. The fact that he hadn't been baptized had placed him apart from the rest of the gang. He didn't have to hear Mass on Sundays and holy days, and he could say words like "Christ" and "son of a bitch" without the need of going to confession afterward. But since his accident, and especially during the bad times at night, he sometimes reflected that it was one thing to have left the Church, as his father had done, and another thing never to have belonged to it at all. Thinking of himself as an outcast from a place totally unknown to him and yet one that should have been his by right, and therefore, by right, his to reject, he picked quarrel after quarrel with his dead father, that neat, sharp-tongued dandy of a man. A barber out of a hill town in the heart of Sicily, he had come to America charged with anticlerical high spirits: priests were lazy, gluttonous, sensual thieves, and the Church was the lie that made them fat and gave them an army of hot-blooded widows to console. "I use-a da reason," his father would say, tapping his sleekly coiffured head. "One an' a-one make two. If God no like, let him strike-a me dead." Which, to the great inconvenience of his family, God soon did—Rocco's father was snipping the hair of a valued client and telling him a complex anecdote about two Greek ladies in a subway train when down he went, to die among his client's severed curls. Why, the little son of a bitch! Rocco thought, remembering his father, dapper as ever, in his coffin, smiling as if to say that the joke had been on him, but no hard feelings. The little dago! For now it turned out that the joke had been on Rocco, not on his father.

Rocco lay dozing, only half hearing the sound of nurses' footsteps in the corridor, the sound of a car starting in the street below. At the open door, he heard a man's voice, tired and hoarse: "If he's asleep, we'd better leave well enough alone."

"No, no, it's very important!"

"Surely you've other patients on the floor who are important to you."

"Rocco's my favorite, Father, and he knows it."

"It never pays to spoil them. They're all alike."

"Rocco's not like *any*one. Wait till you see. He's such a good boy."

"My dear Sister, I had a parish full of them once. I was glad to wash my hands of them. The more you encourage them, the more they take advantage of you."

"Rocco never took advantage—he never even had the chance. His first good job, and he nearly burned to death.

When they brought him in, emergency thought the case was hopeless. I got some holy water ready, just in case. Those first few days, I thought I might have to baptize him myself, whether he wanted it or not."

" 'Whether he wanted it or not'?" the priest repeated, his hoarse voice rising. "Why, you might have been exposing the sacrament to nullity, do you realize that?" He pronounced the word a second time, with relish. "To nullity, Sister."

"I don't care, I'd have done it. I wanted to save him. I still do."

"I wonder if you realize what extraordinary things you've been saying, Sister. It might be wise to forget that young man's soul for a moment and consider the state of your own."

Why, you old bag of wind, Rocco thought, you'd better lay off talking to Sister Louise like that. He stirred under the sheet and gave a loud yawn, and Sister Louise, entering the room, said, "Awake?"

"Yeah, and hungry. I could eat a bear." He pretended not to see Father Regan, who had followed Sister Louise into the room and was standing by the high-silled window that lit the room. He was a man who might be in his late fifties, and his plump pink face looked newly shaved. "What the hell does a guy have to do to get some food around here?"

"Now, Rocco," Sister Louise said, smiling down at him, but with caution signaling to him from her eyes. "Now, you be careful! I've brought Father Regan in to see you."

Father Regan crossed the room to the foot of the bed. His white hair was carefully combed, strand by strand, over the top of his bald head. "Well, my boy!" Father Regan said. "Delighted to see you."

Rocco said, "I been here for weeks."

"Rocco!" Sister Louise said.

Father Regan held up his hand to her. "My dear Sister! I know the type." To Rocco he said, "As a matter of fact, I understood that you weren't particularly interested in seeing me."

"That's right."

"For that matter, that you're not even a Catholic?"

Rocco waited a moment, measuring the risk, then said, "Oh, Christ, no, none of that stuff for me."

Father Regan's plump face trembled with distaste. "Well, Sister! I can see you've been having a splendid effect on this young man! And you expect me to prepare him for baptism? I can tell you that even if he were dying I should hesitate to do so."

At the word "dying," Rocco felt a fresh wave of fear rising inside him. Maybe he had gone too far. Maybe God was real and in the room with them and would be taking Father Regan's side. But Father Regan was attacking Sister Louise, and Rocco was on her side. A crucifix hung from the front of her habit, and he kept his eyes fixed on it, unwilling to lift them to hers. He said to the priest, "I'm not asking for a damn thing from you, so beat it, get out of here!"

"Even if he were dying," Father Regan repeated with satisfaction, and marched from the room.

He waited, he waited, and it seemed forever before Sister Louise whispered, "Oh, Rocco, Rocco!"

He fumbled to take her hand, but she held herself away from him. Rocco said, "He shouldn't've talked to you that way."

"I didn't mind."

"About your *soul*," he said, with childish precision. "Old Fatso's got no right to talk like that about your soul."

"It didn't matter." She glanced at her wrist watch. "I'm late. They'll think I've been kidnapped."

"You're sore, aren't you?"

"Imagine! The afternoon's half over and I've a hundred things to do."

"At me, I mean? You're sore at me?"

Sister Louise turned toward the door. It was plain to Rocco that she would not answer his question, or any question—that she would go away without forgiving him, leaving him there in the room alone with his fear. He raised himself painfully on one elbow and touched her crucifix with the tip of his finger. "*You* do it," he said. "The hell with him."

Sister Louise glanced from Rocco to the bottle of holy water on the table beside the bed. "I couldn't," she said. "It would be a sin."

"I thought you figured it was a sin not to be baptized."

"It is, it's the worst one, it's the original sin."

"Well, then."

"But if you didn't *want* to be baptized—"

"I want it, I want it!"

"For my sake?"

"Yeah, sure."

"That doesn't count."

"O.K., then, for my sake. Jesus, look at us! Fighting like an old married couple!"

"And it isn't enough to want it. You have to believe. Otherwise, I'd be—" Sister Louise groped for the phrase— "I'd be exposing the sacrament to nullity."

Whatever that may be, Rocco thought. Her voice made

it sound so beautiful: nullity. It should be a good thing and not a bad one. He thought of the harpy voices he had lived with all his life—his grandmother, his mother, his three sisters, howling and moaning from morning to night. His father had had to die to escape the racket. Rocco remembered the little dandy seated at the head of the table with his hands to his ears, spitting out curses on all his women. His father, who had given him nothing to believe and so, maybe, disbelieve. Now he was grateful to his father for having left him in a state of sin—the worst sin, Sister Louise had said, the original sin—because he could make her a present of it. Here, take it, he could say, my original sin; it's all yours. "Look," he said, "I believe."

Sister Louise put out her hand toward the holy water. "Not for my sake?"

"Hell, no."

"Dear Rocco. Such language." But she was smiling, and he smiled back. She made him lie down in the bed, and his burns ached from the change of position, but he went on smiling. She was so pretty. He would wait and tell her that later, in case it might be one more reason not to baptize him. He was glad to be outwitting Father Regan, but he would keep quiet about that, too. There would be plenty of time afterward to tell Sister Louise what he had been thinking. His fear had gone out of him. He was going to live to be an old, old, old man.

"Rocco," Sister Louise said, picking up the bottle of holy water. "You mustn't swear when I pour it on you and you mustn't laugh. This is only the short form of baptism, but it'll do till you get the regular one."

"Don't wet the bed," Rocco said. "I wouldn't want to have the nurses talking."

Sister Louise said, "I baptize you in the name of the Father and the Son and the Holy Ghost. Amen." A few drops of water fell in his tangled hair, then ran down his forehead, and Rocco thought, Jesus, it's cold, that water's cold, but he was careful not to interrupt Sister Louise at her task. He waited to feel the original sin going out of him, as his fear had gone, and he felt nothing. Sister Louise might be very disappointed by this lack of change; if so, he would make up some goddam dago lie to keep her happy. Becoming a Catholic didn't mean you had to go around telling the truth all the time.

Fat Girl

Jeanne was a big, soft bolster of a girl, with no sharp edges anywhere. She had sky-blue eyes that would suddenly go blank and, after a few seconds, as suddenly come back into focus, and if this was strange, what was stranger still was the fact that she seemed to be unaware that it was happening. There was also something odd about her pouting mouthful of pearly teeth—either they were exceptionally small and fine or, young as she was, they were false. Her feet were broad and flat-soled, and from a long way off she could be heard marching slump-slump over the linoleum-covered floors of the office corridors. She had a pretty face, with a well-modeled nose and a high, smooth forehead, from which her hair was drawn back in fine, light-gold threads to a bun behind. Men fell in love with her readily, and she was not surprised.

Two years ago, at eighteen, Jeanne got her first full-time job, with a firm of engineers in a building in the East Forties. The firm is a large one, occupying several floors in the tower of the building; from the office windows, you look far out over Long Island, whose distant reaches seem an unpeopled low green wilderness against the sky. Until early this summer, when a number of substantial aircraft contracts were canceled, the firm had enjoyed many years of unbroken prosperity. At the first hint of hard times, it started cutting down on its office staff, and Jeanne was certain to be among those who would be dismissed, more because her dismissal would serve as a warning to other girls on Jeanne's secretarial level that they must hence-forth work harder than they were used to than because the firm was in serious financial difficulties. "We are taking advantage of this opportunity of putting our house in order," the president of the firm noted, not without relish, in a memorandum circulated among his board of directors. "A little bad news can be a healthy thing."

A week or so later, on the very day that Jeanne was given notice, she was battered to death by a young photog-rapher with whom she had been living. (Though the news-papers didn't mention it, an executive of the firm was with her at the time. Roused by her screams, he ran to get help from neighbors, and so may have escaped being murdered himself.) Jeanne's death was shocking for many reasons, not the least of which was the discovery that she had, or appeared to have, no family. The data she had given the personnel office on applying for a job—place of birth, parents, schooling, and the like—had all been made up, perhaps on the spur of the moment. In any event, the body was never claimed by relatives, and after the police were finished with it, it was buried, without a funeral ceremony, in the plot of a family named Archer, in a small cemetery in Connecticut.

People in the office found it incomprehensible that good-natured, slow-moving, slovenly Jeanne could be implicated in a deed so violent and bloody—the weapon the young man used in smashing her skull was a camera tripod, and it did its work badly—but the fact is that her fate was in every way characteristic of her; she died as she did because, up to the very last moment of her life, she was kind, lazy, and accommodating: a fat girl content with her lot, who pleased herself and pleased others.

The two most extraordinary things about Jeanne were her size and her skin, which didn't resemble ordinary human skin at all; it was as if she had been upholstered in yard upon yard of some marvelous translucent fabric, very thin and strong, which had been drawn taut over her abundant flesh and blood and which effortlessly kept in place the clutter of her internal organs. When that silky pinkness was touched anywhere, it went white, then red, and the mark of fingers remained on the spot for a long while afterward. A stranger taking hold of her nakedness with his eyes closed might have supposed that he had come into possession of a bundle of some ancient, sumptuous Venetian bedding, and he would have been every bit as astonished when, from time to time, the bedding stirred of its own accord or gave up a sleepy sigh, as when, at the very start of love-making, a small, pointed tongue emerged from the pale, little-girl lips and set conscientiously to work.

What puzzled everyone at first was not only her size but also her attitude toward her size, which was one of unquestioning approval. She was totally unlike most fat girls, who suffer openly or secretly from their condition; they rarely choose, as Jeanne did, to ignore the problem. More accurately, not "ignore," since for her the problem didn't exist; her body satisfied her just as it was, and if, undressing her in your mind, your lust was given a momentary check by the thought of the thickness of the great thighs guarding the portal of her trunk, or by the thought of the loop of flesh that would surely hang from her waist as she knelt swaying above you in bed, it was, Jeanne seemed to imply, your loss, not hers—let your goggle-eyed adolescent mind busy itself undressing other girls, the skinnier the better. She managed to convey without the least taint of vanity the impression that she believed herself to be a remarkable physical specimen. It was as if she had gathered up every scrap of available information about herself and had fed it into a computer and had then learned, without surprise, that the reading provided by the computer was the single word "Perfect."

Jeanne took exceptional pleasure in eating and drinking. They were activities that she engaged in aggressively, as other people climbed mountains or competed in games. The sight of food and liquor made her eyes shine. Her first meal of the day was a hasty one—so hasty that she often had no recollection of having eaten it and would say later to girls in the office that it was no wonder she felt starved, having had to go without breakfast that morning. It was her own fault that the meal had to be gobbled on the run. She set her alarm clock to go off too late to allow time for all the tasks she knew she ought to perform in the apartment; moreover, when the alarm rang, she frequently turned it off without so much as opening her eyes and, hugging a pillow in her big bare arms, dozed until the second warning system, a clock-radio on a bureau well beyond her reach, filled the room with its clangor. Jeanne would then plunge groaning up out of bed, a cloud of pink skin that smelled of a childish intensity of sleep and, ever so faintly, of the previous evening's cigarettes and whiskey, and stumble through washing and dressing. In that morning rush, it was impossible for her to leave her room as tidy as she hoped to find it on her return. She acted as if she believed in a magic by which inanimate objects would be able to perform their own housekeeping, and the bed that she left unmade in the morning was always a disappointment to her when she came home at night and found it still unmade. As she clumped heavily down the stairs of the apartment house, the taste of breakfast, which consisted of whatever she had managed to find in her closet-sized kitchen—an open Coca-Cola and a couple of brick-hard brownies, say, or, with luck, a leftover hamburger flecked with white grease and all the more delicious for being cold—mingled not unpleasantly in her mouth with the taste of toothpaste and fresh lipstick.

Jeanne was expected to reach the office by nine, but she was always late, in part because she allowed herself too little time to walk the ten or twelve blocks between her apartment house on First Avenue in the Fifties and the office, and in part because she stopped at a delicatessen along the way to pick up a Danish pastry ring and a plastic container of coffee. ("Heavy on the cream," she would say, in her sweet, rather infantile voice.) Reaching the office, she lifted the coffee and pastry out of their brown paper bag and set them on her desk, on a blotter that bore the stain marks of innumerable other coffee containers of precisely the same circumference. With a concentration that turned the simple, necessary acts into a ceremony, she prised the lid off the container of coffee, unwrapped the waxed paper from around the Danish, and sat motionless for a few seconds, enjoying the look of the steam that rose from the coffee and the crisp fragrance of the pastry. She picked up the ring in both hands, the plump little fingers held at a sharp angle to the rest, and bit it off in large chunks, working them as steadily into her mouth as if she were stoking a furnace. Now and again, she would stop to wipe flakes of pastry from her smeared lips and chin, not with the paper napkin provided by the delicatessen, but with her fingertips, which she would afterward lick carefully, one by one. When the Danish was finished and her fingers thoroughly licked, she ran the palms of her hands along the sides of her chair, which was covered with a stout brown furze and which, in the course of her two years in the office, took on a hard, yellowish patina. She ended by brushing any remaining crumbs of Danish from her lap onto the floor and uttering a long-drawn-out sigh of satisfaction. She fed and cleaned herself with the raptness of some outsize domestic animal, staring straight ahead of her and seeing nothing; she didn't like to be spoken to on such occasions, and despite her good nature, she would generally refuse to answer any questions that were put to her, affecting, as a form of politeness, not to hear them.

This was the first of several between-meal snacks that Jeanne treated herself to in the course of the day. The second came shortly after ten, when Amos Archer, for whom she worked as secretary, arrived at the office. Archer would be as breathless as if he had just raced in on foot from Riverdale, though in fact he lived in a single room in a cheap hotel across the street. Sometimes it happened that smoke would be curling up out of the right-hand pocket of his tweed jacket when he arrived. Archer had old-fashioned good manners and believed that nobody should smoke in elevators; on entering one, he would thrust his lighted pipe into his pocket and, as often as not, would forget its presence there until somebody happened to notice the smoke, or until the jacket itself, after smoldering away for a time (his jackets were famously old and threadbare and as dry as tinder), would suddenly burst into flames, which Archer would beat out with his bare hands, shouting "Damn! Damn! Damn!" in a high voice that sounded not altogether displeased with his adventure.

Archer was a good-looking, gray-haired man who, in his fifties, gave an impression of benign senility. He let his glasses ride well down over the bridge of his nose, and he would fix his attention on you over the tops of them, perhaps thinking that this would serve to increase the seeming sharpness of his appraisal of you. What it did, on the contrary, was to make him look dimmer and more elderly than ever—a Foxy Grandpa who had somehow prematurely mislaid his foxiness. Trained as an engineer, he had long since been eased out of any responsibility for design in the firm; though he was listed as one of the vice-presidents, he had been reduced to serving as a sort of office manager, whose duties were supposed to consist of keeping the place in order. It was he who parceled out the chronically insufficient office space and purchased necessary equipment and supplies, and the high-strung ineffectiveness with which he performed these tasks was, for as long as the office remained prosperous, a cherished office scandal—Archer was the example always cited when the senior partners wished to reassure themselves that, big and rich as the firm had grown, it had not lost the common, cranky touch.

Archer and Jeanne suited each other to perfection. They were alike in geniality and incompetence, and from the start their days passed without friction and without accomplishment. As soon as Archer had seated himself at his desk, Jeanne would hurry down to the short-order restaurant in the lobby of the building and ask for tea and a buttered raisin-bran muffin for Archer and coffee and a blueberry muffin for herself. ("Heavy on the cream," she would say again, not for the last time that day.) Scattering crumbs of muffin along his desk and occasionally, with too violent a gesture, overturning his tea—"Goddam silly containers! Why don't they make the bottoms broader than the tops? Why don't they *engineer* them? My underdrawers are soaking!"—he would harangue her passionately from his inner office about the problems heaped on his shoulders by his unconscionable superiors, while Jeanne, in the glass-walled outer office, would sit munching her muffin and sipping coffee, hearing nothing and saying nothing.

Once they had finished their snack, Archer would summon her to his desk and set about dictating memoranda, in extended reply to memoranda received by him from other executives of the company. Jeanne had claimed, applying for the job, to be capable of taking shorthand, but this was no doubt as untrue as everything else she had set down on that occasion; she wrote out laboriously, in a round, childish longhand, the messages that Archer intended to have strike like thunderbolts his innumerable adversaries up and down the hall. He spoke rapidly, in bursts of intricately cluttered phrases, and Jeanne would have been unable to set down six consecutive words as he had uttered them, but her incompetence scarcely mattered; no sooner had he tossed off a sentence than it turned out that he was merely testing the sound of it. "No, no, change that, change that!" he would exclaim, with mounting excitement, for the power of veto, even though it was being exercised only against himself, invariably went to his head. "Make it 'In answer to your inquiry'—no, make it 'In answer to your impertinent inquiry'—no, let's save 'impertinent' for later—make it just 'inquiry'—'inquiry of the seventeenth, let me refresh your recollection concerning the disposition of the . . . ah, the desk and chairs that you have the impertinence to imply'—yes, 'impertinence' is excellent there —'the impertinence to imply were promised you as of the first of the month. Nothing could be farther—further?—farther from the truth. Indeed . . .' "

By one, the usual time at which Jeanne went to lunch, she was again, so she claimed, starved. If she was having lunch with some of the girls in the office, they went to the nearest Schrafft's or Stouffer's, but if, as was more likely, she was being taken to lunch by some man in the office, or by some client of the firm whom she had met, this guaranteed a substantial meal at one or another of the three or four middle-priced French restaurants in the neighborhood. In any event, lunch was always preceded by her first drink of the day: a vodka Martini on the rocks. *"Oh,* but that's *good!"* she would protest, in a tone of astonishment, as if she had never tasted alcohol before and had heard nothing but bad about it. Three or four long swigs and her glass would be empty. Most of the other girls, whose masters were sterner than Jeanne's, would limit themselves to a single drink, but Jeanne had no fear of Archer, and the speed with which she gulped the first Martini allowed her ample time for a second before the usual fruit salad or grilled-cheese sandwiches arrived.

When Jeanne was with a man and he asked if she would like a second drink (his attention having perhaps been called to this possibility by Jeanne's habit of spinning ice cubes about in the empty glass with her forefinger), she would roll her sky-blue eyes and say, "I know I shouldn't, but, oh, Lord . . ." Later, if the man asked whether she would like a glass of wine with her meal, she would roll her eyes again and in the same voice say, "I know I shouldn't, but . . ." And if the man proposed a bottle of wine instead of a glass, Jeanne's spirits would rise in proportion. "That would be *lovely*," she would say, reaching her hand out over the red-checked tablecloth and giving her companion's hand a warm, prolonged squeeze. The palm of her hand would be moist; by this time her smooth, high forehead would be covered with innumerable tiny beads of sweat. "Mr. Archer will be furious."

"Nonsense. He's dotty over you."

"No. Yes. That's true. He's a lamb."

"Who happens to bark like a dog. Yap, yap, yap."

"No, no, no!"

"Yap!"

"Nope!"

Delighted with their wit, they filled the restaurant with a shout of laughter. Heads turned, regarding them.

When she had lunch with the girls, she was back at the office by two-thirty; when she had lunch with a man, she rarely got back before three-thirty and sometimes as late as four. On these exceptionally tardy occasions, Archer would greet her by not greeting her, silence serving him as a sign of wounded feelings, and Jeanne would spend much of the rest of the short afternoon making up to him and forcing him to forgive her. She was, of course, drunk, but less conspicuously so than one might have expected, and, while it was impossible for her to work at anything that required precision (the typewriter keys swam before her eyes in a blur of %'s and @'s), she found a dozen harmless errands to perform between their offices. She would think of questions to ask that required her to seat herself, disheveled and pinkly incandescent, beside his desk, or she would carry in papers to sign that permitted her to hover beside him, her damp bosom grazing his head, and the bizarrely mingled smells of her body—Johnson's baby powder, Arpège, garlic, cigarette tobacco, and the odor of skin and hair—would steadily, relentlessly encircle him. Soon he would be sputtering away on the subject of the intolerable burden he bore on behalf of the company night and day without a word of complaint to anyone, and Jeanne would perceive that she had been forgiven, not for the first time, not for the last.

Sometime between four and five, depending on the hour of her return from lunch, she would pay a second visit to the restaurant in the lobby, picking up two orders of tea, toast, and strawberry jam, with perhaps a couple of slices of pound cake on the side, or a piece of lemon-meringue pie—dishes that she described to Archer as "your special surprises." Archer never tasted them; half a piece of toast without jam, dipped into milky tea, was as much as his stomach dared to encounter at that hour. Jeanne would consume the surprises to the last morsel, saying with the coquettish smile that she used only when she spoke of food, "Waste not, want not." She had a large stock of such sayings, which she squandered continuously throughout the day: "A stitch in time saves nine." "Let sleeping dogs lie." "Least said, soonest mended." She used them like stage money, in lieu of the real thing; they let her hold up her end in conversations without the bother of taking thought, and the pleasure she derived from not thinking became a part of her companion's pleasure, as palpable as the touch of her hand or mouth.

Tea over, it was a matter of scarcely an hour before it was time to stop work for the day. Jeanne's mind would have begun to clear by then, which meant that an energetic befuddlement was replaced by torpor. She enjoyed this lull between periods of drinking; as the first waves of a delectable lassitude stole up her legs and into the stronghold of her body, she would march along the hall to the ladies' room and, kicking off her broad, ugly pumps, stretch herself out on the couch that occupied a third of the little, mirrored anteroom. Provided that she had remembered that morning, in the hurried hurly-burly of dressing, to furnish herself with a handkerchief, she would arrange it daintily over as much of her face as it could be made to cover; otherwise, and more commonly, she would cover her face with a couple of pieces of Kleenex, or, failing that, with a few lengths of the cheap speckled white toilet paper that Archer had ordered no telling how many thousands of rolls of over the years. She held the paper in place with her left arm, which she kept crooked over her eyes to shut out the harsh, naked fluorescent light above her in the ceiling, and to any of the girls who happened in before she fell asleep, she explained that she was taking forty winks. That was one of her usual sayings—"forty winks." She had never been known to say that she was going to take a nap. As the girls went to and from the toilets and sinks, or stopped in front of the mirror to comb their hair and restore their make-up, they chattered together without regard for the bulky object on the chintz-covered couch behind them. They knew that once Jeanne had fallen asleep, no ordinary sound would waken her. From time to time, she would speak a word aloud, or utter a faint moan, in response to some remembered or perhaps only dreamed-of pleasure; then her enormous thighs would part, her legs separating into the upright strokes of an *A* and her plump feet, pink toes packed together inside gauzy nylon, pointing stiffly left and right, like the feet of dolls.

The alarm that served to rouse her from her forty winks was the hubbub of closing time, when the door of the ladies' room was in constant, clattering motion. Jeanne uncrooked her arm, removed the handkerchief or paper covering her eyes, and peered at the ceiling unseeing, as, slowly and with difficulty, she came back into the world. She got up, thrusting her feet reluctantly into her pumps, and made her way into the bathroom proper, where she splashed cold water onto her closed eyelids, dried her face and hands with a dozen paper towels, and returned to the anteroom. She stared fixedly at herself in the mirrored wall, repeating softly, "Oh, God, oh, God." Then she borrowed lipstick and eye shadow from one or another of the girls, made up her face in slapdash fashion, and walked slump-slump to the office, where Archer, unmindful of the hour, was sure to be hammering away on his ancient typewriter, the room blue with smoke.

Teetering in the doorway: "Time to stop, Mr. Archer."

"Stop now? Stop *now?*" A fusillade on the keys, struck at great speed with two fingers. "Just getting started."

"Tomorrow is another day."

"I like working late, after the rabble has gone. Gives me a chance to use my head."

If she happened to have no date that evening, or if the date was a late one: "Come buy me a drink instead."

"You've already drunk too much today."

"You're not my father."

"Old enough to be. Your grandfather, if I'd got into trouble early enough. You were practically falling down when you got back from lunch. Which of my lecherous, aging colleagues was trying to seduce you, goddam the whole mindless lot of them?"

"Nobody."

"Ha! No kneesies, no invitations to a midtown matinee?"

"Just one drink. Then you can send me home."

"Never. Not a drop."

In the end, they would go across the street to a small bar in the hotel where Archer lived, and he would buy her the one drink that she had exacted from him and in return would try to learn from her something about her relationships not only with the men in the office (this as possible ammunition for his running battle with them), but also with the college boys who were, so he instructed Jeanne, her only suitable beaux. Archer had been married twice and divorced twice and had no children. His idea of how a good father ought to behave toward a daughter like Jeanne—and he never for a moment risked assuming any other role—was based on recollections of how his father had behaved toward him and his sisters forty years earlier. He gave her advice, but he had no confidence in it, and he was grateful that she did not laugh at him. He was also grateful that she spared him, surely as much from boredom as discretion, particulars of her relationships with men. When she spoke about sexual matters, it was in general terms, and with unself-conscious candor. One gathered that she felt about sexual activity much as she did about her body: that it was a good in itself and had, and needed to have, no connection with any emotion of love. She spoke of

235

other people's sexual practices with an ease that astonished men of Archer's age. She seemed to assume that anyone who had the ability to go to bed would do so as often as possible and that the choice of a partner was by no means the crucial aspect of the performance; which was to say that it was, after all, only a performance and could be judged accordingly. Sometimes, when she was having lunch with girls from the office and they happened to be seated near a window giving them a view of the street, she would offer comments on one or another of the male passers-by. "That one there, in plaid," she would say. "He'd be great in bed."

"Jeanne, what a faker you are," one of the girls would say, egging her on. "Nobody can tell by looking."

And Jeanne would smile her pearly smile and say, "*I* can."

Four or five evenings a week, Jeanne went out on dates. Her escorts ranged in age from twenty to sixty. The very young men were unmarried, but nearly all of the rest had wives or, at the least, ex-wives. Most of them were commuters, with houses in Westchester or Connecticut, and no doubt their wives were used to eating dinner alone or with the children. Married men in their thirties who took Jeanne out were inclined to be still somewhat uneasy over not catching their habitual trains; to keep their wives from worrying about them, they felt obliged to telephone home that they had been held up in town on business, but they hated to have Jeanne overhear the falsehoods that made it possible for them to be with her—perhaps to be sprawled with her, telephone in hand, on her rumpled couch, with their loafers off and their mouths a smear of lipstick. Sometimes she found the evidence of their discomfiture touching,

as when a young man would wait until she went to the bathroom before picking up the phone and, in a low voice,
telling his wife in the suburbs the squalid, necessary lie.

Jeanne wondered why the young men took everything so
hard. Their bad consciences were a matter of indifference to
her, except to the extent that she was puzzled by their having them. What possible injury could be done to anyone,
directly or indirectly, by a man's taking her to dinner and,
in some cases, to bed? Even if some of them fell in love with
her, what harm? She would never try to take them away
from their wives; she was neither ambitious enough nor
conspiratorial enough to find such an undertaking attractive.
She was lazy and she disliked secrets. The guilty feelings
of the young men were tiresome, which was one of the
many reasons that she preferred going out with older men;
they would have solved any problems in respect to the
structure of their private lives long before. They liked feeling
desire for her, whether they acted on it or not, and they
liked having a companion for whom other men obviously
felt desire. Finally, they liked her because she made no
demands. She was warm and soft and slovenly and cheerful, and these are qualities that young men do not put a
sufficient value on.

The youngest of her regular escorts was a black messenger
boy in the office, who invariably took her to a mock-Irish
pub in the same block as her apartment house and stared
at her over baconburgers and beer for a couple of hours,
scarcely speaking a word (the jukebox, which he fed continuously, took his place as the object she was expected
to listen to, and Jeanne was well satisfied with this arrangement), and the oldest was the senior vice-president of the
firm, a celebrated engineer and no less celebrated woman-

izer, who had had a heart attack a year or so earlier and who was terrified of dying of a second attack. No longer willing to risk making love, he was as eager as ever to be in the presence of desirable girls, and more eager than ever to be *seen* to be in their presence; he would take Jeanne to "21" or Quo Vadis and sit staring at her with something like the same immobile, silent longing as the young black, while Jeanne ate and drank with gusto and from time to time brushed his cheek with her open mouth.

Jeanne lived on the fourth floor of her apartment house. Since it was a walk-up, the vice-president was forced, for his heart's sake, to meet and say good night to her in the tiny ground-floor lobby. Most of the other men in the office felt that they owed it to their manhood to make the climb to her door at the beginning and end of the evening, hoping for much or little according to their natures. It was a stiff climb, and when they rang her bell at the top of the third long flight of stairs, they would be breathing hard. Some of them, aiming to give an impression of youthful vitality, would wait a minute or two outside her door to catch their breath, but, if Jeanne had ever troubled herself with such trifles, the ruse would not have deceived her at all—they had to press the button beside her name in the vestibule of the lobby in order for her to release the lock of the front door, and she could have calculated to the second how long it would take them to reach her floor. In fact, she had no thoughts about them between the time they pressed the button downstairs and the time they pressed the button outside her door. When she opened the door, they began to exist, and when she closed it, they stopped existing: it was as simple as that. If they were visibly winded, she took pity on them, and this was never, as they feared, because she assumed that their momentary fatigue was a sign of diminished sexual power. Her imagination was exceptionally economical; she could entertain a single concern for a long time without feeling obliged to let it lead her into a second or third one. Sometimes, greeting them at her door and, for a wonder, being ready to go out, she would say, "Poor thing, you look exhausted! Don't you want to come in and rest?" And her middle-aged escort, wanting nothing so much as a few minutes' respite in her blowzy living room, would reply pantingly, "Nonsense! Never . . . felt . . . better in my life! Away we go!"

Equally contrary to what Jeanne's admirers supposed was how little she speculated about their bodies. In her presence, the older men fretted to themselves about their approaching or actual baldness, about their jowls and thickening waists, about the bellies that could no longer be sucked in and rendered comparatively invisible. They would hold their heads unnaturally erect to strengthen the line of the jaw, and, seated, they would keep a picture magazine spread on their knees to conceal the flagrant thrust of their pots. At the moment of undressing, they would become as skittish as maidens, turning off lights and taking advantage of half-opened closet doors to hide behind, then making a rush, phantoms of white, rippled, ungainly flesh, for her ill-made bed. Jeanne, who undressed at leisure in the bathroom, would return to find her bedroom in darkness, the man tucked away under the covers and dimly smiling, like a child in a nursery waiting for Nanny's good-night kiss. "But I can't *see* anything!" Jeanne would complain, turning on the light beside the bed and throwing herself down naked beside the man, with only the thickness of the covers left between them. Propping herself up on one elbow, her big body running the length of the bed like an Appalachian range of translucent pinky-white alabaster, she would say, "Let me look at you," and throw back the covers, exposing him. She would contemplate him without haste, reaching out from time to time to touch his body at one point or another and saying, to his astonishment and pleasure, "Nice. Oh, that's nice."

Jeanne's agreeable promiscuity, centered for so many months on the office, was brought to an end when a young man named Ross Fisher fell in love with her. He was a graduate student at Columbia, getting a Ph.D. there for his parents' sake but planning, for his own sake, to become the greatest photographer in the world. They met at a cocktail party one weekend, somewhere in the gusty upper reaches of Riverside Drive, and that was the first thing he ever said to her: "I'm going to be the greatest photographer in the world."

"Do you always say that to people when you first meet them?"

"To girls I do."

"And are they always very impressed?"

"They always say I ought to be analyzed and I always say I've tried that, so then we take it from there. Or we don't take it from there, you know?"

Afterward, neither of them could remember the name of their host, or even why they had happened to go to the party, and Ross considered these facts proof that they had been ordained to meet. Promptly at five the following Monday, Ross was at the office to pick up Jeanne and take her to dinner. He was there on Tuesday as well, and on Wednesday; by then, everyone in the office was aware

that an intense courtship was under way—indeed, Ross
had announced it to the girl at the reception desk. "I'm
courting Jeanne," he said. "I'm going to take her by storm,
you'll see. Once I make up my mind to do a thing, nothing
can stop me."

Even Archer, who seemed to observe so little, soon
became aware of Ross. By the end of the first week, he
was in the habit of nodding to Ross, and by the end of the
second week, he occasionally went so far as to utter a
muffled "Hi" to him. Working his pipe up and down in
his strong yellow teeth, Archer said one morning to Jeanne,
"Not much to look at, but at least he's the right age."

"I hate the babies you want me to like."

"Give him a chance."

"He won't let me not. I wonder what makes him so sure
I won't get sick of him. I always do, his type."

"That young man seems pretty sure of everything."

Archer had been wrong to say that Ross was not much
to look at. He was a slender, small-boned boy, with features
that had the look of having been almost too carefully
chosen. Because he was the same height as Jeanne, beside
her he seemed smaller than he was. It was true, moreover,
that he weighed less than she did, which led to a good
deal of ribald speculation in the office about the ways
and means of their making love. In fact, there was nothing
particularly novel about it. Ross had known but two
or three girls, and they had been as inexperienced and
tentatively exploratory as he. He was enchanted by the
speed and ease with which Jeanne engulfed him. It was as
if the boundaries of their bodies had been abrogated; there
was no beginning or end to him or to her. In whatever
fashion, or sequence of fashions, she led their flesh to be-

come entangled, the feeling on his part was always that of being plunged—weightless, his heart bursting—into an abyss. Making love with Jeanne was by far the most extraordinary physical experience of his life, and sitting beside her afterward at a bar, or across from her at some rickety restaurant table, he marveled at the composure with which, having returned to the world, she faced the world. The tranquil impassivity of that big body had no connection with the fierce engine that had wracked him and wrung him and left him a breathless eunuch, curled in its shadow.

For Jeanne, Ross was a lover like any other. With time, she knew, he would learn to give her greater satisfaction, but what he already gave her was enough for her needs. It was the surprising modesty of these needs that made it easy for her to say that she would try to be faithful to him. At first, it had not occurred to her that this would be a matter of concern to Ross; she was amused and touched by how shocked he was to discover, in the early stages of their affair, that she was continuing to see and go to bed with other men. It turned out that he had not supposed, from what he had read and heard about affairs, that such conduct was permissible. He was still more shocked when, having accused her of behaving unnaturally, she laughed at him. "Unnatural would be *not* going to bed with people I like to go to bed with," Jeanne said.

"I don't want to make love to anyone but you."

"Then you don't have to."

"And I don't want you to make love to anyone but me."

"That's different."

"People who love each other—"

"Oh, Christ! Who said anything about that?"

"You have, in bed."

"Those times don't count. You always beg me to say something then, so I do."

He said furiously, again a six-year-old, "I'll kill you if you go to bed with anyone else."

"Sticks and stones can break my bones, but words will never hurt me."

He burst into tears, and she held him in her arms on the edge of the bed. When he could speak again, he said, "I *am* going to be the greatest photographer in the world, you wait and see. You'll be terribly proud of me."

"If you don't stop that baby talk, I'll never be proud of you."

He curled his fingers into her bare thigh; the skin went white. "That hurt?"

"Yes."

"Now?"

"Yes."

"Want me to stop?"

"I don't give a damn what you do."

"Tell me to stop. Tell me to stop. *Tell me to stop.*"

But she would say nothing. Eventually, he took his hand away, and the red-and-white mark of his fingers was on her thigh for days.

She had intended not to see him any more, but she could never stay angry with anyone for long. She not only went on seeing Ross but agreed to make the experiment of remaining faithful to him. The only condition that she exacted for what he solemnly called her "fidelity" was that he never ask whether she was having sex with someone else. There was no way for him to be sure that her fidelity was absolute, but after a few weeks she allowed him to move into her apartment, and this was assurance of a kind: if she was ever with another man, at least it was no longer in the bed that she shared with Ross.

His presence in the apartment proved a convenience to her, as well as a guarantee to him that he enjoyed privileges in respect to her time and body greater than anyone else enjoyed. For it turned out that Ross had a natural bent for housework. He was as tidy in his domestic habits as Jeanne was sloppy in hers. In the morning, it was he who insisted on their making the rumpled bed that Jeanne would have left unmade until evening, and sometimes when, despite his repeated warnings, she was late for work, he would hurry her out of the apartment and make the bed himself, then carefully wash and dry the breakfast dishes before setting out on the long crabwise uptown journey to Columbia.

Jeanne had no interest in his graduate studies. Her education, such as it was, had sunk in her without a trace; she could read and write and (though not easily) multiply and divide, but she never mentioned a book that she had liked or disliked, and her knowledge of history embraced only such figures as Washington and Lincoln. Once, when Archer asked her to name the fifty states of the Union, with a bottle of Scotch for a prize if she could name them all, she was able to name only twenty-seven, and one of these turned out to be Omaha. Ross was often furious with her for being ignorant. "How can you stand knowing so little when you ought to know so much?" he would ask, looking up from his reading. "I'd hate to have my mind as empty as yours is."

"You can be bright for both of us, baby."

Even his photography didn't interest her. He fashioned a makeshift darkroom out of a closet between the bedroom and bathroom, and spent at least two hours of every day taking and developing pictures, and the most that she would say of the results was "That's very pretty," or "That's ugly. What do you see in such ugly things?" He took scores of pictures of her—a languorous odalisque, always fully clothed, for though she offered to pose for him in the nude, he rejected the offer with a taunt: "You're too fat."

"You never thought so before."

"You're not. Of course you're not. But I want your body to be mine. I don't want anyone to see it except me."

"Lots of people have seen it."

"Never any more."

"Then go back to taking pictures of chimneys and dead trees."

"What a bitchy thing to say. You don't care whether I become a good photographer or not."

She smiled and held out her arms. "Come to Mama."

Trembling with contempt and anger, he went to her.

The day of her death began like any other. She was, of course, behind schedule, and Ross shouted to her as she padded down the apartment-house stairs that he had a seminar that evening and wouldn't be back from Columbia until late. She stopped at the delicatessen and ordered a Danish and coffee ("Heavy on the cream"), which she savored slowly at her desk. Archer came in ahead of his usual time. The cutting down of the office staff had made him uneasy for Jeanne's sake, and he was determined that he and she should be seen to be getting a great deal of hard work accomplished. "I've already had my tea downstairs," he said.

"What a rotten liar you are."

"Listen, you know as well as I do what a panic my witless colleagues are in. They've lost two cents and they whimper like bankrupts."

"I'm not worrying. I'll go down and get us a special surprise. Something gooey."

"No, God damn it, you'll stay here and work." Archer's glasses slid to the very tip of his nose and hung there, and he was too distracted to push them back. "Please, Jeannie," said Foxy Grandpa, and because he had never said "please," and because he had never called her "Jeannie," she sat down beside him with pencil and paper and let him churn up the contents of his In and Out baskets and fire off savage memos to his enemies until, to their astonishment, it was one o'clock.

"Watch the time," he said. "Be back by two."

"Time and tide wait for no man."

"I warn you, they'll throw you out."

"Let's cross that bridge when we come to it."

With a couple of girls from the office, she had lunch at Schrafft's, and perversely she took care to have her usual two vodka Martinis, followed by a glass of wine. When the other girls returned to the office, Jeanne drifted through midtown, window-shopping and enjoying the heat of the sun on her damp face and throat. She got back to the office to find an envelope waiting for her on the desk. It was her notice. Plainly, it had been prepared a day or two earlier, so plainly, she had done well to dawdle over lunch. Coupled with her slight drunkenness, the sensation of having been fired—of having had something harsh and irrevocable happen—exhilarated her. She went into Archer's office to share this unexpected pleasure with him. "I feel—" she began, intending to tell him that she felt like a child let out of school, like a child at a circus, like a child with a red balloon, but seeing his face, she guessed instantly what had befallen him, and in the same breath, but in a different voice, she ended, "Oh, Christ. I'm sorry."

No pipe, no glasses—why had he taken off his glasses? Had it been to keep them from being broken while they stripped him of his badge of office? He said, "They're making me put in for early retirement. I said I'd fight it, but of course I won't. I haven't anything to fight it with."

"Buy me a drink."

"You're already drunk. You ought to be ashamed."

"Now, Daddy-o."

"One drink, then, just to spit in their eye."

In the little bar of his hotel, they sat drinking until after dark. Archer found his glasses in one pocket, his pipe in another. He never stopped talking, having thirty years of grievances to explore. He grew cheerful as he drank, and the worse the grievance, the more uproarious it began to seem to them. Once or twice, he interrupted himself to say, "You don't have to stay and listen to all this dreary vomit, you know," and she smiled and patted his hand on the bar and, shaping the words with care, said, "Jeannie is a very, very, *very* good lis'ner." Around nine, they set out to find a place to eat. Holding tight to each other and tacking with brave abandon from one side of the pavement to the other, they made their way toward a restaurant that Jeanne remembered liking, a block or so from her apartment house. When they reached Jeanne's doorway without having located the restaurant, she suggested that he come up and let her cook supper for them. She worried a key out of her purse, and between them they found the keyhole and unlocked the door. As they started up the stairs, Jeanne warned Archer that it would be a long climb and that he must stop talking in order to save his breath. The stairs proved even more treacherous than the sidewalk. Archer fell to his knees on almost every landing, when the counted-on next step failed to materialize. Occasionally, he took to his backside, bumping his way upward from tread to tread. Jeanne reached the fourth-floor landing ahead of him, and the door of the apartment was already open when, puffing with exertion, Archer arrived. He stumbled past Jeanne into the living room. "Welcome!" he said to her as she followed him in, and then, "Bathroom?"

Leaving the bathroom, Archer took a wrong turn, wheeled into the dark bedroom, tripped over a camera tripod, and crashed to the floor, carrying the tripod and a small table with him. Jeanne hurried to him from the kitchen, switching on lights as she went. Archer was moaning and Jeanne was laughing as she gathered him up off the floor and propped him, a crumpled tweed sack, on the edge of the bed. She peeled off his jacket, trousers, and shoes, and pushed and rolled him onto the far side of the bed. "Take forty winks while I get supper," she said. Archer made no answer. Curled with his face to the wall and holding his bony, bruised knees in his hands, he was already asleep.

Jeanne went to the bathroom to sprinkle cold water on her face. She felt very drunk and very cheerful and only a little sick as yet. Rocking from foot to foot, she stared at her bathrobe, hanging in its accustomed place on a hook on the back of the bathroom door. Even sober, she had room in her mind for but one thought at a time; the bathrobe before her, she no longer remembered her plan for making supper. She washed her hands and brushed

248

her teeth, fumblingly undressed herself, and returned to the bedroom. With a sigh of pleasure, she lay down naked upon the bed and crooked her arm over her eyes to ward off the light. As she fell asleep, she turned on her side and drew up against the soft warmth of her breasts Archer's wiry little body. And there they lay when Ross came back at midnight and walked into the apartment, ablaze with lights, and called her name.

Last Things

Dog and man were almost of an age. By the usual reckoning that a year in the life of a dog is equal to seven years in the life of a man, Jacques was somewhat older than his master; he was thirteen, which is to say ninety-one, and Harry was eighty-five. Jacques had been given to Harry as a puppy, when Harry was already in his seventies. He had guessed at the time that this playful bundle of black curls and needle-sharp white teeth would be the last dog he would ever possess. The thought came to him unbidden and made his heart turn over. Then he felt ashamed. All his life, he had taken care not to spoil things that were good in themselves by trying to measure their duration. He would let the puppy plunge headlong into the future and frolic there, unknowing. Jacques would grow up and reach his majestic prime—for Jacques was a standard poodle, not one of your skittish miniature or toy poodles—and afterward grow old, while Harry, already old, would merely grow older; with luck, they would be having a long life together.

From the first days of their relationship, Harry felt a

special affection for Jacques. In a way that he had never done with any other dog, he gave himself up to the bright-eyed creature somersaulting over a rug or fiercely nibbling on a shoelace as he was held (trembling with pleasure to be held) a prisoner between Harry's feet. He would have seen exceptional qualities in Jacques even if they had not been there, but they happened to be there in abundance, and Harry felt something like a lover's pride in discovering them. He could not keep from calling his wife's attention to Jacques' gifts, even at the risk of turning Jacques into her rival. One day he summoned Laura into the living room from the little study where she spent much of the day knitting sweaters for their great-grandchildren and dozing over television. "Now watch this," Harry said. "Gets the message the first time I tell him something." He bent down and scooped the puppy up in his gaunt, liver-spotted hands, gave him an ardent shake or two in mid-air, and said, "Want to go for a hike, old sport?" Setting Jacques down on the living-room rug, he said, "Well, off to the front door, then. Look lively! Haven't got all day!" Jacques trotted to the door and, propping himself upright against the doorframe, turned his head toward Harry with an impatient air. Harry shook his head in awe. "Never mentioned 'door' to him before today. Lord God, I'd teach him to read and write if I thought it would make him any happier."

"Falling in love with a dog at your age," Laura said, and went back to the television program he had called her from.

In the past, Harry had always resisted teaching dogs tricks, but something in Jacques' nature indicated that he wished to learn as many things as possible—not simply good manners (he had housebroken himself in a matter of days) but accomplishments. He was eager to perform, and it was plain that performing pleased him because it was a sign of the bond that existed between Harry and him. Their audience could see that when Harry and Jacques performed a trick, Jacques was every bit as proud of Harry as Harry was of Jacques. They were comrades, equal in skill, equal in admiration for each other. Jacques learned to weave in and out between Harry's legs as the old man strode briskly across a floor or lawn. He learned to retrieve a slipper when the old man would take one off, hold it under Jacques' nose for a moment, then hide it in some distant, out-of-the-way place. He learned to pluck a handkerchief gently with his teeth from the crotch of a tree trunk seven or eight feet above the ground and return it undamaged to the pocket of Harry's jacket. And he learned to sit on his haunches, as erect as a bishop at High Mass, while Harry asked him, "What would you rather be than a Yale man?" No movement. "Than a Princeton man?" Not the least flicker of an eyelash. "Than a Harvard man?" And Jacques rolled over, paws in air, playing dead.

As he grew out of puppyhood, Jacques particularly enjoyed taking rides in Harry's car. The car was a soiled and moldering Chevrolet, which Harry had purchased at second hand many years earlier, but as far as Jacques' opinion of it was concerned, it might have been a Rolls. When Harry drove downtown on some errand or other, Jacques sat upright beside him on the front seat, looking at first glance, with his big round head held back and the thick hair at his shoulders bunched into epaulets, like some grave dignitary from another continent, or perhaps even from another planet. As soon Harry parked the car and went off about his business, Jacques would move over into Harry's place and remain seated there, staring through the windshield and with paws resting lightly on the steering wheel, until Harry returned. Passers-by catching a glimpse of the dark figure behind the glass were often tempted to nod and say hello to him, and once when Harry left the car in a no-parking zone, a policeman came up and started giving Jacques a piece of his mind.

In the years of Jacques' prime, seemingly reached so soon and so soon to be left behind, Harry slipped imperceptibly into the eighties. He was still vigorous, still alertly in charge of his little domestic kingdom. When a colony of rats moved into a far corner of the crawl space under the house and seemed to thrive on the poison he set out for them, Harry bought an automatic in a pawnshop downtown and found in the garage a rake, to which he affixed with rubber tape an extra-long handle. Pushing his gear in front of him, he inched his way on his belly over the red soil of the crawl space. Now and then he butted his head against a floor joist; sweat started up on his skinny arms. Holding a flashlight in one hand and the gun in the other, he picked off the rats as they crouched in the wavering disc of light, then with the rake dragged their bodies slowly out from under the house and buried them. The exploit was nothing to brag about; to Harry it was a commonplace solution to a commonplace difficulty.

Even in age, Harry moved with the jauntiness of his youth. He continued his long rambles with Jacques and his regular game of golf with three cronies of an age as great as his own. The foursome had played together for decades; the game was so important to them that only illness or unusually adverse weather could keep them from appearing on the first tee at the same hour of the same day every week of the year. The game and the hour or so afterward in the locker room, where, over drinks, they worked out the day's complicated wagers and exchanged a few welcomely familiar dirty jokes, made up the happiest moments of Harry's life. Though he took care not to think about it, this happy time was constantly in jeopardy, for unlike their friends in the community, the Melchetts were almost destitute. They lived in a small frame house on the unfashionable fringe of the country-club section, and for income they had only the checks they received from Social Security and a system of disguised allowances from their three children. One son, for example, paid Harry's dues at the club and the property taxes on the house; the other son was steadily acquiring, at prices Laura and Harry never questioned, the contents of the house, which he left in the Melchetts' possession. Meanwhile, their daughter sent them small gifts of money not only on their birthdays and at Christmas but on Mother's Day, Father's Day, and nearly every national holiday as well, and this practice was both a standing joke in the family and the strictest necessity.

The time came when Harry felt that he could no longer afford to keep a car. The Chevrolet was beyond further repair, and a new car was out of the question, so with his usual cheerfulness, Harry announced that he had decided to give up driving. Though his hearing and sight were excellent, he pretended otherwise. "Deaf and half-blind as I am, I'm a menace to others," he said. "Sometimes I see two white lines down the middle of the road and I try to drive between them, and Lord God!—one of them isn't there at all!" Harry was as inventive as he was cheerful, and what he couldn't do in one way he would find the means of doing in another. A neighbor's son had discarded a bicycle; Harry caught sight of it at the curb before the refuse truck arrived, pushed the bicycle home, propped it up on his workbench in the garage, and in a few days got it back in running order. Soon he was pedaling it over to the country club for his weekly game of golf. The only drawback to this arrangement was that by the time he reached the club his legs ached as much as if he had already played a full nine holes. It was obvious that further ingenuity was called for. Jacques was big and strong, though getting on in years, and it occurred to Harry to rig up a harness by which Jacques could pull him over to the country club without the slightest effort on his part. The exercise would do Jacques good; moreover, from Jacques' point of view it was another trick to be learned, another chance for Harry and him to show off. He indicated by a fervent waving of his tail as he stood up on his hind legs and pawed the air that nothing would please him better than to be put in the harness and start pulling.

All his life, Harry's inventiveness had suffered from a single flaw: in his delight at solving the immediate problem, he rarely foresaw certain remote consequences of the solution. If a towel rack in his bathroom broke, he would open the bathroom window, reach out, and snap off a branch of a nearby tree to serve as a temporary substitute. Where he had been obliged to remove inconvenient twigs, the branch would have a number of sharp stubs. Sooner or later (for with Harry, "temporary" could mean months and sometimes years), he would skid in the course of getting out of the tub and, trying to steady himself, would stumble against the branch, whose stubs would rake his flesh and draw blood in half a dozen places. Or Harry would "temporarily" replace the broken-off foot of a sofa with a tower of used cardboard beer coasters, and after a few weeks an army of carpenter ants with a taste for beer coasters would march up from the crawl space into the house and set about devouring not only the coasters but the sofa as well. In the case of the bicycle, Harry had thought of harnessing Jacques but not of controlling him. In spite of this, their first journey to and from the club was a notable success. As a pair of performers, they were much admired—a big black poodle pulling along at a smart clip a white-haired old man on a child's bicycle. On the second journey, Jacques happened to catch sight of an old enemy of his sharpening her claws in a garden across the street. He took off after her at high speed, with Harry shouting at him to stop and squeezing in vain on the loose brake handles. Jacques leapt the curb, but the bicycle struck it head on and came to a jolting halt. In the same instant, the harness broke, Jacques galloped off after the cat, and Harry shot up over the handlebars and, turning a half somersault, landed on the small of his back in the damp crater of a compost heap. Had he landed anywhere else in the garden, he might have broken a dozen unmendable bones. He lay there marveling at his good luck and smiling up at the undersides of some sunny leaves. After a few minutes, he got up and made his way on foot to the club, where the three old companions awaiting him on the first tee rebuked him vehemently for being late.

As was to be expected, dog and man grew alike with age. When they went out for a ramble, both of them tended to favor their right sides and so kept drifting off course and into the lane of oncoming traffic. Every few yards, they would correct their aim by a sudden jog to the left, making their progress along the shoulder of the road a series of continuous unpredictable tackings. The older they grew, the less heed they paid to traffic. They were pedestrians and, like all pedestrians, felt entitled to the right of way. Without knowing it, they took fearful chances; once, on the state highway in front of the Melchetts' house, a truck, brakes screaming, swerved round them with but inches to spare, and Harry said mildly, "Damn fool. Don't care who they let behind the wheel these days."

Jacques was not only somewhat older than Harry—he was growing old faster. Sometimes when he got up, his back legs buckled under him and he sat down with a look of bewilderment in his white-rimmed eyes. He would cock a leg to piss and start to fall over; gradually he learned to piss like a bitch, sagging forward on all fours. He breathed with difficulty, snuffling and letting spit run from the loose corners of his mouth. To make matters worse, his breath was disgusting. Harry might be taking a nap on the sofa in the living room, and Jacques would totter across the room and lift his graying muzzle to Harry's cheek. Waked more by the stench of Jacques' breath than by his coarse wet tongue, Harry would cuff the old dog away, then reach out and pat him from a distance. Jacques broke wind constantly, with an energy unlooked for in a creature approaching ninety. In winter, he would lie on a big hot-air register in the hall and soon make all the downstairs rooms in the house uninhabitable. In summer, he was expected to spend the day out of doors. Between the garage at the back of the Melchetts' house and the hedge dividing their property from the Coxeys' lay a narrow patch of uphill land, which Harry called his garden. It was a garden only to the extent that every few years he would make an effort to clear the gravelly soil of rocks and prune the branches of the adjacent trees in order to let more sunlight fall on a dozen or so carefully laid-out rows of tomatoes, beets, carrots, and beans. Though the garden rarely flourished, its crisscross of guardian stakes and strings and the brightly colored empty seed packets fixed in place to denote where the different crops were expected to emerge gave the hillside a look of purposeful neatness; it pleased Harry to gaze on it from the kitchen windows as he washed and dried the dishes after meals. Halfway up the slope of the little garden was a grassy knoll, and it was here that Jacques would settle down as if by right, dozing and waking throughout the long, hot days. He liked watching Harry at work with rake and hoe in the garden; he liked watching the birds as they chittered and flung spray from the lip of the concrete bird-bath that stood on the far side of the garden; and he liked intimidating the occasional squirrel that ventured up onto the bath and scattered the birds. When this happened, Jacques would get to his feet and make a single preliminary lunge toward the bath: all that was needed to send the squirrel zigzagging in terror up the nearest tree. Jacques would then grandly subside, lowering his muzzle onto his paws for a well-earned nap. The curious thing was that he stank almost as much out of doors as he did in the house. On windless days, his odor brimmed in the garden like water in a glass. It was a mystery to Harry where the stench came from. Even when Harry washed him in the warm sun and carefully dried him in a towel, Jacques' coat retained an unclean smell, as if he had been rolling in offal. Harry could remember the sweet, herby smell of him as a puppy, when he held him up in his hands and tossed him about. He had been like cinnamon.

Laura would have nothing to do with Jacques and less and less to do with Harry. She was growing feeble, and the strongest things left in her were her hatred of Jacques and her envy of Harry. Nothing angered her like hearing people say how remarkable Harry was. It was always the same word—"remarkable." Nobody ever applied that word to her, even in flattery. Her sight was poor and her hearing was poor and her false teeth made her mouth ache. She would cup her hand in front of her mouth and nose, and breathe out hard, to discover whether her breath was as foul as Jacques'. Her hair was falling out; bare skin gleamed among thickets of thinning white stuff, and it was surely too late to disguise her baldness with a wig. Besides, whom was there left to deceive? Her children? Her grandchildren and great-grandchildren, in whose existence she found it hard to believe? She had not thought at twenty, with all that ropy hair to the waist, that someday her scalp would shine like a speckled egg. She was rotting away, as Jacques was. It seemed as if every day Jacques and she had more in common and she had more to hate him for. From the time he had been a puppy, Jacques had slept in the same room with Harry and her. In his impetuous youth, he had often bounded up into bed and settled down affectionately between them, and she had just as often flung him out. She would not be having Jacques in bed with her, she had told Harry; bad enough to grow old without sharing her husband with a dog. "Now, Laura" was all that Harry had said in reply. He had a disposition so amiable that in sixty years she had never been able to provoke a single substantial quarrel. Patiently, Harry had trained Jacques to stay out of the bed. He had found a space for the dog to sleep on "his" side of the room, as far as possible from Laura. In recent months, Jacques had grown too weak to climb the stairs. He slept now in the living room, close to the sofa that Harry napped on and had long since given the odor of his body to. If I were to die, Laura thought, Harry would move our bed downstairs and be next to Jacques again.

And not from thinking that, but having thought it, suddenly and without so much as a warning pain, Laura died. Harry found her seated in her chair in the study, with the television on. It was early evening; through the window behind her, he could see Venus, low in the green sky. He thought that the television had put her to sleep, as it often did. The easiest way to wake her was to turn off the set, and when he did so and she did not wake, he guessed at once that she must be dead. He felt only a tremor —a skipped pulse beat—of surprise. There she was. She had simply come to the end. From year to year he had felt her envy of him gathering force in her and poisoning her, and because there had been nothing that he could do to prevent it, he had responded in his usual fashion, by pretending that it did not exist. No doubt this had increased her bitterness toward him—she had always felt that he showed too little respect for her emotions. How far apart they had drifted with age! It was so different from what he had expected when they were young. It must have been different for Laura, too, but for a long time now she had taken care not to speak of such things. She kept her feelings to herself, as if to punish him for his earlier disregard for them. From time to time, and more rarely with every passing year, she would lash out at him in a gust of anger, and it was plain that she wanted him to do the same, but he never did. He faced the storm of her anger in silence, and waited for it to pass. He had been a disappointment to her on those occasions and on so many occasions. He stared at her sitting there, her mouth ajar. There would be plenty of time later to think about all the things she had failed to forgive him for. Perhaps he would think about them; perhaps not. It was a question of the cheerfulness of remembered things. Some of the past went on being of help to him, but most of it no longer mattered. Laura had done right not to live another day. If he had died before her, what a mess she would have made of their affairs! It had always been his duty to keep order in their lives. He liked having everything just so—"a place for everything," as his father used to tell him, "and everything in its place." He wanted the daily business of the world to proceed evenly, without fuss. He abhorred loose ends, and he would be sure to leave none behind when his time came. What was his inventiveness but a way of accommodating as quickly and easily as possible to things that had gone wrong, or threatened to go wrong? With luck, it was a way of making things go better than they had before. Always one had to say, "With luck."

Harry went out into the hall to telephone Lawrence, his elder son. A lawyer in his late fifties, Lawrence lived with his wife and children in a city a hundred-odd miles away. Harry dialed the number and stood waiting for someone to pick up the phone. His children were no longer very vivid to him. Sometimes in his recollection of them they started to fade away into their own childhoods; at other times he thought of them as older than he was. The truth was that they were not as interesting as they might have been. None of them was a patch on Laura in her best days. He could talk to Lawrence, but Paul he had

261

despised for thirty years; Harriet, who had been pretty
as a child, was plump and officious, and made angry wise-
cracks about people whose names meant nothing to him.
The voice that answered the phone was tired and middle-
aged, with an edge of asperity that reminded Harry of
Laura. Harry said, "Son, this is Dad, and I'm afraid I've
some bad news. Your mother. Yes, peacefully. In her
sleep. No, it's all right, I can handle everything at this
end. Tell Harriet and Paul, and I'll see you here tomorrow.
I don't want you children out on the roads at night."

He called the undertaker and went into the pantry and
poured himself a drink of Scotch and water, not so much
because he needed one as because he felt it would be
expected of him. When, in a few minutes, he would walk
next door to tell the Coxeys of Laura's death, they would
think it strange that he could face the long night without
a stimulant. How little people knew about each other!
He had never taken a drink when things were going wrong
—he drank only when he was already happy, as in the
locker room at the country club, among friends. Besides, Laura's death was not in the nature of something
that had gone wrong. It was something that a stranger
weighing the facts might think of as having more good
in it than bad. All the bitterness and envy that had been
choking Laura had gone out of her, and out of the world.
He went into the study and sat down across from her.
Contrary to what the Coxeys would suppose, it was not
horrible to see her there. She had the look of a ramshackle
toy, too small ever to have been a real woman, much
less to have been the Laura of his first encounter with
her—that slender girl, with long, wheat-colored hair and
pearly skin, who carried herself with such extraordinary

pride. For him, there had been many Lauras since then, and no doubt for Laura there had been many Harrys, each less precious than the one before. He heard then, in the study, the voice of the first Laura, speaking her first word of love to him. Holding his face between her hands, she had said to him softly, "Ah, boy! Boy!" It was a long time before she gave up calling him that, and her giving it up had nothing to do with his wrinkled face and white hair. When she stopped, it was because she had stopped loving him.

They had fallen in love at college—ignorant, passionate virgins, reveling in their bodies and full of wonder at their appetites. In those days it was unthinkable for young people to go to bed without being married; their ardor made them ache, but even this was pleasurable, being so soon to be assuaged. For, young as they were, and reckless as early marriages were thought to be, their families were delighted with the match and urged them not to trouble themselves with a conventional long engagement. Since there was plenty of money on both sides, Harry had no need to prove himself financially. They married at twenty-two, in her parents' big summer house by the sea, and set off on their honeymoon in a car that was the wedding gift of his parents—a glinting, intricate plaything of brass, nickel, leather, and wood. Jack Treanor, a college friend of Harry's, had offered them for their honeymoon the use of a hunting lodge on his family's estate in the Smokies. Treanor, because he loved men, would not be marrying, but he had a temperament ideally suited to marriage; throughout the wedding festivities, it seemed that he was as much at the center of them, and brought as much joy to them, as the bride and groom. He was a spruce, pink-cheeked, and generous young man, who fell in love with women every bit as eagerly as he did with men, but for whom women meant friendship and men excitement and a bodily devotion; when Laura and Harry, in their sky-blue Locomobile, went putt-putting away down the oyster-shell drive, Treanor felt an almost irresistible longing to leap up onto the running board and accompany them. He was in love with Laura and could not say a word.

To many of Laura's and Harry's relatives, the honeymoon journey into the unfashionable mountains of Tennessee was an adventure as arduous and perhaps as dangerous as a dash to the North Pole. The roads were mainly of dirt, and every fifty miles or so there was certain to be a flat tire. Laura and Harry would listen with cheerful resignation for the pop of burst rubber, the whoosh of escaping air; then they would clamber down laughing, jack and tools in hand, to change the tire, crank up, and be off again into the wilderness. Was not Harry inventive, resourceful, capable of making much out of little? Was he not sure to be sweet-tempered and cheerful even in adversity? And was it not for these qualities among others that the willful, mercurial Laura loved him?

They were an exceptional couple, and they knew it. If the most ordinary good fortune had befallen them, they would have led exceptionally happy lives, but it was not to be, or not for long. On their return from their honeymoon (the lodge in the Smokies having been safely reached, their bodies having violently acquainted themselves with each other), they set up housekeeping in a pretty and ample five-room apartment in New York, with an Irish maid who endangered the smaller chairs and tables with her dusting. Harry began his career as a runner in the family bank; he was finding his way as his father and grandfather had done before him. The first baby came, less because they wished him to do so than because it hadn't occurred to them to prevent his coming. After two years, there was another boy, whom Laura found a whining nuisance, and when, a scant year later, a daughter arrived, Laura instructed Harry that henceforth he was to take every possible precaution. Being Harry, he made an effort to look on the bright side; surely, he thought, there was some way to make a condom a less grisly-looking object, but for once his inventiveness failed him. The hateful thing remained what it was: disfiguring, repellent to touch, indestructible. Soon all the rivers and oceans of the world would be full of them. Still, it never crossed his mind that the burden of contraception should be placed upon Laura; bad enough, he reasoned, that women were responsible for bearing children without their being responsible for not bearing them.

Harry had a camp built in Laura's name at his parents' place in the Catskills. Nearly every weekend all summer long, they would invite three or four couples up to share their limited quarters. They ate and drank and swam and slept *al fresco,* with continuous mild flirtations but with no affairs. How innocent they were, even in their amorousness! Nobody nowadays would credit how childlike their good times were. People said of Laura and Harry that they were the handsomest couple ever, with the most beautiful children ever, and the naturalness with which they accepted such compliments was also childlike. The first Laura and Harry had been the bride and groom; the second Laura and Harry were this splendid young couple, and they, too, were soon to vanish.

Unexpectedly, the family bank was threatened with failure, in part because of certain gross errors of judgment on the part of Harry's father. As soon as the bank examiners had left his office, that jolly, incompetent man went home, wrote half a dozen letters of apology to members of his family, and drove up into the mountains, where he drowned himself in his favorite trout stream. Harry, being by then a teller, resigned from the bank in order to save it further embarrassment. By coincidence, a financial depression followed the trouble at the bank, and jobs were far less easy to come by than Harry and his friends had supposed; the letters of recommendation they wrote in his behalf were read and filed away and forgotten. It took him nearly a year to find a job that sounded feasible: a company that manufactured an unusual kind of steam turbine was in need of a crack salesman, and in the light of Harry's bent for mechanics, it was agreed that this would be just the thing for him. And so it was, for two or three years; by then, it had become clear that what made the turbine unusual was precisely what made it unreliable. The company went bankrupt just as Harry was completing the design of a device that would have assured the turbine commercial success. Harry took out a patent on his improvement, of course too late. It was the first of several patents he took out, none of which aroused more than momentary interest in the business world.

When the crash came, Harry and Laura and the children were living on Long Island, in a big, run-down house on the North Shore. Harry's family had lost the bulk of its fortune in the bank debacle, but Laura's father had grown continuously richer throughout the twenties. He had insisted on paying the children's tuition at boarding school;

he had also given Laura a considerable allowance for clothing and entertainment, and had seen to it that she had a new car annually. He had always encouraged Laura and Harry to live beyond their means, though he would have protested that the exact opposite was true—that he was constantly urging them to be more provident. Whenever Laura's extravagance got her into trouble, she would turn to her father, who would first deliver a pleasantly incoherent lecture on getting ready for rainy days and then write out a check far more than sufficient for her needs. The crash, in wiping him out, left him without purpose. All his life, he had expressed affection through money, and when for the first time this was no longer possible, he took to his bed and within a year had died of a broken heart.

At the time, Harry was a partner in a trucking firm in New York. The firm had only recently begun to show a profit, and it was doubtful whether, with a continued high overhead, it would be able to survive a prolonged depression. Though now in early middle age, Harry was by some years the youngest of the partners, and when it became obvious that someone must be encouraged to walk the plank, Harry was the first to volunteer. He arranged to be bought out by the other partners for a small sum; they thanked him in tears, feeling like Judases. Harry assured them that he was in excellent spirits. And it was true, for he had no fears in respect to the future. He was genuinely puzzled by the panic he observed all around him. It had never occurred to him that he would fail at anything for long. Bad times might come, but bad times would pass. "Live every day of your life," he would say, "but live it a day at a time." And people would nod, not so much in agreement with Harry's maxim (on examination, wouldn't it perhaps turn out to be nonsense?) as in envy of his equanimity. He acquired the habit of signing letters, not "Yours truly" or "Sincerely yours," but "Take it easy," and he meant it.

Laura proposed that they sell the house on Long Island, add the proceeds of this sale to the sum that Harry had received for his share in the trucking firm, and go abroad to live until the depression had run its course. Household expenses would be wonderfully reduced if they were to rent a place somewhere in France or Italy, far from the habitual temptations of party-giving and party-going. There would be no more costly keeping up with the Joneses, because there would be no more Joneses. Harry noted mildly that it would be unlikely for him to be able to find work abroad, in countries where he could not even speak the language. Laura countered by saying that it appeared unlikely for him to be able to find work in America—better men than he were walking the streets, if not actually selling apples in them. Harry accepted her appraisal of him with his usual reasonableness. The point was that whether there were jobs or not, he had to be ready to be struck by lightning. Laura produced another trump: it would be such an advantage for the children to live abroad and complete their education there. They would become cultivated citizens of the world, speaking who could predict how many languages and finding themselves at home in half a dozen capitals. Harry agreed that the prospect was a pleasing one; what he objected to was that once he got a job he would be permitted only a few weeks of vacation at most and would therefore be separated from his family for long periods of time. "I call that selfish," Laura said. There was no suitable answer to that, or none that Harry cared to risk making. If he disliked Laura's plan, he disliked even more having to disappoint Laura. "Have it your way," he said.

"No, no! I want you to be as excited about the project as I am," Laura said. "Otherwise, the children and I won't go."

Harry mustered the necessary smile and said, "All right. I am very excited."

"Cross your heart," she said, exultant as a child.

Still smiling, Harry crossed his heart.

Laura found the south of France less economical than she had been led to believe. From Nice, she dropped a postcard to Harry saying that she and the children were pushing on into Italy—she had heard rumors of how dirt-cheap life in Milan could be. A week or so later, a postcard showing the wedding-cake roof of Il Duomo let him know that the family found Milan impossible and was pushing farther down into the boot; Laura had met some American tourists who were full of praise for Rome. Sure enough, in Rome Laura succeeded in locating an apartment on the top floor of an old *palazzo* in the Via Gregoriana. It had terraces on three sides, with a panoramic view of Rome, and when the cannon was fired at noon on the Janiculum, it made the crystal prisms of the chandelier in the drawing room go chink-chink. The card was signed, "Love from all, L.," and Harry read it over three or four times with feelings of pleasure and irritation. Glad as he was to find Laura in such a sunny mood, he was in need of some hard facts: what did the apartment cost, what was the price of food in Rome, would the children find it difficult getting into the proper schools? He wrote Laura that evening from the small, suffocating hotel in the West Forties where he

269

was spending the summer. "Please answer the following
questions by return mail," he instructed her. "And please,
darling, *not* on a postcard. The information I seek is important, because things are getting worse here instead of
better, and every day I have a number of fresh decisions
to make. I have leads on half a dozen jobs—you can't keep
a good man down!—though nothing firm as yet. Only bad
news in respect to the house. I've cut the asking price in
half, but still no takers. It seems there are hundreds and
maybe thousands of big houses for sale on the North Shore,
most of them in better shape than ours. Considering the
amount of the mortgage payments we have to make, the
amount of property taxes we pay, and the amount of equity
in the house that will be left above the mortgage if the
asking price keeps being cut, by the end of the year the
wise thing may be to let the bank foreclose the mortgage.
This will mean a total loss for us, but if I went on pouring
into the house the remains of the money I got for my
partnership, we might well end up with neither house *nor*
money. I know you find all this kind of business talk boring,
but look at things my way for a moment. There are no
chinking prisms in this rotten hotel room. Not that I am
complaining, or not much. There can be times, you know,
when nothing goes right, no matter how sensibly a man
behaves. I am trying hard to be sensible here in New York,
and I hope you will try hard to be sensible in Rome.
Answer the questions in sequence, as fully as possible, like
a good girl."

His first answer to the letter was a cable: "OH GOD STOP
WHAT A WET BLANKET YOU ARE STOP LOVE LAURA." The
second answer came a couple of weeks later and confirmed
the fears that had been aroused in Harry by all those chink-

ing prisms. The apartment at the top of the old *palazzo* was as expensive as it was charming; the children's schools were also expensive; and though food was cheap, Laura was paying the wages of the cook and maid who came with the apartment. Life in Rome was costing only a few hundred dollars a year less than life on the North Shore; meanwhile, Harry had meals to buy and a weekly hotel bill to pay. For a third of what it had cost, he sold their camp in the Catskills to a still-wealthy cousin. Most of that money went at once to Rome. Harry found himself dividing the sum in his bankbook by months, then weeks, then days. Meeting on the street a man whom he recognized as a customer of the trucking firm, he asked him point-blank for a job.

The man said, "I got nothing at your level."

"Any level."

"You wouldn't take it."

"Try me."

"Harry, I'm sorry—it *is* Harry, isn't it?"

"Try me!"

And so from a near-stranger on a street corner he successfully begged a job as a night watchman in a big truckers' depot in the Bronx. The job paid forty dollars a week. He wrote Laura and the children that he had found a temporary executive position of little importance. As soon as he had put aside money enough for a steamer ticket, he would be giving up the position and joining them for a holiday in Rome. They would be having a regular old-fashioned family reunion. Meanwhile the house was lost, as he had feared it would be. He put the furniture in storage and moved into a room in a boardinghouse in Mott Haven. For a year and a half, in boots and lumber jacket, he walked the grease-spattered floors and dark alleys of the depot. His hours were from midnight to 8:00 A.M., six days a week, and on Sundays he slept all day, not moving. Later, he never mentioned to Laura and the children how he had passed that period of his life. It was not so much that he was afraid they would feel sorry for him; he was afraid they would feel embarrassed for themselves—Laura because she had been enjoying herself when he had been miserable, and the children because they seemed to require a loftier image of their father than that of a night watchman. For Rome, though it failed to give the children a second language, succeeded in turning them into snobs. When the time came, they were sorry to return home; with a gesture here, an anecdote there, they were ever after to convey the impression that, though Americans in America, they were nevertheless in what amounted to exile.

Two things brought Laura and the children home. The first was that Jack Treanor encountered Harry late one afternoon in New York and invited him to stop by their club for a drink.

Harry, smiling: "Not mine. Yours."

"My God, you weren't thrown out? Peaceable Harry?"

"Resigned."

"Money trouble?"

"Just so."

"Oh, hell. I'm the only man I know who still has pots of money. Oh, hell." Treanor was genuinely distressed whenever he was brought face to face with the fact that he was incomparably richer than anyone he knew. Unlike most rich people, he was capable of imagining what it must be like to be without money. Having inherited his wealth, he felt keenly the unfairness of the advantages it brought him, but so far he had found no practical means of mitigating this unfairness. If he were to give away his entire fortune, rendering himself as miserable as he supposed every impoverished person must be, it would bring no greater happiness to others, since the sum—he had worked it out with care—would amount to about twenty-five cents for every person in the country. He paid his taxes with relish and handed out capital in chunks to worthy causes, but more chunks kept piling up: Himalayas of money, unconquerable. Sick with dismay, he stared sidelong at Harry as they entered the bar. He was certainly not looking his best, poor Harry. Oh, hell! Treanor had remained spruce, pink-cheeked, and youthful; he had kept the same attractive lover for ten years and, tempted though Treanor was to fall in love each day, he had found it easy to be faithful to him. He had made the lover happy in the simplest way possible, by buying him anything he wished. Considering his opportunities, Fletcher was far from greedy. Good clothes, good jewelry, a car—they were all so many toys. As Harry lifted his drink, Treanor was shocked to see that the rims of Harry's fingernails were black. Under questioning and with his accustomed cheerfulness, Harry began to describe his job at the depot, his quarters in Mott Haven. Treanor drank three Martinis in quick succession, to keep himself from picturing too clearly the nature of his friend's plight. Dear Harry, of all people! He thought of his years of unbroken domestic happiness and then of Harry alone, in a single dreary room in . . . wherever Mott Haven might be. Oh, Christ, Christ! By chance, he was in need of a manager for a couple of family enterprises in the small town in Tennessee where the Treanors, a hundred-odd years ago, had begun putting together the first modest pieces of their now formidable empire. These enterprises—a coal company and a soft-drink distributing company—were the not very profitable souvenirs of that earlier time, which Treanor retained in part out of sentiment and in part to remind himself and the remaining distant members of the family that once there had been Treanors who stumbled awake in the dark and who sweated like animals to get ahead. He had had it in mind to put the running of the companies into the hands of some young go-getter in Felix, but, his face flushed with alcohol and the happiness of an inspired good deed, his brain bursting with a single feverishly repeated word, he offered the job to Harry. Harry accepted it at once. Treanor said, "You don't think you ought to talk it over with Laura and the children first? Felix is a small town, a *Southern* small town. It isn't New York, it isn't Rome."

"No matter. It's my chance. I can't thank you enough."

"Oh, hell!"

"If it weren't for you—"

"My dear, *dear* Harry! Not a word!"

Later, falling tipsily asleep beside Fletcher in a bedroom at the club, Jack remembered the word that had raced through his mind at the moment of his being kind to Harry. Laura. He had come so close to begging her to touch him as they danced at her wedding. So close, so close! He smiled into the dark, marveling, not for the first time, at how many people one person can be.

The other thing that brought Laura and the children home, though Laura herself would never know it, was a cable to Harry from their second son. It reached Harry just as he was writing to tell them about his new-found job in Felix. It read, "MOTHER BEING IDIOTIC STOP ADVISE YOU

COME STOP PAUL." Harry sat motionless at the foot of his bed, his writing materials scattered on the blanket beside him. He was aware at once of what the words were intended to tell him. Simply as information, the message seemed to alter nothing in his mind. He felt his ordinary calmness, but when he tried to go on writing the letter, to his astonishment he discovered that his hand was trembling violently. He said aloud, "Ah, the shit! The little shit!" He struggled to protect Laura against their son by obliterating the cable; it did not exist, it had never existed. In vain. There was no way not to possess the knowledge that Paul had conveyed to him. Laura, Laura! Over the long period of their separation, he had sometimes wondered whether, given the opportunity, she would not wish to have what he thought of (and what she, too, would be sure to think of) as a little fling. And of course opportunities would have arisen. She was a good-looking, spirited woman; she adored parties and the admiration of others. Rome was surely full of men eager to make love to her, and whatever decision she had reached in respect to them she would have weighed intelligently and at length. The last word that anyone could ever apply to Laura was "idiotic." If she was reckless, she was reckless only after taking thought and measuring the cost; she liked long odds, and on the occasions when she miscalculated, she took care to be a good loser. And now that priggish boy was seeking to punish her—*daring* to punish her! Harry felt himself coolly excluding Paul from his heart. He perceived that the process of exclusion would be easier than he had expected; up to then, he had never thought to measure how little he cared for Paul. Parenthood was a strange business and often an unsatisfactory one; luckily, it allowed for a greater variety of responses

275

than the world pretended. He could see no reason ever to forgive Paul. Meanwhile, he had no intention of going to Rome and confronting Laura. He wanted her to do whatever it was she had chosen to do; the matter was as simple as that. He would not answer Paul's cable, and he would never mention it to Laura. He picked up a sheet of note paper and placed it on the cover of a book that, balanced on his knees, served him as a sort of writing table. His hand had stopped trembling. "Dear Family," he wrote. "Good news at last!"

Felix, Tennessee. County seat of Townsend County. Founded 1781. Alt. 1623 ft. Pop. 19,736. Birthplace of Zebulon Tracy, thirteenth Vice President of the United States. Chief industries: lumbering, textiles, tourism. Rotary, Kiwanis, Lion's Club.

The town lay on the western slopes of the Smokies, in coves and open meadows that dropped in a series of natural terraces to a tributary of the Ohio. As in most Southern towns, the streets extended in a grid from a central square, in the middle of which stood a pillared and domed county courthouse. The "nice" part of town—the so-called country-club section—lay at a distance of several miles from the congested downtown district. The club and golf course had been built on land that had once been part of the Treanor estate. Jack Treanor himself lived with Fletcher and half a dozen servants in the old Treanor mansion on a hillside overlooking the town. The mansion was a nineteenth-century castellated Tuscan villa, reputed to contain a hundred rooms, and was referred to locally as the Castle. All it lacked was a ghost; as Jack said, the Treanors had been a merry and untroubled lot for generations, and haunting was not in their line.

When Harry came to Felix, he rented an apartment on the opposite side of town from the Castle. The section was a near-slum, the apartment small and dark. Harry was aware that Laura and the children would dislike it intensely, but it had the advantage of being both cheap and handy; the two offices where he would be spending most of his time were within easy walking distance, in an even worse section of town. As the moment approached for the family to join him, Harry assured them by mail that their new home would be only temporary—not, he added, his usual "temporary," but really and truly and on a stack of Bibles temporary. Having put in twelve or fourteen hours at his two jobs (for the work in each case was new to him, and he had much to learn), he would come home late to the apartment, with its roaches scuttling along the baseboards and the silverfish in the sinks, and set about covering the stained, sea-green walls with fresh coats of paint. He painted everything white, thinking to make the little rooms look as bright and cheerful as possible. Too late he saw with dismay that he had caused them to resemble a series of harsh little hospital cells. He would tumble into bed at two or three in the morning, sick with fatigue but thinking, at least it's clean, or cleaner than it was. "Lord God!" he would say aloud, in the echoing bedroom, "I'm making a start," and fall instantly asleep.

Though forewarned, Laura and the children were shocked by the meanness and bleakness of the apartment and, by extension, of Felix as well. The apartment was plainly not on the Via Gregoriana, and Felix, as Jack Treanor had urged Harry to advise them, was not Rome. Still, since the children would be away most of the year at the state university, the weight of the general domestic dismalness fell upon Laura. "Just let me get my feet on the ground," Harry would say. "As soon as we can, we'll look around for something else."

"I cannot live like this," Laura said, in a sullen monotone. "I cannot, I cannot, I cannot."

"All I ask is six months. Maybe we'll find a place in the hills outside town, where the young folks are beginning to build."

"There are no young folks in this town," Laura said, "and I am not surprised. There are no old folks, either. There are just the people like us. Leftovers."

"Now, Laura."

"If only you'd taken the trouble to see how we lived in Rome!"

"I'm sure it was wonderful, but it couldn't have lasted. My partnership money was running out. This is where we belong now."

"*I* belong in this cretinous town? Harry, how little you know!"

"You'll see. It's not so bad."

Perhaps to the surprise of both of them, Harry turned out to be right. For Laura was not sullen or skeptical by nature —on the contrary, she was nearly always tempted to think better of people on first meeting them than, on further acquaintance, they turned out to deserve. In middle age, she would give her heart away as readily as she had done as a girl; no less girlish was the astonishment she felt when the recipients of her affection took advantage of that gift. Unlike Harry, she had not schooled herself against the ordinary disappointments of life. Plunged as if for the first time into the depths of despair, within a few days, and again as if for the first time, she would joyously embrace the world. She was quick to respond to the least hint of criticism ("WHAT A WET BLANKET YOU ARE"), and she wore praise like a brooch on her bosom, boldly. "Dear foolish roller coaster!" Harry said to her once, in mingled alarm and admiration. "Dear sturdy track!" she said in reply. That was in their good days, before the misadventures of old age began.

As for Felix, it was a far pleasanter place to live in than a stranger impatiently working his way through the traffic in Courthouse Square was apt to suppose. The town was not merely what the Chamber of Commerce called it: "Gateway to the Beautiful Smokies." It was strikingly clean, with broad streets of rosy brick under tunnellike leafy trees, and in summer a breeze smelling of wild flowers blew in from the miles of open meadows to the west; rimmed on three sides by mountains, in winter it gathered up sunlight in such a fashion that a heavy fall of snow during the night would have vanished utterly by noon. Many of the residents of the town had moved south to Felix after the crash, looking for a place where rents and the cost of food and help were low, and the need to make good less frantic than up North. Newcomer Harry aside, it appeared that even the hardest-working men in Felix found time in the late afternoons for a round of golf or a couple of sets of tennis, with, afterward, a plunge in the club pool and a long drink on the terrace, in the twilight, doubly blue, of the gaudy parasols. There was still good hunting and fishing to be had in the neighboring wooded coves, dark with pine and rhododendron, and all winter from Courthouse Square one looked up and saw skiers like grains of brightly colored dust drifting at random over the snowfields, between the taut loops of the tows.

What helped Laura make her peace with Felix—what

led her even to forgive Harry for the horrible, white-walled rabbit hutch that he had brought the children and her to as if it were a palace—was the renewal of her friendship with Jack Treanor. She remembered at once that Jack had thought her the perfect bride. She remembered, too, how he had wished to be allowed to accompany Harry and her to his family's lodge on the heights beyond Felix, in order to share their honeymoon with them. What a strange young man he had been, and how lovable! He was no less lovable now, and the strangeness was gone; or, rather, it had never existed, for she saw that what she had taken for strangeness had been simply the difficulty for her of encountering something unfamiliar. What beautiful but silly young creatures they had been, buffeted by feelings they did not suppose existed and so had not even thought to examine and (no doubt) primly reject! In those days, she had been far from weighing risks and counting odds; she had not known how to measure, even on the simplest terms, the limits of the possible. It was plain to her now that there ought to have been some means by which she and Harry and Jack could have pitched themselves headlong into one another and broken, each in his own way, each for his own good, the bonds of their infantile, unintentional selfishness. Instead, she married, giving herself in ignorance to ignorant Harry. Some aura of a promise unfulfilled hung over the three of them and deepened their relationship. They were all together at last, as Jack had wanted them to be. Whenever Laura and he met, they hugged each other like lovers, and Harry and Fletcher were expected to look on indulgently from the sidelines, as if transformed without warning into the parents of some infatuated young couple. Jack saw in Laura the girl she had been, living on miraculously unchanged; he paid her the compliments—whispered, passionate, occasionally obscene—that he had failed to pay her all those decades ago, in the festive house by the sea, and Laura found no difficulty in accepting them.

For the first time in twenty years, Jack gave a ball in the high-ceilinged gilt-and-crystal ballroom of the Castle, announcing to all Felix, with the unchallengeable authority of a thunderclap, the arrival as permanent residents in town of his friends Laura and Harry Melchett. Invitations to the ball and gossip about the guests of honor went hand in hand. One had to admit that the Melchetts were something of a puzzle. They lived in who knew what squalor in a section of town that few members of the country-club set had ever driven through, much less visited, and Harry's place on the lowest rung of the Treanor ladder of jobs— a rung so low (peddling coal? peddling soft drinks?) that many people were learning of it for the first time—was certainly unworthy of a man of Harry's age and appearance, but because the Melchetts were Jack's friends, the unsavory address and plebeian job would have to be set down as some form of acceptable eccentricity. For in Felix the stamp of Jack's approval was a *laissez-passer* through every imaginable barrier of money and class. There was also the fact that Laura and Harry were so obviously people of breeding; in Felix they were not alone in having come down in the world. Distinguished members of the depressed *rentier* class—Forbeses from Boston, Brainards from Hartford, Delafields from New York—peopled the woods that encircled the golf course, playing house in cottages that they might once have deemed unsuitable for their chauffeurs.

The ball was, as it could not have failed to be, a triumph. The society editor of the Felix *Courier* described it as "easily the most notable event in Felix's history. The Astors in their prime would have found much to envy." At five in the morning, Laura, Harry, Jack, and Fletcher sat having the last of several nightcaps, in the room known as the small study. This room adjoined a much larger room, known as the office; the office adjoined the paneled library, which opened in turn onto the three-storied great hall of the Castle. Fletcher was a small, lithe man of thirty, who affected a lower-class accent and vocabulary and who liked to make fun of the scale of the opulence on which Jack and he lived. On his first visit to the small study, Fletcher had asked, "Where in Jesus' name am I? And what are all them goddam knives and forks?" The room had been decorated twenty years earlier by Jack's father with the trophies of an African safari; on the dark walls gleamed masks, spears, guns, and heads of animals. On becoming familiar with what he called "my father-in-law's things," Fletcher learned to admire them and soon undertook to add to the collection. He hung a dart board in the small study and mastered the stunt of flipping a short African knife, end over end, into the heart of the board. He had a weakness for startling Jack's guests with unexpected gestures; it was his way of having, in the square world of Felix, what amounted to the last word.

For a wonder, Fletcher had enjoyed the ball as much as the others. "A very successful cruise," he said, to tease Jack. "Two probables and a possible. Felix is stumbling backward into the twentieth century."

Jack laughed, not hearing the words. All four of them were happy and talked out; they sat staring into space with dazed smiles, each unwilling to be the first to bring the evening to an end. Laura, lying back in the deep leather couch under the dart board, began to fall asleep, and Jack, seated beside her, reached over to nudge her awake. Being drunk, his aim was uncertain; his hand slipped down past her bare shoulder and into the V of her dress and rested there. Eyes closed, seemingly fast asleep, Laura reached up and took his hand between her hands and held it tight against her breasts. For some seconds, Harry, Fletcher, and Jack himself gazed at his hand, lying half-hidden in Laura's hands, then Fletcher, getting up, said, "O.K., baby, God damn it, bedtime!" Jack scrambled to his feet, saying, "Please don't be angry with me. I can't *bear* for you to be angry with me!" Jack was in love with everyone he had ever known or would ever know; he would fall in love with the first person to come to the Castle tomorrow. That was his failing, but surely it wasn't a thing he deserved to be punished for. He burst into tears and fell at Fletcher's feet, hugging Fletcher's knees and kissing the black stuff of his trousers.

In the first ten or fifteen years of their life in Felix, Harry worked as hard as any long-dead Treanor. By six, he was up and at the coalyard, where he spent the morning taking orders, weighing the loads of coal on the trucks, dispatching the drivers, and keeping the drivers' wives and girl friends from swiping coal out of the open bins in the yard, sometimes in baby carriages and at other times in somebody's borrowed or stolen car. Harry spent the afternoons at the soft-drink plant, again taking orders, dispatching drivers, and preventing petty thievery on the part of his employees and their innumerable relatives. The theory was that since the bulk of the coal business was in winter and the bulk of the soft-drink business in summer, it should be possible to make use of roughly the same amount of help and equipment all the year round in the delivery of two unlike but complementary products. In practice, no such efficient use of men and machines was achieved. The companies having been unprofitable to begin with, they were accustomed to paying the lowest wages in town and so were left with the dregs of the local employment market— wiry little mountaineers of remarkable strength and cunning, armed with knives and guns and almost totally illiterate. They drank beer and white mule all day and much of the night, and they fought their kin with equal relish over trifles and treasures: a tin cup moved six inches out of its usual place on a shelf might lead to a shoot-out between father and son, and so might pressing a claim to one or another of the womenfolk they held more or less in common. Between shootings and stabbings, Harry was sometimes called on to arbitrate a dispute where the prize at stake was a sallow, aging girl in her teens, already half-toothless, with a baby whimpering in her arms. Arson, rape, incest, and murder were all commonplaces among the men at the yards, and the law was careful to look the other way except when by bad luck a stranger happened to be gunned down in a tactless outbreak of family hostilities in the heart of town. The men respected Harry; even in his sixties, if a crew in one of the yards was shorthanded, Harry would pitch in and help load coal or cartons of soft drinks onto the waiting trucks. As evidence of their respect for Harry, the men stole from him only in emergencies. Prompted by the insurance company, he was sometimes obliged to swear out a warrant against one or another of his workers, but the thief on being convicted bore no grudge; as soon as he had served his time in prison, he would insist on coming back to work for Harry. Once, glancing about the coalyard, Harry noticed that every man on the place had a record; no wonder he was finding it difficult to buy insurance.

In the best of circumstances and working no matter how hard, Harry could never have made a success of the two businesses. For one thing, coal was giving way to oil and gas, and the advisers to whom Harry was answerable two or three rungs up the ladder of Treanor enterprises had no intention of going into new fields. Similarly, the soft drink that Harry sold—P. J. Cola, named after some long since forgotten small-town druggist—was a pygmy beside the big companies that had swept into town and, armed with what seemed, by Harry's standards, unlimited budgets for advertising and counter displays, battled each other to divide ninety per cent of the market, leaving half a dozen tiny companies to scrabble for what remained. With his gift for tinkering, Harry would manage to keep his trucks on the road years after they ought to have been junked; with his gift for neatness, he would worry his books into order night after night, paying not a penny more in taxes than the law required. In vain, and he knew it. The corporation accountants had doubtless been told that Jack Treanor would like to keep the old companies running, even at a loss, provided the losses remained small enough not to catch the eyes of cranky stockholders. When the accountants hummed and tapped their pencils against their teeth, Harry perceived that for as long as Jack lived he had a fighting chance; after that, they would show him no mercy. Still, he would not give up. He projected budgets for four years hence, five years, six. From time to time, some unexpected and welcome thing happened—a contract, say, for the heating of a large private sanitarium—that made it look as if perhaps he would soon be winning in business instead of always losing. Those were the good days, and life was a matter of stringing together as many good days as one could. The bad days took care of themselves and were sometimes, Harry admitted, his own fault. Harry was not much surprised when the sanitarium went bankrupt, leaving all its bills unpaid. Why else had its treasurer turned to Harry, a stranger? But why had Harry given him credit? Not even to Laura would Harry have dared to confess the truth: because the treasurer seemed like such a nice, confident young man. Because he reminded Harry of himself a long time ago.

Among the welcome things that happened was that Laura found them a house they could afford to buy. It was close to the district where most of their friends lived, but since it faced a state highway roaring with traffic night and day, and since the highway was scheduled to be widened within a few years, with a consequent shearing off of much of the lawn in front of the house, the property had gone begging for months. Harry did not fear the noise of the traffic—"Lord God! Aren't I getting deafer by the minute? A nice, steady hum might be just the thing to help me sleep"—and he rightly predicted that the widening of the highway would fall many years behind schedule. To his astonishment, Laura (extravagant Laura!) had managed to save up in pin money over the years the thousand dollars necessary to make a down payment on the house; the rest of the purchase price would be taken care of by a mortgage, the interest on which would be no greater than the rent they were currently paying. The house was a square wooden box, with a single red-brick chimney rising out of the

middle of the roof. It had the droll look of being not quite
life-sized, but the rooms were ample enough for Laura's
and Harry's purposes. With the children long since grown
and living at a distance, Laura and Harry would have the
luxury of a guest room, where one or two grandchildren
could be put up during their summer vacations. Laura
would be where she belonged at last, within a few minutes
of the country club and her friends and the nicest shops
in town. Possession of the house would give them what
amounted to a fresh start. They were nearing their seventies,
but for Harry the words "fresh start" were far from having a
comic ring. "I'll carry you over the threshold," Harry said
on their first day in the house. "Don't talk nonsense," Laura
told him. "You'd fuse every disc in your back. Bring in a
carton of dishes if you're feeling all that strong."

With characteristic zest, Harry threw himself into the
cleaning and painting of the new house. Laura chose the
colors, and Harry splashed them on. He laid asphalt tile
on the kitchen and bathroom floors. He rigged up a shower
above the tub. He divided a single upstairs closet into two—
one for linens, the other for brooms, dustcloths, furniture
polish, and the like. ("A place for everything, and everything
in its place.") Because the land ran uphill behind the house,
it turned out that drainage would be giving them trouble;
a day's rain, and the crawl space under the house became a
sea of red mud. Harry was delighted to learn of the problem.
There was nothing he enjoyed more than building drains.
A man who could cause water to go where he wanted it to
go, instead of where it had always previously gone, had
mastered a skill of considerable importance. When Harry
dug a trench, keeping the sides just so by an occasional
quick paring movement of his shovel and calculating to a

nicety the pitch at the bottom of the trench (he favored a generous half-inch to the foot, which allowed for uneven settling), Harry felt like some heroic aqueduct builder of ancient times, dominating nature by the simplest means: clay tiles, sand and gravel, the manipulation of gravity, the sweat of one's brow. During their first summer in the new house, Harry constructed a labyrinth of ditches, carefully backfilled and graded, along the rear lines of the house. Catch basins with heavy iron grates set in concrete aprons were located at regular intervals, flush with the ground. Their next-door neighbors the Coxeys would look out in wonder night after night to see Harry at work by the light of the kitchen windows—an old man with white hair standing in the bottom of a ditch and tossing shovelfuls of dirt high over his head. Laura explained to the Coxeys that digging was one of Harry's hobbies. She added that he had others of an equally unusual nature; nothing he was seen to be doing about the house was to alarm them, ever. The drainage system was ready by fall. During the first hard storm that followed its completion, Harry stood out in the driving wind and rain and shouted in exultation as he observed his drains swallowing up with ease the hundreds of gallons of water that came rushing down the hillside into them. The soil in the crawl space under the house remained as dry as gunpowder; no wonder it was later to become a favorite nesting place for rats.

Harry had expected Laura to dote upon the house; instead, it was he who did so. Again and again he would praise it for some trifling but agreeable attributes they had not known it possessed—for example, the scores of daffodils that leapt up out of the scraggly, untended lawn in spring,

288

or the view from their bedroom window, which drew the
eye up and away from the dreadful highway to where,
through a cleft in the nearby hills, one caught a glimpse of
a single distant peak of the Smokies, bearing, even in June,
a blazing cap of snow. Surely someone had admired that
view before them; surely someone had planted those daffodils with love. But Laura in her feelings appeared to remain at a distance from the house, and Harry wondered
(though in silence—more and more it was the case that
he would not risk talking with her about such matters)
whether the good fortune of acquiring the house had happened, for her, at a moment when questions of good or bad
fortune had stopped counting for much. There were things
that if one had to wait overly long for them were not worth
having; it might be that Laura, growing old, had exhausted
her gift for plunging upward, seemingly without injury, from
despair into joy.

Harry, as he would learn, was wrong; the question was
not one of age, but inattention. For many years now, as much
emotion of happiness as Laura was capable of feeling was
aroused in her, not by Harry, but by Jack. Absurd to feel
this emotion so late, absurd to feel *any*thing so late, but
there it was, like a great stone in the pathway; no getting
around it by pretending it didn't exist. To be old and passionate was macabre; very well, she would be macabre. The
facts were unbecoming but inescapable, and she faced them
daily without flinching. From the evening of the ball at the
Castle, she and Jack had been lovers. And not lovers. It
was a relationship that flourished and became all the closer
because it was incomplete. What remained unfinished in
it—their not having gone to bed together—served to hold
it together during the first years; afterward, it was a trifle,

or they treated it like one. Laura had hesitated to make love less out of consideration for Harry (she had learned in Rome, overnight, how little that cost her) than for Jack, who had invested so much of his life—but how willingly! oh, with all his heart!—in being true to Fletcher. And Fletcher, though he cared so little in principle for fidelity that he had rarely been faithful to Jack for longer than a week at a time, nevertheless counted on Jack's unshakable fidelity to him.

Little by little, Laura, Jack, and Fletcher worked out a new set of relationships, in which, without his knowledge and with his name having scarcely been mentioned, an equitable place was found for Harry. Jack and Fletcher would go on being lovers, Laura and Harry would go on being man and wife, and Laura and Jack would be lovers in every respect except that of sex. Laura acquired in Jack's life the place and perquisites of an official mistress. She assumed the role so gradually that it gave no offense to the puritan custodians of the private and public morals of Felix. There would surely have been those who considered Laura a great advance morally over Fletcher; in any event, it came to be the case that she was always at the Castle. At luncheons and dinner parties, it was the expected thing to find Laura beside Jack, welcoming the guests as they arrived and bidding them good night upon their departure. It was she who chose the menus, ordered the wine, arranged the flowers, hired and discharged the servants. In the Castle, Laura lived as she had hoped to be able to do in the apartment high above the tawny Via Gregoriana. What a difference to have Jack praising the consequences of her extravagance, instead of, like poor Harry, groaning over them! With his usual enthusiasm, Jack egged her on. He had never seen such attractive linens, such pretty china—where on earth had she found them? In the cupboards of the Castle itself? How extraordinary! She must keep on rummaging about. But she must buy lots of new things as well.

Laura's high rank at the Castle cost Fletcher nothing. Before her time, he had rarely consented to spend an entire evening with Jack's Felix friends. When he did so, it was generally to play pranks on them—to pretend at dinner, for example, that he was trying to seduce some awkward undergraduate, whose grimly heterosexual father, helpless prisoner of his good manners, would be glaring at Fletcher in silent indignation from a few seats farther along the table. Old Laura had brought the place to life; it was amusing at last, and to add to the amusement, Fletcher experimented from time to time with washing and scrubbing up some disreputable young drifter and passing him off as a flower of the Old South. The young man would always be introduced as a Beauregard and would always be said to have come from the Tuscaloosa branch of the family. Afterward, Fletcher would take the young man up to bed, and Jack would accuse them at breakfast next morning of having no hearts. Fletcher would protest that they had invited Jack to join them and that he had turned them down. Jack would have no recollection of this exchange; drinking, he blacked out earlier with every passing year. Over the long, sunlit table, he could only smile benignly back and forth between them and say, "Oh, hell. Oh, hell."

As for Harry, he was as much pleased by the position that Laura had made for herself at the Castle as Jack, Fletcher, and Laura herself were. Even in the days when they were among the smart young married couples in New York, it was always she who had prompted their party-giving and party-going; Harry was content to spend evening after evening at home, repairing appliances (the pleasure it gave him to extract a child's bent toy from the depths of a vacuum cleaner!) and tinkering with gadgets. Now, as he neared seventy, working at two jobs, he needed his sleep. He got up at five in the morning, and he worked long past dark, and he was satisfied to fall into bed as the grandfather's clock in the hall downstairs was shaking the house with the clamor of nine. At that hour, Laura and Jack would be just leading their guests in to dinner, and Harry, pulling up sheet and blankets and making himself cozy in the warm cave of the bed, thought as his eyes fell shut of how little he envied them. Some time after midnight, Jack's chauffeur would bring Laura home; Harry would wake to the sound of the big Cadillac being maneuvered back and forth, back and forth, in the narrow driveway behind the house. Harry would hear Laura's clear voice—after fifty years, still the voice of a girl—saying, "Good night, Joe!" and the chauffeur replying, "Good night, ma'am, thank you, ma'am," and the back door of the house opening and closing; and he would be asleep again before Laura had climbed to the top of the stairs.

The arrangement, because it was so pleasing to them all, might have gone on unchanged for years. "With luck," Harry would have added, in his usual way of touching wood, but at a moment trivial in itself, they were suddenly without luck, and the good times came to an end. The indirect cause was, as it happened, a stranger—a young pickup of Fletcher's, whom he encountered one morning in the bus terminal just off Courthouse Square. The boy had never been to Felix; he was passing through on his way to Knoxville. He was broke and hungry and sick of hitching, and he wanted someone to stake him to a ticket. Fletcher treated him to a Coke at the terminal and then to a hamburger at a quick-and-dirty on the square. He was a good-looking boy, with well-kept teeth and a smile that he might have learned from watching old Westerns on television; a three or four days' growth of beard lay like a smudge of light-brown dust on his fair skin. It turned out that he was in no particular hurry to reach Knoxville. He smiled his TV smile. He reckoned that one day would do as well as the next. Fletcher invited him up to the Castle for a swim. Before the swim, he helped him shave and bathe. He doused him with lotions, decked him out in tight black silk trunks and a silk dressing gown, and led him down to the pool, where Jack lay on a towel sun-bathing and having a drink before lunch.

"Jack, this is David. David, Jack." On principle, Fletcher kept introductions short; there were few last names in his life.

"My dear boy! Fletcher, make David a drink." Jack propped himself up on one elbow to admire the newcomer. The sun gleamed in the thick white curls of Jack's chest. His lean, well-oiled body looked twenty years younger than it was. "David is one of my favorite names. You'll stay for lunch?"

David smiled. He looked away into the distance and then back. He said that he reckoned he wouldn't mind.

Fletcher was captivated by the performance. He had spent much of his life appraising the aptitudes of young men. "Tell me who writes your stuff," he said.

"Sir?"

"And 'David'—whose stroke of genius is that?"

The boy ran his tongue over those exceptionally white teeth. "Sir?" he asked again, taking no chances.

"No matter. Let me make you a vodka Collins."

"Yessir, that'd be—"

Fletcher put a hand on David's arm, which was covered with fine golden hairs warmed by the sun. "Real nice?"

"Yessir, *real* nice."

Jack said, "Fletcher, stop being such a bitch. The boy's enchanting. David, go swim while I tell Fletcher here how to behave in polite society."

Very early the next morning, after the happiest night that Jack had ever spent in the Castle (for he was right: the boy *was* enchanting), Fletcher, having passed out at dinner, roused himself to find Jack's and David's rooms unoccupied. He came upon them at last, making love on the black leather couch in the small study. For a little while yet, they would be unaware of his presence. He liked having the power over them of their unawareness; it was a power that could be manipulated by being turned into a prank, and to Fletcher pranks were irresistible. It occurred to him to startle Jack and David by performing his celebrated parlor trick; he would take the short knife from the wall and hurl it end over end into the dart board over their heads. Perhaps because he was drunk and newly awake, but perhaps also because of something in the surfeited eyes and perfect smile of the boy locked in Jack's arms, his aim was faulty. He shouted a warning, of course too late. The knife sped past the boy and straight into Jack's astonished face.

People who live into their eighties tend to have small funerals. There were fifteen or sixteen people at Laura's brief service in church, and among this number would have to be included the usual portion of unaccounted-for strangers. Afterward, at the cemetery, there were only the immediate family and the neighboring Coxeys, themselves now growing old and infirm. Laura was being buried in the new section of the cemetery, which had the advantage (even in cemeteries, one speaks of advantages) of placing her among friends. It was consoling to Harry and the children to think that her grave lay between the graves of women with whom she had played bridge and chatted at the country club for thirty years. In the old section of the cemetery— if, as the sexton said, she had been lucky enough to get into it—Laura would have lain among people she had never known. Higgledy-piggledy in the lumpy grass, the old Felix families jostled each other, and of all the names carved on those tilting eighteenth- and nineteenth-century stones only one—Treanor—would have had any meaning for Laura. In a big plot on the highest point of land in the cemetery, among a score of parents, grandparents, great-grandparents, uncles, aunts, and cousins, filling with but inches to spare the last available space, lay Jack. After fifteen years, the flat marble slab into which his name and dates had been cut showed surprisingly little wear. The pink-veined marble had an unyielding hardness and shininess to it, as if it were bound never to weather into the mossy obscurity of its fellows. Jack would surely not have chosen such a stone, but because he had left no immediate family, the executors of his estate had faced their task with more than the usual seriousness; they had wanted to make sure that in death Jack would have what he always had in life: the best of everything.

The young minister who conducted Laura's burial service wore his hair extremely long. A fresh breeze blew in off the meadows to the west as he stood reading beside the open grave, and he was obliged to hold the Bible in one hand and keep his unruly hair in place with the other.

Shortly after arriving in Felix, he had prepared for these occasions an assortment of snippets of psalms that seemed appropriate to the geography of the region; he found that the snippets went down better with most members of his congregation in their moments of grief than the usual grave-side references to dust and ashes. If you stopped to think about it, ecology was what the psalms were all about. Drat that wind! he thought, and read aloud, strands of lank hair snapping like halyards against his cheeks: "Great is the Lord, and greatly to be praised in the city of our God, in the mountain of his holiness." Ordinarily, upon mention of the word "mountain" he would gesture toward the adjacent Smokies; today the gesture was out of the question. He read faster and faster: "I will lift up mine eyes unto the hills, from whence cometh my help. . . . As the mountains are round about Jerusalem, so the Lord is round about this people, Amen." He snapped shut the Bible, pulled a tweed sports cap from his pocket, fitted it carefully onto his head, tucked the ends of his hair in under the rim of the cap, shook hands with the white-haired Harry and his three gray-haired children, shook hands with the frail Coxeys (were they of his congregation? would he soon be burying them as well?), waved a cheery good-bye to the undertaker and his assistant, bundled himself into a bright-red open English two-seater, and, with a spurt of gravel from behind the wheels, raced off down the grassy lane of the cemetery onto the main road. Shepherding the little funeral party into a couple of waiting limousines, the undertaker clicked his teeth in disapproval of the vanished man of God. "Damn swinger!" he said, but under his breath, out of respect for the living and the dead.

The Coxeys had invited Harry and his family to lunch.

Weren't they right next door, and wouldn't everyone be in need of something to eat and drink, and perhaps especially to drink, after such an ordeal? Certainly Harriet, Lawrence, and Paul would, but not Harry. He had something more important in mind. It was a beautiful day, and the golf course would be lying there all afternoon half-empty, and he was determined that Lawrence and Paul should take advantage of the opportunity. He and Harriet would follow them around in a golf cart—he might even play a few holes with them for old times' sake. Over their whiskies, the children were shocked: play golf on the very day of their mother's funeral? Harry glanced from one to another of them, his blue eyes wide with incredulity. Why on earth shouldn't they play golf? What did they suppose Laura would want them to do? Sit there and drink and mope? When had that ever been her style?

"Many people would think we were showing a great lack of feeling for Mother," Lawrence said, asserting his right as the eldest to serve as the family spokesman.

" 'People would think'!" Harry mocked him. "At your age, my God, Lawrence, are you still worrying about what people would think?"

"*I* would think," Paul said. "Harriet would think. The whole idea is quite unsuitable, and—I may add—quite like you. You will never think things through. I've no clubs, no golf shoes, and I am, besides, no longer that much interested in the game."

"I'll go over to the house and see what we can use for clubs," Harry said. Before they could make a protest, he darted off at his usual jaunty pace. They would all be heading home that evening, and good riddance; meanwhile, he had no intention of letting them spend the afternoon discussing his future. He knew perfectly well what they were thinking. In the name of being sensible, they would plead with him to sell the house, put the proceeds into an annuity, and then turn himself over to the keepers of some gruesome nursing home, to die by inches of having nothing left to do. Well, Lord God Almighty! He wouldn't give a straw for their sensible suggestions. He had a hundred worthwhile projects to carry out, or a thousand. Everywhere he turned, he encountered unfinished tasks. Some of them he had put off because he looked forward to doing them; others he had put off because he dreaded them. The task he dreaded most he had put off longest, but soon he would face it, as sooner or later he faced everything; he would not let those nagging old-maid children take his responsibilities away from him. He fumbled about in the front hall closet. The leather trim of his golf bag felt dry to the touch. He hauled it out and looked over the clubs: good enough for an afternoon's sport. In the pocket of the bag were half a dozen balls and a few wooden tees, left over from the time, a year or so earlier, when he had played his last game. Since then, he had been content to make his way once a week to the locker room of the club and sit sipping a beer and listening to the players as they tramped in from the eighteenth green, sweating and protesting that they would never take a stick in hand again.

With the bag slung over his shoulder, Harry started back across the yard to his neighbors'. The Coxeys would be serving lunch on the porch, on a side of the house away from the heavy traffic, and Harry heard their voices long before he reached the bottom step of the porch. He caught the word "valiant," spoken by Mrs. Coxey, and something in her tone made him feel sure that the word was being applied to him. He straightened his shoulders in spite of the bag, lightheaded with pride. Valor was what soldiers possessed, and since childhood (it had been his secret since childhood), he had tried to exercise the discipline of a good soldier. His earliest memory was of being told that he had been named for a soldier—a brother of his father's had fought in the Civil War and had died, poor young man, in some miserable swamp west of Richmond; Harry was Harry for that dead soldier's sake.

"Valiant?" Paul said. "Oh, come. Stubborn is more like it. Right or wrong, he never gives up."

"Our difficulty," Harriet said, "is that there are times in life when a person *must*. And this is one of them."

Lawrence said, "I don't think we should be trying to thrash these matters out behind his back."

"In any event, I won't be making a spectacle of myself at golf," Paul said. "We've far more important things to do this afternoon."

"Just what the doctor ordered!" Harry said, dragging the bag thump-thump up the porch steps. "Balls, tees, a regular pro shop!"

"Father," Harriet said, "nobody wants to play golf. After lunch, we want to have a nice long talk."

"Nothing to talk about."

Harriet assumed the patient air of an adult about to reason, not for the first time, with an intractable child. "Plans for your future," she said.

"I already got my plans. Nothing has changed because of Laura."

"You can't go on living alone in that house."

"You think I wasn't alone there these last few years?"

Paul said, "What an absolutely rotten thing to say about Mother."

"Another county heard from," Harry said. He seated

himself on the top step of the porch and accepted a plate of food from Mrs. Coxey. Mr. Coxey busied himself pouring wine out of a gallon jug. "When I need the advice of any of you children, I'll ask for it. Laura as good as died when Jack Treanor died. Then the executors came along and shut down my poor little companies, and maybe I could have died, too, right on the spot, but I didn't. I hung on and here I am. Damn lucky for you I outlived Laura."

"Look at it from the financial point of view," said Lawrence, wishing to be seen to take part in the discussion.

"Lord God, I don't cost you all that much! When I die, you'll sell the house and each of you can get back then whatever you've had to lay out so far. You're a lawyer—I'll sign any damn paper you please. Paul's got all the furniture ticketed already. Maybe you'll show a little profit on me if I don't go rattling on to ninety. I'm sure as hell not going to die just to make things easier for three middle-aged, sour-faced children."

"Now, Father," Harriet said. He who had never provoked a quarrel in his life was plainly seeking to provoke one now.

"He's impossible," Paul said. When Paul was angry with someone, he would refer to him only in the third person, as if he were no longer present. "No use trying to reason with him, I assure you."

Mr. and Mrs. Coxey fluttered about in dismay, passing dessert and coffee. They had not intended to provide the occasion for a family quarrel. Exchanging glances, they agreed silently that, while they must not take sides, they were certainly on Harry's. Mrs. Coxey did her best to convey this information to Harry by offering him a second helping of cake.

"No more talk," Harry said. "If anything comes up,

we'll handle it by phone. If you're not strong enough to play golf, better pack up and hit the road. You got a lot of driving ahead of you. Nothing takes the starch out of a man like a funeral."

All three of the children wished to indicate that they considered this remark in extremely bad taste. They began to speak at the same moment and were joined by the Coxeys.

Lawrence: "You've no call—"

Harriet: "Poor Mother—"

Paul: "He—"

Mrs. Coxey: "More cake?"

Mr. Coxey: "This pot is Sanka."

Harry got to his feet, eyes shining. What a world of good his riling of the children had done him! He felt like a twenty-year-old. Tomorrow he would start getting the house ready for winter. The dust would fly; he would work longer and harder and better than ever before. As the children stared, he teetered back and forth on the outer edge of the top step of the porch, then started to perform a jaunty, shuffling dance.

In the days that followed, Harry surpassed himself in feats of ingenuity. For years he had put off repairing the back porch of the house, a corner of which had settled at a dangerous angle. Harry borrowed an automobile jack from Mr. Coxey, raised the porch, removed the defective pier, and built in its place a new foundation of brick and concrete. "Good for a thousand years," he said to Mr. Coxey, giving the foundation a kick. A thousand years was Harry's invariable estimate of how long any handiwork of his could be expected to endure. From another neighbor he borrowed an aluminum extension ladder, with which he was able to carry out one of the tasks he enjoyed least: the annual cleaning out of the gutters along the second-floor eaves of the house. What irritated Harry was the inefficiency of the process; he had to keep shifting the ladder again and again, a few feet at a time, as he proceeded along the four walls of the house. A far better method of dealing with the problem now occurred to him—one that called for the ladder to be put in place only once and mounted and dismounted only once. Armed with a forty-foot length of stout nylon clothesline, Harry clambered up onto the pyramidal roof of the house. He fastened one end of the line around the chimney that rose from the apex of the pyramid and the other end of the line around his waist. As safe as any Alpinist, he made his way down the shallow slope of the roof, squatting on his haunches to dig the dead leaves and other débris out of the gutters and hurl them in clods to the ground. The Coxeys caught sight of him from the far side of the hedge dividing their properties; Harry's body seemed to dangle like a puppet's against the sky, unsupported. Alarmed as they were on his behalf, they knew better than to raise objections; they held hands and whispered "Tch! Tch!" and were there to congratulate him when, his labors at an end, he stepped off the bottom rung of the ladder. "You didn't feel the least bit dizzy?" Mrs. Coxey asked, making old eyes at him. Harry was trembling with fatigue, and a vein throbbed like mad on his temple; no matter. He tossed back his head and said in scorn, "I like heights."

Once Harry's ordinary seasonal chores had been completed, he set to work digging in the little uphill garden behind the house. Because the garden had been neglected for the past year or so, there was much to be done; the Coxeys guessed that he must be planning to put in a crop of winter rye, for spading over in the spring. But the Coxeys were wrong. He was facing at last the task he had put off month after month since long before Laura had died. In a way that he could never have conveyed to others, he had felt with Laura's death an unexpected and astonishing increase in strength and appetite. At a moment when most of his friends (and certainly all three of those dreary children) would assume that he was getting ready to slip out of the world, he felt himself coming fully and passionately into it: into himself and the world together, alone without a trace of loneliness. Still, there was no telling how long this sense of well-being might last. For all he knew to the contrary, it was an exaltation that many old people felt in the last few moments before they suddenly crumpled up and went smash into death, as a light bulb quickens and flares up at the moment of burning out. Whatever the case might prove to be, he had promised himself that he would leave no loose ends behind.

Every day for several days, Harry took his long spade from the garage and dug for an hour or so in the cool of the morning. It was a wonder to him how stones worked their way up through the soil year after year—always the same bountiful crop to be disposed of! He made a little cairn of stones at one side of the trench, on the grassy knoll that had always been Jacques' favorite observation post. Someday the stones would serve to line a dry well or fill a low place in the driveway. When he had cut and shaped the trench to his satisfaction, he went into the house and took from the desk in the study his old pawnshop automatic. Having made sure it was loaded, he went into the living room to fetch Jacques. For weeks now, the old dog had been unwilling to leave the house. It was as if with age he had grown afraid of the outdoors. Morning and night, Harry would drag him by the scruff of the neck into the yard, trying to keep him from soiling the house and himself. Incontinent, stinking Jacques! Harry remembered how, as a puppy, Jacques had learned in a few days to housebreak himself; he had gamboled and frisked with pleasure over the trick of relieving himself whenever his master wished. That dear creature, coiled like a spring between one's hands, had become a lump of matted curls, sluggish and slobbering. The tongue with which he licked Harry's hand hung permanently from his lower jaw. He would stare up at Harry in worship, then his eyes would go vacant, and he would begin to doze.

The tugging and coaxing required to get Jacques out of the house always left both Harry and Jacques exhausted. Moreover, no sooner was he outside than, beset by invisible enemies, he struggled to make his way back into the safety of the darkened living room. He would butt the screened kitchen door with a paw until he had forced it open a crack; little by little, sometimes failing and having to start afresh, he would work away at the crack until it was wide enough to admit a leg, then a shoulder, then his entire body. Spent with the effort, he would fall inside the door and lie panting on the kitchen floor.

Harry found Jacques by the living-room fireplace. A puddle glinted mirrorlike on the brick hearth behind Jacques. Harry gripped the old dog at the shoulders and pulled him gently to his feet. He took a firm grip on Jacques' collar and pulled him slowly, slowly, through the hall and kitchen. Jacques heaved and groaned; once they reached the bright sunlight of the back yard, he began to whimper. "Now, boy," Harry said. "Be a good boy,

Jacques." He drew the old dog up onto the grassy knoll beside the trench. Grateful not to be tugged at any longer, Jacques lay down, gave a lick or two to Harry's hand, and fell asleep. Harry measured the trench and the dog with his eye; he had judged everything so accurately that there would be only inches to spare. Seating himself beside Jacques, he took the automatic out of his pocket and placed the muzzle against Jacques' ear. He looked away from Jacques toward the house and pulled the trigger. The report was much louder than he had expected. Jacques seemed to take a single leap sidelong away from Harry, then there was no movement at all. Harry put the gun back in his pocket and, kneeling on the grass behind Jacques, began to push the heavy body down the slight grade to the trench. He had calculated on gravity to help him, and so it did, but the body was heavier than he had estimated. Harry sweated hard, forcing the inert mass of dark hair down the slope toward the trench. At last the body began to slide of its own accord. He watched it drop into the bottom of the trench, followed by a rain of light-red pebbles. Harry scrambled to his feet and started shoveling earth back into the trench. He could feel his heart hammering. He was going to faint. No. With each shovelful of soil he lifted, he heard himself saying silently, *No*. The trench was filling. Now it was level with the weeds in the surrounding garden. Soon it began to form a mound above the garden. He smoothed the mound with the back of his shovel. He was very strong. He would finish the job in good time. He would leave everything just so. When the Coxeys came hurrying through the hedge, they saw Harry stamping with vigor the soil above the buried dog.